p20

D1713894

PRAISE FOR BOXING AND THE MOB

"Jeffery Sussman has written a riveting book that captures the entanglement of boxing and the mob. The sport of boxing is made for the mob as much as it is for the kids fighting their way out of poverty. Once you start this book, you will not put it down."—Bruce Silverglade, owner of Gleason's Gym

"Boxing's culture of corruption is legendary. It's a great sport that was at the mercy of professional gamblers and mobsters who predetermined the results of matches by fixing fights for much of the twentieth century. That dark chapter has waxed and waned over the years and is the subject of Jeffrey Sussman's exciting and engaging book Boxing and the Mob. Boxing, without a central governing body to oversee it, will, as Sussman cogently asserts, remain corrupt and malodorous."—Robert Ecksel, editor of www.boxing.com

"Mr. Sussman's offering is a sure bet to capture the appreciation of anyone with an interest in boxing and the mob. His account of the influence of Frankie Carbo and others who controlled the sport is a history lesson, written in an entertaining style that reminds one of the great boxing writers of days past. The book is a knockout!"—Anthony Celano, retired NYPD detective squad commander

"Wow! Jeff Sussman did one heck of a job investigating the mob and boxing. Great read!"—Jerry Palace, retired NYPD detective

"I loved Jeffrey Sussman's previous books, but this one may be his best yet! While reading this book, I honestly felt that I was in the same room as Carbo, Palermo, and many others during point-blank discussions. He also makes you feel the pain of the fighters who had to go along with 'the deals' that were beyond their control. This book is truly the history of the mob's involvement with professional boxing. I couldn't put it down! This is a must-read."—Bill Calogero, host of the Talkin' Boxing with Billy C. television and radio program

BOXING AND THE MOB

BOXING AND THE MOB

The Notorious History of the Sweet Science

Jeffrey Sussman

ROWMAN & LITTLEFIELD
Lanham • Boulder • New York • London

Published by Rowman & Littlefield
An imprint of The Rowman & Littlefield Publishing Group, Inc.
4501 Forbes Boulevard, Suite 200, Lanham, Maryland 20706
www.rowman.com

6 Tinworth Street, London SE11 5AL, United Kingdom

British Library Cataloguing in Publication Information Available

Library of Congress Cataloging-in-Publication Data

Names: Sussman, Jeffrey, author.
Title: Boxing and the mob : the notorious history of the sweet science / Jeffrey Sussman.
Description: Lanham, Maryland : Rowman & Littlefield, 2019. | Includes bibliographical references and index.
Identifiers: LCCN 2018048723 (print) | LCCN 2018059910 (ebook) | ISBN 9781538113165 (Electronic) | ISBN 9781538113158 (cloth : alk. paper)
Subjects: LCSH: Boxing—Corrupt practices—United States--History. | Organized crime—United States—History.
Classification: LCC GV1136.5 (ebook) | LCC GV1136.5 .S87 2019 (print) | DDC 796.830973—dc23
LC record available at https://lccn.loc.gov/2018048723

To my wife and best friend, Barbara

CONTENTS

ACKNOWLEDGMENTS

I remain indebted to Stephen Spataro, the East Hampton reference librarian, whose ability to reach deep into the Internet to find out-of-date newspaper and magazine articles is a skill worthy of admiration.

I am grateful to my editor, Christen Karniski, for her approval and support of my authorial ambitions, and for her incisive editorial judgment.

My good friend, Stephen Scott, encouraged me to write this book, and for that and his ongoing interest, I am grateful.

I am grateful to former New York City organized crime detective Anthony Celano, who directed me to important source material for this book.

Not least, I'd like to thank my wife Barbara, who lights up my world with the generosity of her being, plus she knows how to spell every word in the dictionary.

INTRODUCTION

I first learned about fixed fights when I was 13 years old. At my Bar Mitzvah party, which was held in the grand ballroom of the Commodore Hotel (now the Grand Hyatt Hotel), my father introduced me to one of the 250 guests. The man, in an elegant gray sharkskin suit set off with a black silk tie, was my father's uncle, a former bootlegger, named Irving. I never saw him after that night. He apparently kept such a low profile that even today you can't find any information about him on the Internet.

Here's what my father told me about him:

> During prohibition, he made millions of dollars smuggling illegal liquor from Canada into the United States. His wife, whom he had met while smuggling booze across the border, couldn't have children. They adopted two boys; one became a successful surgeon, the other a prominent lawyer. Irv's wife died, and he married my aunt, Cele. She was a widow and had a son named Teddy, who was a little slow. Irv owned a warehouse in Harlem where he kept his trucks. After prohibition ended, he turned the warehouse into a garage and gave it to Teddy to run. It's a big garage, maybe five stories. Teddy makes a nice living from it. During his lifetime, Irv worked closely with a New Jersey gangster named Longy Zwillman, who controlled the entire state. You know why he was called Longy? Because he had a big one. You know what I mean? Just kidding. Anyway, one day, Longy was found hanging by his neck from a rope in the basement of his house. He must have been dangling for quite a while because his tongue had turned black and his face was purple. No one knew if he

had committed suicide or if the mob had gotten rid of him. He was a tough guy who beat a lot of raps. But he wasn't tough enough at the end. Longy's action was taken over by Willie Moretti. He was the guy who helped kick-start Frank Sinatra's career by threatening night-club owners to hire Sinatra. Then Moretti had the chutzpah to de-mand kickbacks! Moretti also held a gun to a band leader's head—I think it was Tommy Dorsey—and demanded that he release Sinatra from a contract. With a gun to his head, he obliged. Just remember: Never get into bed with the mob. They'll rob you coming and going.

Anyway, back to Irv: During the mid-1930s, he was indicted but never tried for the murder of Dutch Schultz. Irv and the Dutchman were in a hot competition to see who would be the beer baron of northern Manhattan. The Dutchman was a psychopath, a cold-blooded killer. He wanted to kill Tom Dewey, the DA. That made the mob very nervous. Although the Dutchman had killed or bought off a lot of competitors, he lost the war: He was assassinated in some chop house in Newark. Ironically, it didn't do the mob any good, because Dewey came after them and sent bushels of them to prison, and maybe a dozen to the electric chair. But the Dutchman's death was good news for Irv and some other mobsters, for they cut up the Dutchman's action, and those who didn't go to prison thrived. Irv was a smart guy who actually paid a PR guy to keep his name out of the papers. His partners were pleased, because no one except for the psychos wanted publicity. Irv wanted the world to think of him as a quiet country squire. He had a big mansion next door to Averell Harriman's place. Irv once invited me up to his estate. He had a pair of Dobermans who kept sniffing around me. They were very obedi-ent: When he told them to stay or sit, they remained that way until he called them. My family was poor in those days. A dog was a luxury we didn't have. And being sniffed at by a pair of attacked-trained Dobermans was a little unnerving. Still it was a memorable experi-ence for a poor guy to have lunch in a gangster's mansion. He knew that we were poor during the Depression, but he never offered me a job or gave me handout; however, he did give me tips on fixed horse races and boxing matches. He would tell me to bet $75 on a Jack Sharkey or Primo Carnero match, and I would walk away with $750. That was a lot during the Depression. Unfortunately, he didn't give me more than four or five tips a year. While it was nice to get theses relatively small windfalls, it wasn't enough to live on, so we remained poor right up to the outset of World War II. That's when my dad won a garment factory in a poker game. One thing I learned from Irv and my dad was never bet on anything unless you know the outcome. Only bet on a sure thing. Gambling is a sucker's game. Betting on a fixed fight was never a gamble.

My curiosity about fixed fights was ignited that day. I asked my father how many fights were fixed, and he replied,

More than the public realizes. You know all you have to do is pay off one fighter and tell him to bet that money on his opponent, and he will clean up. It is especially appealing to washed-up boxers, guys on their way down, and to guys who are second-raters, guys who know they'll never fight their way to the top of the pyramid. You know boxers have no unions, no pensions, and many of their managers steal their money. So if a guy is smart, he'll take the money and move on. It's better to have money in the bank than mush in your head.

I didn't have any further inside knowledge about fixed fights until the 1980s, when I was doing publicity for Olympic gold medal boxer Howard Davis, a welterweight. I got to know a fight promoter and asked him about fixed fights. He assured me that none of Davis's fights were fixed, and I believed him, especially after watching Davis in the ring. The promoter said,

Sometimes it's easier to fix the referee rather than the fighter. A referee can separate fighters before a knockout punch is coming; he can separate fighters when one of them is an inside fighter; he can call a foul on one fighter and not another; he can pull them apart when his guy looks like he's taking too many punches; he can begin a knock-down count late. There are many things a referee can do to affect the outcome. And, for insurance, you can also fix one of the judges. Look at how many people argued for years about the long count in the Tunney–Dempsey fight. Was it fixed? Was it on the level? I think it was fixed. You know the referee wouldn't start counting until Dempsey went to a neutral corner. When Tunney knocked down Dempsey, even though Tunney didn't go to neutral corner, the referee started counting right away. That was an obvious one. The ref favored Tunney. But as bad as it was, it wasn't as obvious as Jake LaMotta giving it away to Billy Fox. Some guys are no good at faking a loss. And some of them are not believable when winning a fixed fight. Just look at Primo Carnero. He couldn't punch; he was awkward; pushed his opponents away. Yet, he won enough fixed fights to become the world champion, and the poor guy had all his money stolen from him. He walked away broke. The same thing happened to Blackjack Billy Fox and others.

Because boxing matches are so easy to fix, the sport has always attracted mobsters, professional gamblers, and con artists. They have existed in the shadows of boxing for as long as people have bet on the sport.

In the 1880s and 1890s, there were "fight stores" in various cities and towns throughout the United States. New York and Chicago had the largest concentration of such stores. In his book *The Big Con: The Story of the Confidence Man*, David Maurer writes,

> The fight store swindle worked, briefly, like this. The mob consisted of one or more ropers [the person who brought in the sucker to be swindled], an insideman, a doctor, two prizefighters, and several minor assistants. The roper traveled about the countryside (usually not far from the store) and steered a mark in whenever he could find one. He posed as a disgruntled secretary to a millionaire sportsman, often a railroad executive, who ostensibly traveled about the country in a private [railroad] car with a prizefighter, his personal doctor, a trainer, and staff of servants. In order to indulge his sporting instincts, he would match his fighter against any other fighters . . . and of course he bet heavily on the fight.
>
> The roper told the victim that he had been selected for a part in this scheme because he could be depended upon. The roper's problem was this: He had been abused and neglected by his employer, who, he says, is really an old skinflint. He has decided to quit his service—but not before making some money for himself. The next fight, for which he is now making arrangements. . . . He has contracted with his employer's fighter to take a dive . . . in the 10th round. His employer will bet heavily on his own fighter. He, the secretary, cannot personally bet against his employer; hence he needs someone with money who will bet heavily on the other fighter, then divide the proceeds. It's a sure thing. [1]

As soon as the victim had been convinced of the reliability of the scheme, he was sent home to empty his bank account and bring back the money. The money that both parties bet was placed in a locked satchel, and the victim was asked to hold on to it until the fight was over and the winnings could be distributed; however, just in case the victim could not be trusted, he was given a satchel that contained cut-up newspapers. The millionaire railroad executive had secreted the satchel with the money in a hidden closet. After several rounds of boxing, during which the millionaire's fighter was apparently losing, an unexpected event occurred: The millionaire's fighter suddenly hit his opponent with a devastating shot to the heart. His unfortunate opponent dropped to the canvas, pig's blood spilling out of his mouth. The millionaire's doctor would rush into the ring, apply his stethoscope to the chest of the flattened fighter, feel for a pulse, and declare—sadly, oh so sadly—that the poor man was dead. The millionaire took possession of the satchel containing only paper and wished the victim better luck next time. The confused, dazed victim nodded and began to walk away, when the millionaire, the roper, and the doctor loudly warned everyone present that they should immediately leave, for prizefighting was illegal, and if the police arrived, they would all be charged with accessories to manslaughter. The victim fled, often cursing his bad luck but not suspecting that he had been set up.

But it was not until the twentieth century that the fixing and betting was controlled by organized criminal syndicates, rather than mendacious entrepreneurs. And two of the most notorious mobsters, Owney Madden and Frankie Carbo, were leaders in organized crime.

Madden had heard the stories of how a baseball game had been fixed and hundreds of thousands of dollars were won by a coterie of gamblers controlled by a criminal genius and mastermind of many gambling ventures. The man was Arnold Rothstein, and he was celebrated or hated, depending on your point of view, as the man who had fixed the 1919 World Series. He was also known as the man who organized crime in the United States, a visionary who taught and mentored such young criminals as Lucky Luciano, Meyer Lansky, Frank Costello, and Bugsy Siegel. They were the men who would control organized crime in the United States for decades.

Rothstein's right-hand man was Abe Attell, the former featherweight boxing champion from 1906 to 1912. While being tried for being Rothstein's bagman, he convinced the jury that it was another man named Abe Attell who was the real culprit. He walked out of the courtroom and continued working as a professional boxing trainer and gambler who always knew which fights and which boxers to bet on, for he was in on the fix, if not the actual fixer. He made his money the easy way.

This book is about the intermarriage of mobsters and boxers, of fixed fights and the millions of dollars earned by mobsters through the 1960s, right up to the time when Frankie Carbo and his minions were given long prison sentences.

THE MAN WHO FIXED THE 1919 WORLD SERIES

The man who fixed the 1919 World Series was an avatar of mystery, a man known but unknown, a man of power and a man to be feared. He was the father of organized crime, the man who turned gambling into big business. He was Arnold Rothstein, the son of well-educated upper-middle-class Jews, whose connections in Manhattan constituted manifold spheres of influence. Instead of entering an honest profession, Rothstein was attracted to the city's underclass of criminals. He disliked school, for the demimonde was where excitement was brewed. He believed that it intoxicated all those who partook of its pleasures. As Rothstein's biographer, Leo Katcher, points out, "What did he need of schools when there were such places as gambling houses, pool rooms, and the prop room of Hammerstein's Victoria Theatre on the corner of 42nd Street and Seventh Avenue? There was a dice game in the prop room every Monday."[1]

By 1925, Arnold Rothstein had obtained mythical status to such an extent that F. Scott Fitzgerald created a fictionalized version of the notorious criminal mastermind.

In *The Great Gatsby*, Fitzgerald writes,

> He's quite a character around New York—a denizen of Broadway.
> "Who is he anyhow, an actor?"
> "No."
> "A dentist?"

"Meyer Wolfsheim? No he's a gambler." Gatsby hesitated, then added coolly, "He's the man who fixed the World Series back in 1919."

"Fixed the World Series?" I repeated.

The idea staggered me. I remembered, of course, that the World Series had been fixed in 1919, but if I had thought of it at all I would have thought of it as a thing that merely happened at the end of some inevitable chain. It never occurred to me that one man could start to play with the faith of 50 million people—with the single-mindedness of a burglar blowing a safe.

"How did he happen to do that?" I asked after a minute.

"He just saw the opportunity."

"Why isn't he in jail?"

"They can't get him, old sport. He's a smart man."[2]

Arnold Rothstein was the son of Abraham Rothstein, an orthodox Jew, so honorable that he was known as "Abe the Just." Abe was a successful businessman whose word (to use a cliché) was considered his bond. It was said that he never did a dishonest thing in his life, never bet on a baseball game, a horse race, or a boxing match, never mind ones that had been fixed. His wife "felt that Abraham never made a light promise, for a promise became debt. And he believed in paying his debts."[3]

Katcher describes Abe as follows:

He was a man of simple, fixed belief. He believed in the Law. The Law of his faith and the law of his country. He was a disciple of orthodoxy. He was a good man.

A testimonial dinner was given in his honor in 1919. It marked his efforts—and success—in settling a major dispute in the New York City garment industry. He had been chosen by both sides to act as arbitrator because both sides trusted him completely.[4]

The honorableness that Abe exuded was something Arnold felt compelled to rebel against. How could he possibly live up to such exacting standards? He said, "I gambled just to show my father he couldn't tell me what to do."

"Gambling was a sin," Abraham said. Arnold paid no attention. What did his father know anyway?[5] He would be the cynical rogue that his father would find worse than distasteful. The routines of Abe's life were as defined and predictable as a schedule of daily high school classes, and so—rather than submitting to such a boring routine—Arnold quit school, quit his parents' world, and sought out adventures that would make him rich and powerful.

Arnold's dislike of his father, mother, and siblings began when he was a small child, as is related in Katcher's biography. Rothstein's mother, Esther, took two of Arnold's siblings on a visit. Arnold wanted to go too, but Esther left him at home, without an explanation. Arnold retreated into a dark closet, where he gave vent to his self-pity. His father heard him crying. When Abe opened the door, seeing his son folded up like a fetus, he asked his sobbing son what was wrong. Arnold claimed he was hated by both of his parents. That's why he had been left behind. No one wanted to be with him. No one liked him. Abe, distressed by Arnold's wanton sadness, attempted to reassure his son that he loved all of his children equally. Of course, his parents wanted to be with him, but Esther could handle only two children on such a visit. Abe could not explain why Arnold was not chosen to accompany his mother. Arnold did not buy his father's attempted explanations. He despised his father for lying to him. From that moment onward, Arnold would live a life in rebellion of his father's values; his actions from childhood through adulthood would cause his father anguish and ultimately cause his father to disown him.

Arnold found his opportunity at age 16. He wandered into a seedy pool hall on the Bowery populated by gamblers, hustlers, pimps, petty thieves, and the women who were attracted to them. Some of the women lived off the earnings of the thieves and hustlers. Many others, in thrall to pimps, supported their servitude by prostitution. Arnold watched them with fascination and guiltless pleasure as low-stakes pool hustlers fleeced tourists and young men from uptown who had been out for a night of excitement and slumming among the demimonde. Arnold had found his métier, the sawdust on the floor, the aroma of cheap booze in the air, and the implied lawlessness of the place. These were to be Arnold's people; they would become his tutors, and—when he became master of their world—they would become his employees.

Although having been a disappointing academic student before dropping out of school, Arnold had a natural gift for numbers. He could figure out long odds and percentages in his head. He could perform complicated long division and multiplication. He could recite to himself a series of concomitant sporting events, each with different odds. The manipulation of numbers was as natural for him as it is for many people to hum the melodies of songs stored on the hard drives of their brains. Gambling would be Arnold's world, his career, the thing that completely engaged his intelligence and imagination; however, unlike other gamblers, he would bet only on sure things, on guaranteed outcomes.

He was quick-witted and smart, and attracted the attention of Big Tim Sullivan, the political boss of the Lower East Side and the Bowery; Big Tim was also a gambler and entrepreneur who had ownership stakes in theaters, saloons, gambling dens, and brothels. Big Tim told Arnold that with his ability to do complicated mathematical problems in his head, he should focus his talents on gambling, on opening a gambling casino. According to Katcher, "He saw a successful future for [Arnold] not in politics, but in gambling. . . . That business takes brains."[6]

It's better to control the actors in the game than to be one of the actors. And since Arnold was only interested in sure things, a gambling casino was the best thing: The edge was always with the house. You didn't have to cheat the customers, for they invariably lost. Just let them play, and eventually they'll go home broke. To make it easy for Arnold to graduate to running a casino, Big Tim would help finance the venture for a piece of the action. He would be Arnold's silent partner and known protector.

Big Tim was a lord of Tammany Hall, and Tammany was a consortium of lordly politicians who controlled politics in Manhattan for generations. It had made all of New York its fiefdom. It began by helping poor Irish immigrants get jobs, primarily with the police and fire departments, but as the ethnic composition of the immigrant population changed, Tammany politicos helped all residents who could return their favors. Among those who could change the outcomes of lives, Big Tim was a powerhouse, and he was as corrupt as any stereotype of a politician with his hands in the till, in the sugar bowl of public funds, and the pockets of criminals who needed his protection. He controlled much of the East Side not just by his ability to generate jobs and protect illicit businesses, but also by using the services of local gangs to enforce his rules. In addition, he made police precincts outposts for maintaining the status quo. While cops were ostensibly commissioned to keep order, they were rewarded for looking the other way, for letting gambling houses and brothels flourish without interruption. The payoffs were enormous, and cops who earned wages slightly above the poverty level were known to have six-figure bank accounts. They were also expected to let the rewards of graft flow upward into ever more powerful hands, and there were no hands more powerful than those of Big Tim.

Tim learned quickly that all politics are local and that his power was locally generated. Nevertheless, he decided to give U.S. Congress a shot. According to historian David Pietrusza, "Sullivan served briefly in Congress, finding it dull aside from his campaign to capture the congressional pinochle championship. He left after one term."[7]

He took many of his colleagues down the hustler's road, relieving them of thousands of dollars in all-night card games. He told a New York City reporter that congressmen were so poorly regarded in Washington that people would tie their horses to them as if they were nothing more than hitching posts.

Washington, DC, did not excite Big Tim; for him the real exercise of power would always be exerted through Tammany Hall. Tim enjoyed the fruits of power, the respect of his constituency, and the opportunities to cash in on his power. In New York City, he was surely a big man, Big Tim Sullivan, but in Washington, he was just plain Congressman Sullivan. In New York City, he took in oodles of money, investing in real estate, theaters, amusement parks, brothels, and gambling casinos. Washington, for him, had been a poor southern city built on a swamp. Before the creation of air-conditioning, it was the worst place to be in the summer. There were clouds of flies and mosquitoes. According to Pietrusza, Big Tim half expected to find rattlesnakes outside of his office. Washington was nothing like New York. Where were the vast populations of immigrants in need of his help? Washington, with its pretentious Roman Empire–style architecture and generous supply of noble monuments, seemed like a museum. It was not the hustling, bustling, crazy city that truly defined him.

New York was his city, and his control extended over vast swaths of neighborhoods and businesses, both licit and illicit. His tentacles stretched from the mayor's office to local police precincts. He could arrange for the appointment of judges and police commissioners. He could get a poor immigrant a job as a city street cleaner. His word was law, and his grip on power and those who paid tribute and obeisance to him was as certain as Caesar's. He dealt with all manner of people, but he especially enjoyed the company of gamblers, showgirls, and mad-ams. Those people, as well as law abiding citizens, knew that they could come to Big Tim with their problems, and if it was in his power, he would solve their problems. Oftentimes, it would cost them something, for in the world of politics, favors are repaid with favors, and sometimes cash. And if Big Tim was anything, he was a political and free-market entrepreneur. He was smart enough to know not to put his name as owner of establishments that were unlawful; for such places, he hired men or women to front for him, and they were handsomely rewarded.

His thousands of constituents didn't care if he played fast and loose with the law. They loved him, not for his crooked ways or unbridled entrepreneurship, but for his unbounded generosity. Poor neighbor-hood immigrants from eastern Europe, Italy, and Ireland were the peo-ple who kept him and his minions in power. He repaid their reliability at the polling places by getting them jobs when they were out of work. He could find employment for them in city agencies or private estab-lishments. If a beat cop wanted a promotion and needed to pay off a desk sergeant, captain, or lieutenant, Big Tim would lend him the mon-ey with the understanding that the cop would pay off the loan with the graft he collected, usually from protection money. If you needed a recommendation to be hired by one of the city's big life insurance companies or one of the banks, see Big Tim. If you needed to borrow some money to get your kid out of jail, see Big Tim. If you were behind in your rent, see Big Tim. If your family was too poor to buy warm winter coats, see Big Tim. If you needed a delivery of coal to keep your bleak tenement apartment warm in winter, see Big Tim.

It didn't matter who you were, where you came from, or what relig-ion you professed. Tim had no prejudice against any of the recent immigrant groups that populated the teeming streets of the Lower East Side of New York in the early years of the twentieth century. Jews, Italians, Poles, Irish, and Africans were all his constituents. At Thanks-giving and Christmas, he made sure that none of his constituents went hungry. Free turkeys by the thousands were distributed to the homes of the poor. And Big Tim didn't forget the derelicts who populated the Bowery flophouses. Each of them, drunk or sober, was given a hearty Christmas dinner, as well as new shoes and woolen socks to keep their feet warm during the cold winter on the street. For all of that and so much more, Big Tim could expect his constituents to elect the men he picked for public office. And he often picked himself to serve in state-wide offices. From 1887 to 1893, he served as an assemblyman in the New York State Assembly. From 1894 to 1902, he served as senator in the New York State Senate, and then served again in that office from 1909 to 1912. He served as a U.S. congressman from 1903 until he resigned in 1906. He gave U.S. Congress one more chance to prove that it was worthy of his teeming imagination and was easily elected in 1912, but he failed to finish his term due to ill health.

Big Tim had time-honored methods for making sure elections were sure things: If recalcitrant and ungrateful constituents would not vote the Tammany party line, Tim would engage the services of his favorite gang leader, Monk Eastman, a Jewish thug who terrified everyone who got in his way. Eastman controlled a gang of more than 100 violent men, each of whom were adept with clubs, blackjacks, brass knuckles, guns, knives, and axes. They were Big Tim's unofficial police force. When not working on behalf of Big Tim, Eastman's gang offered its services to those who needed a debt collected, a business partner elimi-nated, a business incinerated for the insurance money, or even the disposition of a spouse. The gang's prices ranged from the modest to the exorbitant, depending on the services rendered: a broken leg, a broken jaw, death by gun, death by knife, death by drowning, death by defenestration. They, along with other New York gangs, for instance, the Plug Uglies, the Hudson Dusters, the Gophers, the Dead Rabbits, were the precursors of the notorious Murder, Inc., organization, which was a subsidiary of organized crime that carried out murders for hire.

Although violence was always an option for Big Tim to use on the way to the ballot boxes, he preferred more imaginative methods. For example, large numbers of his constituents wore beards, and those who didn't were encouraged to grow beards about a month before election day arrived. Big Tim's Tammany workers would escort the bearded voters to their polling places and have them vote as instructed. Once that was done, the bearded voters would be escorted to a barber shop, where their beards were shaved off, leaving only their mustaches. The mustachioed voters were then escorted back to their original polling place, where they would vote a second time. Once that was completed, the voters made a third visit to their local barber to have their mus-taches removed. Unrecognizable and clean shaven, they were permit-ted to vote a third time. For their exercise of democratic principles, the tertiary voters were given a few dollars and a free glass of beer in one of Big Tim's saloons.

And it was Big Tim who would guide the young Arnold Rothstein onto the golden road of big-time gambling. Big Tim always had an eye for upcoming talent, and he had judged the young Arnold Rothstein not as a political operative in his employ, but as a brilliant gambler who could contribute to Big Tim's wealth. He would not only finance Arnold's first gambling house, but also put him in contact with those best able to advance Arnold's ambitions. In addition, he would be Arnold's mentor and advocate. Their arrangement lasted for years, until Big Tim started to suffer from tertiary syphilis. As his mental faculties descended into paranoid confusion and he thought others were out to get him, he was placed in a mental institution and then removed to his brother's house, where he was kept under close guard. He managed to escape, but the police were not notified for 10 days. His corpse was finally discovered next to railroad tracks and taken to a morgue. He was not identified and so was set to be buried in Potter's Field as an anonymous pauper. Just before the body was to be shipped, a policeman identified it as Big Tim. Even the Bronx coroner, a political appointee and friend of Big Tim's, did not (or had chosen not to) identify the body.

Big Tim's face, though rigid in death, was easily recognizable. He sported diamond-stud cuff links with the initials TDS. He was outfitted in an expensive, bespoke men's suit. It was hardly the attire of a pauper. Apparently, Big Tim's paranoia and constant blabbing about his criminal connections and sources of income had caused the anxiety level of his former associates and partners to shoot up to feverish levels. Big Tim's enemies had reported his indiscrete revelations and confessions to political reformers, and they wanted to end the corruption of Tammany Hall. Fearful of losing its grip on power, as well as being indicted for various crimes, Tammany and its cohorts knew that the big guy would have to be silenced. He had served his purposes well, and now he was silenced for the benefit of those who had profited from his former position of power.

Big Tim's demise had no effect on the activities of Arnold Rothstein, who was now known simply as Rothstein or A. R., or the brain, or the Big Bankroll, for the circumference of his bankroll was growing wider by the day, if not the hour. He had modeled his career and defined his ambitions not on the example of Big Tim, but on a successful society gambler in New York who counted the rich and powerful as his clients and friends. He was named Richard Canfield, and he ran the most elegant, most desirable gambling house in New York; it attracted many members of high society, both men and women, who gambled away hundreds of thousands of dollars each week. Their huge losses never seemed to bother them. It was the thrill of gambling that excited them, and since they had more money than they might ever spend, the loss of hundreds of thousands of dollars was insignificant. Those were the people Rothstein wanted to patronize his casino. He wanted to supplant Richard Canfield.

On the way to realizing his dream, Rothstein had opened small gambling joints, but he was now ready to ascend into the hierarchy of gambling. He had long ago grasped that the house always has an edge, and it would be only the dumbest owners who could not make a profit. And Rothstein's profits would continue to multiply. He had owned a series of gambling houses, each one a little more elegant, a little more upscale, and a little larger than the previous ones. He had leveraged his winnings and his real estate holdings, and opened a posh gambling house in a West Side town house. He hired beautiful showgirls to steer their rich patrons to his house. The girls would receive a percentage of the house's winnings, although many of the girls complained that Rothstein had shortchanged them. Nevertheless, they kept steering the trade to Rothstein.

As successful as Rothstein's gambling enterprise was, it was not enough for him. There had to be other sources of illicit wealth. He wanted as many sure things as he could lay his hands on. Gambling for sure things was his main modus operandi, the guiding principle of his illegal activities. And so the Big Bankroll also became the biggest loan shark in New York. He lent money to bookmakers, thieves, brothel owners, fences, blackmailers, con artists, drug dealers, anyone who couldn't get a legitimate loan. He made sure that collateral would be available to repay any of their losses. If collateral was not available, the lender would have to buy insurance from Arnold's recently formed insurance company. In many cases, the insured would not be permitted to cancel their policies and so had to continue paying the premiums. Even without writing insurance policies, Rothstein charged exorbitant interest rates, sometimes as high as 48 percent. And what amazed those to whom he loaned money was his ability to keep the loans and the interest rates, and the names of his customers, in his head. As a backup, Rothstein kept the information in a small, black notebook. When customers did pay off their loans, Rothstein pulled out the notebook and wrote that so-and-so's loan had been repaid. Next to the name was the amount of the loan and the interest paid added to the total amount. And if someone reneged on a loan and was not insured, Rothstein would badger the person into repaying the loan. If that didn't work, he would call upon thugs in his employ who would collect the full amount due, but not before leaving behind a generous quantity of bruises as a warning not to stiff the Big Bankroll again.

In 1907, Rothstein had met showgirl and actress Carolyn Green (née, Greenwald), who had a small part in a play, *The Chorus Lady*. Standing 5-foot-4, she had an attractive figure, a pretty face, silken reddish-brown hair, and warm blue-gray eyes. Rothstein pursued her as if she were a gambling debt. Through guile and subterfuge that culminated in a forthright declaration of love, he finally won her consent to marriage. Of her husband, Carolyn stated, "He was quiet, well-spoken, with a nice smile. I had no idea he was a gambler, for he looked like a successful young businessman or lawyer."[8]

She later said,

> Arnold, at that time, was a slim young man with a white, sensitive face, brown, laughing eyes, and a gentle manner. I cannot emphasize too much this gentleness of manner, which was one of his most alluring characteristics.
>
> He was always extremely well-tailored and presented a most dapper appearance, noticeable even on Broadway, where it was the fashion to be well groomed.[9]

Carolyn, having accepted his proposal of marriage, was presented with a large diamond engagement ring. The diamond may have been gaudy, even ostentatious, but she wore it with pride and often brought her hand to her face just so others wouldn't miss it. Now that they had agreed to marry and set a date, Rothstein thought his parents should meet Carolyn. He said, "I've got to take you there. Believe me, it doesn't matter what they say or think. It doesn't make any sense, but that's the way it is. It's something I have to do."

He brought her to their home to be evaluated by Abe the Just. After customary introductions, Abe, Esther, Carolyn, and Arnold sat in silence in the living room. Arnold's mother, after a few moments, left the room without saying and word, and Abe subsequently cleared his throat. The sound of his father clearing his throat reminded Arnold of a teacher commanding attention from young students. His father asked if Carolyn was Jewish.

Carolyn responded, "My father is Jewish and my mother is Catholic. I have been brought up as a Catholic."

"But you will change your religion if you and Arnold should marry, will you not?" asked Abe.

She did not drop her eyes from his. "No, Mr. Rothstein." [10]

She added that she enjoyed attending church, found it a refuge from the hustle and bustle of theater life, and communion was an important part of her weekly ritual. Abe kindly wished her and Arnold well but said he could not approve of the marriage. It was the Law: A Jew should not marry out of the faith. He said he had now lost a son. On their way out of the house, Arnold told Carolyn it didn't matter. He had expected it but thought he should give his father a chance to be flexible. He assured her that they would still get married and that he had no intention of living his life by his father's rules, which he had found so stifling as a teenager.

On August 12, 1909, Arnold Rothstein and Carolyn Green were married. The marriage would be marked by Arnold imposing his own stifling rules on Carolyn. She was no longer permitted to pursue her acting career, and she had to remain at home at night while Arnold was about town wheeling and dealing.

At the news of his son's marriage, Abe Rothstein tore his garments and covered the mirrors in his house with a black shawl. He wrapped himself in a tallith prayer shawl and recited the Kaddish, the Jewish mourner's prayer for the dead. He told his family that he had not gained a daughter as he had hoped, but that he had lost a son. [11]

The marriage of Carolyn and Arnold Rothstein had taken place in Saratoga, New York, during the height of the racing season. Saratoga attracted the richest gamblers on the East Coast, men who bet tens of thousands of dollars on a single race. Many of them arrived in their private railway carriages. Arnold loved Saratoga and would open one of the town's most opulent gambling casinos; however, before he was able

to do that, he violated one of his own rules: He bet on races not knowing the outcomes. He suffered huge losses. Not quite shamefaced, he
asked Carolyn if he could pawn the large diamond engagement ring he
had given her. She agreed. A few days later, having not only recovered
the money he had lost, but also doubled that original sum, he redeemed
the ring and returned it to Carolyn. He told her it would never happen
again.

In fact, Arnold lavished considerable sums of money on his wife. He
gave her furs, jewels, and open-ended charge accounts at New York's
finest, most elegant stores. He made sure she never wanted for anything. But the only thing he wouldn't provide was his presence. He
spent his nights at his gambling operations, doing business at his reserved table in Lindy's restaurant on Broadway and pursuing those who
owed him money, no matter how small the amount. Rothstein did not
operate from an office, although the companies he controlled had sufficient space for him to carve out a large, well-appointed office befitting
Mr. Big. Instead, Lindy's became his unofficial place of business. It was
there that he met with gamblers, politicians, cops, Broadway producers,
assorted crooks, and journalists. Two journalists were numbered as
close friends. One was Herbert Bayard Swope, city editor of the *World*,
who was not only regarded as one of the most accomplished journalists
of the era, but also known as a devoted enemy of William Randolph
Hearst, the high priest of yellow journalism. Swope had served as Rothstein's best man at his wedding in Saratoga. The other good friend was
celebrated journalist and author Damon Runyon, who was so enthralled
by Rothstein's ability to control the world of gambling that he invented
the character of Nathan Detroit, based on his good friend, and who is a
primary figure in the musical *Guys and Dolls*.

The world Arnold Rothstein inhabited (and to some extent created)
from his table at Lindy's completely and utterly absorbed him. His
home life with Carolyn brought little romance and even less sexual
activity. According to Katcher, "No matter what else she was to him, she
was never completely a wife. Never completely a woman of flesh and
blood. She was an idealization, a statue. The conflict took its toll on him.
Nearly always it made him psychically impotent."[12]

The marriage rapidly iced over in the dark winter of their discontent,
and although the marriage continued until Rothstein's death by bullet
wound, the couple agreed to live apart. Rothstein lived in a luxurious

suite of rooms in a hotel he owned, while Carolyn resided in a fancy Fifth Avenue apartment. Rothstein paid the rent; paid for a full retinue of servants; and paid for Carolyn's expenses, including her annual cruises to Europe, where she satisfied her sexual longings with her lover. Although Carolyn referred to herself as an actress, the closest she got to the stage was to sit in the third row, center of the Broadway shows she frequently attended. Following Rothstein's death, she married her European lover. He was more than 20 years her junior, and when she no longer lavished financial largess on him, the marriage crumbled.

Rothstein, too, did not abstain from having affairs. He had an ongoing affair with Bobbie Winthrop, a former showgirl, who committed suicide in 1927. The other woman with whom he had a long-term relationship was a sometime actress and showgirl, Inez Norton. Arnold loved her and left her a sizeable portion of his estate in his last will. The litigation about Arnold's bequests went on for years after his death. But following Arnold's death and assured that money from his estate was forthcoming, Inez decamped for Hollywood to pursue a career as an actress. The career was stillborn. Inez did enjoy success seducing wealthy benefactors who found her sexual allure irresistible. She seduced a young Chicago banking heir into proposing marriage, but when his father learned of the prospective union, he squashed their engagement. Inez merely pursued other likely targets.

Showgirls and minor actresses had always been part of Rothstein's arsenal for attracting the world of suckers. Many of those women, whose theatrical careers were short-lived and tenuous, supplemented their incomes by steering wealthy, naïve gamblers into the Rothstein den of gambling. If particularly attracted to one of the steerers, he would invite one of them into his bedroom. For Rothstein, the actresses and showgirls were commissioned sales agents who could also provide ersatz affection or genuine sexual gratification when and if necessary.

Other than beautiful showgirls, the only other creatures that absorbed Rothstein's attention were thoroughbred racing horses. Since racing was the sport of kings and Rothstein thought of himself (to use the title of Nick Tosches's book about Arnold Rothstein) as the "King of the Jews," he wanted to be considered a great racing magnate. Rothstein wanted to be treated in the media like all the millionaire sportsmen who owned stables and raced their mounts on the country's premier tracks. He wanted to be considered the king of racetrack gamblers and an owner of some of the best thoroughbreds in the country.

He measured himself against the fabulously wealthy August Belmont Jr. Rothstein and Belmont each had Jewish fathers. While Rothstein neither denied nor hid his Jewish roots, Belmont pretended to be as much a WASP as those who had landed at Plymouth Rock. Instead of being the son of a Jewish father, Belmont preferred that the world know that he was the grandchild of his maternal grandfather, legendary Commodore Perry. Belmont raised and raced some of the most outstanding thoroughbreds of the time. He was president of the exclusive Jockey Club. He disliked Rothstein and his world of fixed races, corrupt jockeys, and drugged horses. He thought of him as a vulgar parvenu, a sneaky Broadway character whose means of making money descended to the sordid world of fixed races, corrupt jockeys, drugged horses. Belmont once confronted Arnold at the racetrack and stated, "You know what people are saying, Arnold. And what they're thinking. Half the country believes you were the man who fixed the World Series."[13] Thereafter, whenever the two met, their mutual antipathy was palpable.

Belmont felt so strongly about Rothstein that he attempted to have him banned from the Belmont Park Racetrack, home of the famous Belmont Stakes. Rothstein threatened a lawsuit. Before their respective lawyers could square off in court, the two antagonists reached a compromise: Mr. Rothstein could attend races on weekends and holidays only. Weekdays were reserved for the haute monde, the ruling class of racing; however, on one weekday, Belmont was surprised and angered to see Rothstein at the Belmont racetrack. According to David Pietrusza, Belmont strode over to Rothstein, accused him of not keeping his part of the bargain, and demanded to know why he was in attendance on a weekday. Rothstein smiled and responded that it was a holiday.

"What holiday?" demanded Belmont.

"You should know," said Rothstein. "It's the Jewish holiday of Rosh Hashanah."

Belmont angrily stammered an inaudible response and strode away. Rothstein called out Happy New Year, but Belmont, grimacing, did not turn around to respond.

Rothstein continued to visit the track and decided that he would buy his own stable and have his horses compete against Belmont's and those owned by other millionaires. He named his stable Redstone, a literal translation of Rothstein. As the owner of a stable of racehorses, he was privy to inside information and also could determine which horses were likely winners. To affect the outcome of a race, he could tell his jockeys to hold back his own horses while he bet on others. Or he could pay off other owners' jockeys to hold their horses back. He did it by not only bribing jockeys, but also drugging horses that were favorites to win. In some cases, when neither bribery nor drugs were the means to ensure a favorable and profitable outcome, Rothstein would resort to other methods. One of those methods was known as sponging: A sponge was inserted into each of a horse's nostrils, limiting the horse's capacity to breathe. With insufficient oxygen, the horse could not gallop at a fast enough pace to win a race. At the end of such a race, the horse's jockey would quickly and surreptitiously remove the sponges from the horse's nostrils.

In the years to come, Rothstein would win enormous amounts at racetracks. On one occasion, he collected more than $1,350,000. Knowing that he only bet on sure things, it was suspected by bookies that Rothstein had fixed that and other races. To confuse the bookies, throw them off the scent, and maintain odds in his favor, he would ostensibly bet against himself. He would make sure such bets were widely reported, while his larger bets on a sure thing were quietly placed with a wide range of bookies, so as not to alert them that a race was fixed and that once again, he was betting on a sure thing. Even without winning more than a million dollars on a race, Rothstein was happy to walk away with sums that ranged from $100,000 to $800,000.

In short order, he developed a reputation as not only New York's premier gambler, but also the shrewdest, most savvy gambler in the United States. People from news dealers and shoeshine boys to bank presidents and CEOs wanted to know what the Big Bankroll was betting on. He never let them know. If word had leaked out that Rothstein had bet on something, the hordes of others who would have followed in his footsteps would have turned the odds upside down and Rothstein would have been denied a big payday. His bets were executed with as much secrecy as possible; however, he was not above having his minions issue false rumors about whom he had bet on just so he could drive up the odds in his favor. People often spoke in whispers about A. R.'s bets, thinking they had rare inside information.

As Rothstein's wealth and influence grew, he attracted the talents of young and up-and-coming racketeers, hungry young men who wanted to model themselves on the Big Brain, the Big Bankroll, the Man to See, the Fixer. The three most promising of these young hoods were Francesco Castiglia, better known as Frank Costello and, years later, the Prime Minister of the Underworld; Maier Suchowljansky, better known as Meyer Lansky; and Salvatore Lucania, better known as Lucky Luciano. All three had been friends since their teenage years, and all three would come to control organized crime in the United States until their deaths: Costello in 1973, Lansky in 1983, and Luciano in 1962. Rothstein tutored his protégés on every aspect of successful criminality and taught them how to dress as conservative businessmen, how to speak, how to hold their knives and forks, the gentlemanly way to pull out a chair for a woman, and the proper etiquette for every occasion. Rothstein was their finishing school.

He had an organizational mind, and he taught his protégés how to organize crime and control it in the United States. As such, today he is known as the father of organized crime in the twentieth century and beyond. He could have been a graduate school professor at Harvard Business School, for his knowledge was profound and far-reaching. He taught his protégés that there was no benefit in multiple gangs warring with one another. He delivered lectures on how the world that employed the gangs of New York, Monk Eastman's gang, the Hudson Dusters, the Plug Uglies, were all destined for self-destruction. Modern gangs, by contrast, could each be profitable if they neatly divided their territories, settled disputes through a board of directors, and controlled the prices of contraband so one gang would not be underselling another. While price fixing is against the law, organized criminals operated in a world where everything they controlled was fixed. They combined the ingredients of oligarchy, plutocracy, and totalitarianism, and produced a style of governance that brooked no protests, no deviation by its members from the imposed rules.

The ultimate sanction was, of course, death. And murder, even among bosses, would only be necessary if they refused to settle their differences through diplomacy. Rothstein instructed them that if they acted in concert like large corporations, complementing and supplementing one another's activities, their profits would be enormous and not attract the prying eyes of the law. He predicted that they would generate profits as large or larger than those of America's largest corporations. It was during his heyday, decades later, that Meyer Lansky was heard bragging to a cohort on an FBI wiretap that they were bigger than U.S. Steel. Through Rothstein's leadership his protégés would control bootlegging; drugs; gambling; loan sharking; prostitution; labor unions; construction; the garment industry; trucking; and numerous banks, brokerages, and insurance companies—and, of course, many politicians. Rothstein passed along the lessons of his experiences with Big Tim Sullivan. Having judges and politicians on one's payroll would ensure a certain amount of safety.

While he is regarded as the father of organized crime and was known as the country's most successful gambler, Rothstein is even better known in history as the man who supposedly fixed the 1919 World Series. That event seemed to spearhead the fixing of many other sporting events, including the easiest of all to fix: professional boxing.

The story of the fixing of the 1919 World Series is complicated by many contradictory pieces. Did Arnold actually fix the series outcome, or did he benefit from knowing that others had fixed the outcome? There are numerous threads to the story, but most experts agree that he had knowledge of the fix and, in some ways, contributed to it. Did players on the Chicago White Sox approach gamblers about fixing the series? Did the gamblers then seek out Arnold Rothstein and his big bankroll to put up the $100,000, a number of players demanded?

Eddie Cicotte, the White Sox's premier pitcher, sought out Joseph "Sport" Sullivan, Boston's best-known professional gambler. Cicotte proposed that Sport pay the team members $100,000, $10,000 for each of the 10 players he would enlist to the throw the Series. Sport agreed but said he didn't have $100,000. He informed Cicotte that the only gambler who could come up with that amount of money was Arnold Rothstein. Chick Gandil, the White Sox's first baseman, conspired with Cicotte to enlist key players in their scheme to fix the Series. Players were angry that team owner Charles Comiskey was underpaying them. The six additional players who went along with the plan were outfielder Shoeless Joe Jackson, third baseman Buck Weaver, outfielder Happy Felsch, shortstop Swede Risberg, pitcher Claude Williams, and utility infielder Fred McMullin. Although there were eight conspirators, Cicotte and Gandil still demanded a payment of $100,000 before the Series was to begin. Cicotte also asked Sleepy Bill Burns, who was a former baseball pitcher and wildcat oil speculator, to put up some of the $100,000. Burns agreed that the conspirators could make a great deal of money from fixing the Series, but he, too, was low on cash. Burns, like Sport Sullivan, thought Rothstein should be asked for the money. Thinking that having another gambler in on the fix would attract Rothstein's interest, Burns asked Bill Maharg, a retired boxer, to participate. Maharg was as enthusiastic as the others, and he agreed that they should ask Rothstein for the necessary funding. As a former boxer, Maharg knew Rothstein's sometime bodyguard and friend, Abe Attell, who had been the world featherweight boxing champion from 1906 to 1912.

Maharg and Burns met with Rothstein at his hotel in New York. They outlined their proposal and told Rothstein that eight players had agreed to throw the World Series, if they were paid $100,000 on the morning of the first game. Rothstein said he wasn't interested. In fact, he made a big public display of announcing that he would not participate in such an unholy, unsportsman-like undertaking. He told the two men to leave. A few days later, Attell informed the duo that Rothstein had changed his mind and was now on board.

The three gamblers met in Cincinnati at the Sinton Hotel, where Attell was working with about 25 other gamblers, each taking bets that Cincinnati would lose the first game. When Burns and Maharg asked Attell for the $100,000 for the players, Attell said the money was all out on bets and so could not be distributed to the players. Instead, he said the players would get $20,000 after each game that they lost to the Cincinnati Reds. When that offer was reported to Cicotte and Gandil, they agreed to accept it.

Not trusting the intelligence of Burns and Maharg to manage the fix, Rothstein sent Sport Sullivan and another gambler, Nat Evans, to oversee events in Cincinnati. Rothstein gave Evans $80,000. Of that sum, Evans kept $40,000 for betting and gave the balance to Sport, who kept $30,000 for his own betting. Cicotte, who was scheduled to be the starting pitcher for the White Sox, had refused to participate in the scheme if he didn't receive his share (i.e., $10,000) before the first game. Evans handed over the money, 10 one-thousand dollar bills in an envelope. None of the other players received anything. After the first game, Attell promised Burns and Maharg that the players would get some money after the second game: It was being wired directly from A.

R. Maharg and Burns insisted that the players would not go along with the plot, if they weren't paid. Attell gave them another $10,000. When the two gamblers said that was not enough money to satisfy the players, they were told that was it. The players would not see any more money until the Series was over. Attell then insisted that the players should win the third game so that the odds would not be so lopsidedly in favor of Cincinnati. Gandil kept the $10,000 for himself, and told the duo that, rather than winning the third game, the Sox would lose it to pay back Attell for stiffing them. The duo bet $12,000, all the money they had, on Cincinnati to win. However, the Sox won the game, and so Burns and Maharg, reduced to borrowing money for their train fare, went home broke, disillusioned, and disgusted. They had been gambling out of their league.

Sport Sullivan became worried that the Sox would win the fifth game, thus endangering the gamblers' best laid plans for a large payday. He arranged for $20,000 to be delivered to Gandil, who distributed the money: $5000 to each of four players: Shoeless Joe, Happy Felsch, Rosberg, and Williams. Neither Weaver nor McMullin received anything.

The conspirators expected another payoff, but since not receiving anything, they won the sixth and seventh games, sending the remaining gamblers into a whirlpool of sweat-soaked anxiety.

Knowing that the promise of more money rang hollow with the players, Rothstein and Sport Sullivan decided it was time to enforce their instructions upon the players. For $500, they retained the services of a Chicago hood, a short stocky man who wore a black bowler hat as solidly as a London banker. In his subdued gray suit, he indeed looked like a banker. All he needed was a black rolled umbrella; instead, he carried a snub-nosed .38. On the evening before game six, the hood approached the pitcher, Lefty Williams, who was scheduled to pitch the next day. In a low, snarling voice, the hood told Williams that he better give up a bushel of runs in the first inning. If not, he would be a dead man, and so would his wife. The next day, Williams sent pitches from the mound to home plate that were like kissed invitations: Please hit these out of the park. Williams gave up five runs in the first inning, and the Reds won the game 10 to 5.

Disenchanted bookies paid Rothstein and his minions millions of dollars. As a gambler par excellent, Rothstein's reputation soared. He was the "Big Fixer," the "Brain," the "Big Bankroll," the man to whom all small-time gamblers would have to pay obeisance.

As news of the fix gained currency in the media, Abe Attell blamed the fix on Rothstein, who claimed it was all Attell's idea. In his excellent biography of Arnold Rothstein, David Pietrusza quotes Attell. To wit: "You can say that the story placing the responsibility upon me for passing the $100,000 to the White Sox is a lie. It looks to me that Rothstein is behind the stories, and I am surprised at this, because I have been a good friend of Rothstein.

"He is simply trying to pass the buck to me. It won't go. I have retained a lawyer to take care of my interests, and in a day or two I will tell what I know about this thing in a story that will shoot the lid sky high."[14]

Rothstein's usual attorney, the brilliant William Fallon, was retained to defend Attell and Sport Sullivan. While doing so, he claimed he was not working for Rothstein. A number of reporters and bookies winked at that claim.

Following Rothstein's exculpation, he issued a statement that included the following:

> The whole thing started when Attell and some other cheap gamblers decided to frame the Series and make a killing. The world knows I was asked in on the deal, and my friends know how I turned it down flat. I don't doubt that Attell used my name to put it over. That's been done by smarter men than Abe. But I wasn't in on it, wouldn't have gone into it under any circumstances, and didn't bet a cent on the Series after I found out what was underway. My idea was that however things turned out, it would be a crooked Series anyway and that only a sucker would bet on it.[15]

That statement, no doubt, caused snickers and smirks all along Broadway. No wonder that Daman Runyon based Nathan Detroit on Rothstein. He was too good of a character not to become a fictional hero of *Guy and Dolls*. Rothstein was perceived as the premier gambler of the world.

While Rothstein, Attell, and Sport Sullivan walked away from the Series with money in the bank and no dark legal clouds hanging over their heads, the eight Sox players were not so fortunate. They had each signed a confession about their wrong doing, but during their criminal trial, the confessions vanished. No one knew how or when. But there was talk that Rothstein had paid to make the confessions disappear. The eight players were as free as birds flying out of a cage. Their glee, however, was short-lived, for the new baseball commissioner, Kenesaw Mountain Landis, banned them from professional baseball for the rest of their lives, their ghosts appearing only in *Field of Dreams.*

Rothstein may not have bet on baseball again. Lining up eight players was almost as difficult as corralling a herd of cats. It was difficult and expensive. The expense was not only in fixing the games, but also paying legal expenses after the Series, as well as bribes to politicians, prosecutors, and judges. In boxing, by contrast, all one had to do was bribe one fighter or maybe two judges. Such an easy alternative to the 1919 World Series appealed to Rothstein.

He and his fellow gamblers bet on various boxers and were only rarely fooled into betting on a loser. Rothstein's biggest opportunity came his way when Jack Dempsey, the "Manassa Mauler," was scheduled to fight former U.S. Marine Gene Tunney. The odds favored Dempsey, who was one of the hardest-hitting heavyweight champs of the twentieth century, or as Roger Kahn referred to him, a "flame of pure fire." Just before the fight, Dempsey was suffering from food poisoning, and so he was unable to give his all in the ring. Anyone who bet on Tunney was sure to clean up. The bookies, promoters, and even the fans all thought Dempsey would enjoy an easy win. He was stronger and more aggressive that Tunney. He had battered lesser opponents into bloody submission. His punches were more powerful than anything Tunney could throw. So, when Tunney won the bout by a unanimous decision, observers were shocked. Not Rothstein: He won $500,000 on the fight. Reporters noted that Rothstein and Attell had been milling around, talking with Tunney's manager. As David Pietrusza writes, "We also knew that Abe Attell and Arnold Rothstein were on the scene, among the handful of observers predicting a Tunney victory. A. R., prominent at ringside, won a fortune on the long shot, Tunney. Attell was everywhere."[16]

Rothstein continued to clean up on his gambling venture until 1928. Following a poker game at the Park Central Hotel in Manhattan, in which he reportedly lost more than $300,000, Rothstein was shot by fellow gambler George McManus. Rothstein, believing he had been cheated, refused to pay. For years, he had been known as someone who was either slow to pay his debts or not pay at all. Anger toward Roth-stein was boiling, and word on Broadway was that one night, an angry winner would shoot the belligerent welcher. With a bullet in his gut, Rothstein stumbled out of the hotel, asked for a taxi, and died shortly thereafter. The Roaring Twenties would come to an end the following year, as the stock market crashed. But for one Rothstein associate, Abe Attell, little had changed. He was still cutting deals, fixing fights, and winning large sums from artificially lopsided odds on important boxing matches. The world of boxing had beckoned Attell since boyhood, first as a pugilist, then as a gambler, and he would play a part in the sport for the next four decades. Whenever there was a championship fight to fix, Abe Attell managed to be present. No one could keep him away.

2

FROM BOXER TO BAGMAN TO GAMBLER

The story of Abe Attell is at times a bright red thread and at other times a nearly translucent one that runs through the many-colored fabric of the history of much of twentieth-century boxing. He was a champion boxer, a bagman and enforcer for Arnold Rothstein, and a gambler who had a thumb on the scales of many fixed fights.

Although Abe Attell is primarily remembered as the man who helped Arnold Rothstein fix the 1919 World Series, he had previously been the world featherweight boxing champion from 1906 to 1912. He and Benny Leonard were the prototypes for hundreds of Jewish boxers who echoed the duos' ring successes. But unlike Leonard, Attell was deeply involved in gambling. And like Arnold Rothstein, Attell learned to bet only on sure things.

Any history of boxing in the United States in the twentieth century would have to shadow the career of Abe Attell, for his presence unlocks the secret of many fixed fights. At ringside, in boxing gyms, at training camps, Abe Attell was a presence that indicated something was not on the level. Follow Attell, learn what he was betting on, and do the same. Unless he was placing deceptive bets to change the odds on a fight, he was betting to win. If one bet as Abe did, chances are one would have made a handsome profit.

From his early days of poverty through his brutal ascent to the pinnacle of the boxing establishment and becoming one of boxing's leading fixers, Abe Attell's journey was a long road that started in dire poverty not far from the city dump in San Francisco and ended among New York's sporting millionaires.

Young Attell, like many poor boys, had been motivated by an intense desire to escape poverty while earning the respect of those who had been contemptuous of the Attell family's poverty and mean existence. The humiliations of poverty started within a few years of Abe's birth in 1883. His father died, leaving a wife and 12 children to scrounge for crumbs of nourishment and finance. The widow Attell was reduced to taking in her neighbors' laundry and earning a pittance that left her hands red and raw. Laundry was done by hand, using a scrub board and harsh detergents. She would work day after day, hour after hour, as long as there was dirty laundry in her hands. Some garments, after being scrubbed in a portable washtub, were wrung through a pair of mechanical rubber rollers that were operated with a hand crank; other larger garments, like sheets and towels, were pinned to a clothesline and dried by the sun. Young Abe loved his mother and honored her hard work, and he hated the people for whom his mother labored. One can imagine his resentment that his mother had to clean the garments of others while she could barely afford to clothe her own children. Why should his mother, who so loved and protected and fed her brood, have to suffer the indignities that befell her? Abe needed an outlet for his boiling anger and his fierce desire to get even with a world that ignored the plight of such poverty-stricken families as his own. His hatred and fierce anger found an outlet through a pair of ferocious, clenched fists.

According to a story that Attell told to interviewer Monte Cox and related in *Max Baer and Barney Ross: Jewish Heroes of Boxing*, one summer afternoon Abe spotted a neighborhood boy using a dirty tree branch to beat the sheets that his mother had just hung up to dry. The branch was leaving dirty streaks on the clean sheets. Volcanic rage erupted in Abe, and that rage spewed forth into an uncontrollable attack. He tackled the offender with burning ferocity. His small, tightly clenched fists pounded the face of his opponent, drawing blood and raising bruises. The two boys rolled around on the dirt, trading blows, gouging, kicking, biting, and cursing. While the other boy yelled each time Abe landed a blow, Abe was impervious to pain. The more he fought, the hotter his anger. He could not stop, until his mother dragged him away from his beaten opponent. Once inside their shabby shack of a home, she attempted to wash away the dirt and cuts on Abe's face, but he broke free and ran outside to deliver more blows to his shocked, defeated, and sorry opponent. Abe's mother again dragged him inside, this time bolting the door and not letting him escape again. Abe was furious that his mother would have to wash those sheets again.

Life was brutally unfair to his mother, his siblings, and Abe himself; he was determined to exact a price for their unfortunate fate, even if it would ultimately mean cheating those who had been born comfortable and secure. That fight at the laundry line was the beginning of an almost inexhaustible capacity to not only inflict punishment, but also withstand any punishment meted out to him. Fighting would be his modus operandi for escaping the confines and humiliations of poverty. He would begin by fighting on the streets of San Francisco and then in boxing rings throughout the country. As a boxer with impressive skills, he would even the score and gain victories that would bring him and his mother thousands of dollars.

But before he could become a professional fighter, Abe led a gang of juvenile delinquents through the streets of San Francisco. They were like a pack of wolves, looking for likely targets to mug. When not mugging others, they would go into battle like warriors against other young gangs. Abe loved it. For him it was warfare as sport. He didn't care if he came home bruised and battered, although the sight of him left his mother distraught. Abe's nose was broken so often that it looked like a caricature of a nose.

While running with a gang offered plenty of excitement, Abe needed to earn money for himself and his mother and siblings. He became a newsboy, hawking papers from the busiest corner in downtown San Francisco. It was a prized corner, and every newsboy in the city wanted to own it. Abe was not about to part with his franchise. Whenever another newsboy attempted to take over Abe's territory, Abe fought the boy as if his life depended on it. He never once lost a battle for the corner. As champion of his corner, he developed a reputation as a tough, mean kid who would fight anyone, regardless of size, just so he could maintain ownership of his territory. Newsboys in general knew not to mess with the kid they called the "Little Hebrew." It was better to have a less-profitable corner than a bloody, broken nose.

However, there was one boy, not a newsboy, who was determined to steal Abe's reputation as the toughest kid in the neighborhood. His would-be opponent went by the name of "Kid Lennett." He was a proficient boxer, regularly testing his skills and winning bouts. In particular, he liked to box at the Beer Garden, a bar and boxing ring run by a former middleweight boxer named Alec Greggain. The Beer Garden was a popular hangout for boxing fans. Greggain served up beers and staged amateur boxing matches. A beer was one dollar, and a ringside seat for a boxing match was two dollars. Spilled beer and spilled blood often ran together.

Greggain, a talent scout for promising young pugilists, was always on the lookout for young boxers he could put in his ring, kids who would excite his customers and bring in the bucks. He offered boys 10 dollars if they could whip an opponent of the same age. But first he would test a boy to see if he had a naturally combative personality. He would walk the boy into the center of his boxing ring, turn his back on the boy, then suddenly whirl around, striking the boy with a heavy fist to the chin. The boy would, of course, collapse onto the ring's canvas. Upon regaining his senses, the boy would either flee from his mad attacker or strike back, ignoring Greggain's size and strength. Such a boy would be chosen for a three-, four-, or six-round fight. When it came to young Abe's test for combativeness, he not only sprung up from the canvas like a hot-headed jackrabbit, but also attacked Greggain with such ferocity that he had to be pulled off, still swinging his small, rock-hard fists and spewing out a stream of curses. Greggain was impressed with the tough little street urchin who refused to back off. While Abe was still issuing a litany of curses, Greggain offered the kid a shot at beating the supposedly unbeatable Kid Lennett. Abe became momentarily quiet, even pensive. Then he grinned with excitement. Now he had the opportunity to prove he was tougher than Kid Lennett—not only tougher, but also on the way to being $10 richer than he was when he first entered the Beer Garden.

Greggain warned Abe that the Kid had won his last 10 bouts. Abe didn't care. He said he would knock the Kid's block off. Greggain said he would give Abe $10 if he won and $15 if he knocked out the Kid.

Excited at the prospect of winning $15, Abe headed home, clenching and unclenching his fists. When Abe told his mother he was scheduled to fight at the Beer Garden, she insisted that he call it off. She didn't want her son to be beaten to a pulp. Abe said not to worry. Furthermore, he would win $15, which meant his mother wouldn't have to take in laundry for two weeks. She could relax, go for walks along the water, and sit and watch the fishing boats. She said nothing. She knew Abe was determined and nothing she could say would dissuade him.

Abe prepared for the fight by shadowboxing in the yard behind his home. He skipped rope, using an old clothesline. He filled an old burlap bag with mud, hung it from a tree branch, and, with his hands bandaged, used it as a heavy bag. He ran up and down the hills of San Francisco. He was prepared, he was ready.

The day of the fight came, and Abe was raring to go. He entered the ring, fists raised in premature triumph, then briefly shadowboxed in his corner. The referee called the boys to the center of the ring, gave them their perfunctory instructions, then sent them back to their corners. The bell rang, and the boys advanced. Initially, Abe kept out of range of the Kid, avoiding his swings, sizing him up, looking for weaknesses and strengths. Having done so, he closed in and delivered a left to the Kid's head, and a right to his chin, and the kid flopped on the canvas. The Kid had to be dragged back to his corner. Water was splashed on his face, and his shoulders were vigorously rubbed. He looked stunned, dumbfounded; what had happened?

The Kid, slightly subdued, came out of his corner as the bell sounded for round two. His confidence seemed to return, and he launched a vicious, wild swinging attack. His determination, however, was interrupted by a sharp uppercut from Abe that sent the Kid to the canvas for the second time. The Kid no longer flopped and gasped: He just lay there, unconscious, his tough-guy reputation shrunk, if not erased.

For Abe, that first knockout was a signpost pointing to a career in the ring. Years later, he would conclude his career as one of the 10 best featherweight champions of the twentieth century. First, he would have to prove himself against far more accomplished fighters than Kid Lennett. Abe would develop a reputation as an unbeatable young amateur by winning one fight after another at the Beer Garden. He always tried for a knockout, for he wanted that $15 prize money. From those knockouts, Abe had earned a thousand dollars, after only one year. He turned over the money to his mother, who wept at what her son had done for her.

While Abe was a hero for those who bet at the Beer Garden, he was also a disappointment to them, for his skills made him unbeatable.

Everyone only wanted to bet on the Little Hebrew, but the odds so inordinately favored Abe that it was hardly worth betting on him. Bet $10 on him and you would collect a dollar. So, the game shifted to betting on in which round Abe would knock out his opponent. There, the odds were more even, but it was rare for a fight to go into a third round. While Abe was sharpening his skills as a boxer, he was also learning the ins and outs of gambling, shifting odds, and fixing outcomes. He never agreed to lose a fight, but he would let a bookie know, for a price, the round in which he would knock out an opponent. Whether he ever paid off an opponent is unknown.

As successful as he was at the Beer Garden, Abe knew he was unskilled compared to professional boxers. Yet, he wanted to become a pro to earn the big bucks he knew champions commanded. Between boxing and gambling, he figured he could lift himself and his mother out of poverty. Abe told boxing interviewer Monte Cox that he had seen a "cartoon of some boxers in the *San Francisco Chronicle*," adding,

> I would like to have my picture in the paper someday, so I started boxing as an amateur; they were four rounds back then. I learned the fundamentals as an amateur, but I didn't really learn my trade until I was a pro. In the beginning I tried to knock everybody out and won my first five pro fights by knockouts. But, I decided I was getting hit way too much and decided to really learn to box.[1]

Having learned the fundamentals of professional boxing and sharpened his skills against numerous aspiring pros and several over-the-hill pugs, Abe agreed to fight the featherweight champion, George Dixon. The odds were decidedly in Dixon's favor, for no one expected young Abe to outpoint such a skillful pro. Not even Abe placed bets on himself. Yet, after 15 rounds, the judges declared the fight a draw. It was an amazing accomplishment for a rookie fighter against an admired champion. Abe knew he was on his way. He spent a year further honing his skills, becoming ever more talented, delivering fast combinations, and learning the art of not getting his face beaten to a bloody pulp. Abe readily understood that a good part of boxing was not only inflicting pain on one's opponent, but also avoiding being hit, for a lucky punch could easily send one to the darkened land of the unconscious. He didn't want to be considered another boxer's good luck charm. Furthermore, he didn't believe in luck. Boxing was hard work, and it required a lot of practice and testing oneself against others.

When Abe and Dixon met for a rematch in Denver, fans and bookies did not know what to expect. Would it be another draw? Would the tested champion finally prove his superiority and deliver a knockout blow to the young challenger? Or would the rookie prove he was truly a pro and ready to take the title from Dixon? The fight was long and brutal. Abe displayed the skills that would soon make him famous as a fighter who was determined to win every bout that came his way. After 15 rounds, Abe was declared the winner. He had outpointed the champ, who had to give up the crown to the tough young kid from San Francisco. Abe was 17 years old and grinned his toothy grin of jubilation and raised his narrowly muscled arms in triumph. He was determined to hold on to the title for the next 10 years, earning enough money to support himself and remove his mother from her life as a laundress. Although no longer doubtful of her son's career path, Abe's mother was not free of a sense of dread that her son would get hurt in the ring. Nevertheless, she attended many of his fights to not only reassure herself that her son would survive unhurt, but also to cheer him on. And if a fan of one of Abe's opponents cursed her son, she wacked him with an umbrella or a rolled-up newspaper. She was also pleased to receive the money Abe had won by betting on himself. He always bet a few dollars on his mother's behalf.

The Attell family finally had something that made them proud and enough money so that the widow Attell's work as a laundress had permanently ceased. The family's pride extended beyond the mother and migrated rapidly to two of Abe's brothers. In fact, so impressed were Monte and Caesar Attell by their brother's success that they also became boxers, although neither one scaled the same heights as Abe. The three Attell bothers became known as the "Fighting Attells," threesome siblings practicing the sweet science. From 1909 to 1910, Monte held the bantamweight championship title; Caesar, try as he did, was unable to garner a title for himself.

From 1906 to 1912, Abe fought against every opponent that was offered up to him. For his fans, the opponents were courageous and willing human sacrifices, for none could possibly emerge as a winner. On February 22, 1912, Abe finally lost the featherweight title to Johnny Kilbane, but he refused to hang up his gloves: They had been his means of success. He continued fighting until 1917, when he realized he no longer had the speed and timing necessary to avoid being hurt. He had fought 172 bouts and won 125 of them, 51 by knockout. By mid-century, boxing chroniclers and historians rated him as one of the top 10 featherweight champs of the twentieth century. Some even ranked him as the very best. For those who witnessed his feats in the ring, there was no one who compared to the Little Hebrew.

Now it was time for Abe to embark full-time on a new career. The conclusion of Abe's boxing career was the beginning of his career as a professional gambler, and the man who taught him the ropes outside of the ring was, of course, Arnold Rothstein.

Tom—a retired doctor who had been privy to inside information from his father, a professional gambler who worked for Frank Costello, one of Arnold Rothstein's protégés—gave the author a fascinating account of Abe Attell during a luncheon at an Italian restaurant in the Bronx. Tom enjoyed relating stories of his youth, when he had been an avid boxing fan. Since Tom's father controlled much of the gambling in New York and Abe Attell was a professional gambler, it was natural that they both knew and did business with one another. While savoring a plate of pasta vongole and a glass of red wine, Tom relayed his story about Abe Attell:

> Abe was a great friend of my dad, and I got to know him when I was growing up. He stood about 5-foot-4, but he was an intimidating little guy. According to my dad, Abe would stand up to guys well over six feet: which is why he was able to intimidate the players on the Chicago White Sox. Abe could set his face with that cold, hard, unblinking gangster stare that could make someone feel as if he were about to be wacked. It was natural for Arnold Rothstein to use Abe to carry out his plans with the White Sox.
>
> He didn't talk about it [Rothstein and the fix], but I asked and he finally told me that Abe became Rothstein's muscle for intimidating the Chicago White Sox players into throwing the World Series. The players were paid off, but not all of them, just the key players, and they didn't get all of the money they had been promised. You know, Abe was indicted for helping to fix the game. At trial, this guy showed a lot of chutzpah. He convinced the jurors that he was the wrong Abe Attell. It was another guy with the same name, and the jury bought it. Amazing!

Tom believed boxing and gambling were in Abe's blood. He lived and breathed both. Tom continued,

> During the 1920s and 30s, he managed a fighter named Marty Goldman, who fought in two divisions: welterweight and lightweight. Goldman was a Brooklyn guy and a pretty good fighter; he had a lot of wins by knockouts. I heard that Goldman was owned by Damon Runyon and was popular with two of the writer's friends, the columnists Ed Sullivan and Walter Winchell. Incidentally, those two guys hated each other. I used to see him fight in the Garden and at Yankee Stadium. With the columnists cheering him in print, he was a pretty big draw. Everybody connected with him made out very well.
>
> My dad went to Abe's wedding. It was ironic: After all his fights with Irish kids [newsboys] who didn't like Jews back in the old days in San Francisco, Abe married an Irish woman named Mae O'Brien. His first marriage, I heard, didn't turn out well, but he and Mae were good together. They opened two bars and restaurants, one on the east side, the other on Broadway; both attracted a lot of fighters, fight fans, gamblers, athletes, sportswriters, and some Broadway hotshots. I used to see Abe and Mae when I went to the fights at Madison Square Garden. Abe was a friendly guy who couldn't stop talking. He should have had his own radio show. I once told him that, and he said his face was perfect for radio: banged up, scarred, and with a big broken nose. He was the kind of guy it was fun to be around.
>
> A lot of people turned up for his funeral in 1970. He was 86 or 87. Most fighters are gone long before they can reach that ripe old age. But, you know, he was one of the great ones, an example for many Jewish fighters who came after him. People who knew him, when asked, always smiled and spoke kindly of him. He left his friends with many pleasant memories. Of how many people can you say that? He was one of a kind.[2]

One thing Tom didn't mention or know about was that Abe had owned a successful shoe store, an odd business for a gambler to own. One can hardly imagine this hard-as-nails boxer/gambler fitting shoes onto the feet of women shoppers. And perhaps it didn't quite suit his self-image. Did mob guys laugh at the fierce Little Hebrew down on his knees, or sitting on a bench, pressing a shoe onto a woman's naked foot? As many observers thought, Abe's shoe business would not be long lived, and sure enough it mysteriously burnt to the ground. Abe was accused of arson so that he could pocket the insurance money; however, no one could ever prove that it was arson or that Abe had anything to do with it. There was talk that he paid off the insurance investigator. Regardless, Abe was glad to be rid of the shoe business. Bars and restaurants were more to his liking. He opened two: one on Broadway named for himself and the other on East 51st Street, named for his wife, Mae O'Brien. Both were regularly patronized by gamblers, fighters, fight promoters and managers, sportswriters, and sports publicists. In his Broadway establishment, he hung a pair of his old boxing gloves over the long mirror behind the bar. There were autographed photos of a number of champion boxers but—of course—no photos of gamblers.

After Arnold Rothstein and Frank Costello, Abe's closest associate was notorious gangster Owney Madden, who owned the heavyweight boxer, the towering 6-foot-7 Primo Carnera. Owney also owned several lesser-known pugs, guys who were human punching bags who would climb into rings and fight up-and-comers just so Owney could clean up with the bookies. With their flattened noses and cauliflower ears, they were guys who needed some savings before they retired from the sweet science.

But it was Primo Carnera who was Owney's golden goose, and Owney did not hire only over-the-hill pugs to fight his champ: He hired well-known and respected boxers, and paid them enough to make sure they would each take a dive. Among those who lost obviously fixed bouts were such notables as Jack Sharkey, Tommy Loughran, Ernie Schaaf, and King Levinsky.

Owney and Abe were determined to make Primo, the "Ambling Alp," as he was known, the world champion. They, like master gambler Arnold Rothstein, would only bet on fixed outcomes. Owney would give Primo just enough spending money to keep him happy but cheated him out of a fortune in earnings. Of course, that didn't satisfy Owney's greed: He also earned an additional fortune by betting large sums on his Primo to win.

To keep the scam on track and make the giant heavyweight look somewhat competent in the ring and perhaps convince skeptical fans that Primo was a genuine boxer, Abe was brought in to teach Primo the finer points of boxing: jabbing, ducking, sidestepping, throwing a right cross and an uppercut, and so forth. As a result, Primo began to throw punches that resembled those thrown by a real boxer. Yet, he remained an object of derision, and nothing Abe could do would erase that opinion. One only had to observe Primo pushing an opponent away from him when he should have been throwing lefts and rights.

It finally came to an end when Owney's thugs failed to succeed in threatening Max Baer to throw his title fight with Primo. Knowing it was time to get rid of a disappointing investment, Owney and his men discarded Primo as if he were nothing more than foul-smelling garbage.

Poor Primo: He refused to believe his fights had been fixed. He genuinely believed he had legitimately fought his way to the top of the roster of heavyweight boxers to win the world heavyweight championship. Such proclamations, as often happened, were met with either derisive laughter or smirks.

Primo ended his boxing career without a cent. Thanks to Max Baer, however, Primo had a second career as a professional wrestler and was paid enough money to retire in comfort.

Abe was involved in not only the sad, sordid career of Primo Carnera, but also gambling on every heavyweight, middleweight, and welterweight championship fight from the 1920s through the 1960s. No one knows how many boxing matches Abe had a hand in fixing. He became a ringside fixture, talking secretively with judges, referees, and promoters. His friends and associates throughout his life were gangsters, boxers, promoters, trainers, and managers: a fraternity that controlled boxing and fixed some of the most celebrated fights of the twentieth century. Abe's era was a time of great fighters: Benny Leonard, Jack Dempsey, Joe Louis, Max Baer, Barney Ross, Henry Armstrong, Sugar Ray Robinson, Jake LaMotta, Willie Pep, Carmen Basilio, Gene Fullmer, Muhammed Ali, Sonny Liston, and others. How many of their fights were fixed? No one knows. What is known, however, is that gamblers, promoters, boxers, managers, and trainers made out like bandits from the time of Arnold Rothstein right up through the time of Sonny Liston. And Abe Attell touched all of their careers. The millions of dollars they made were generally laundered into legitimate businesses so the IRS and FBI would not be able to gain proof of ill-gotten gains.

Boxing was a great wealth generator for those in control, and little Abe Attell could always be found at the center or on the periphery of the action but never on the outside of the circle. He had come a long way from the fierce, desperate newsboy on a San Francisco corner fighting for his livelihood and the rescue of his mother from a life of depressing poverty to being a member of the Ring Boxing Hall of Fame, the National Jewish Sports Hall of Fame, the International Jewish Sports Hall of Fame, the World Boxing Hall of Fame, the San Francisco Boxing Hall of Fame, and the International Boxing Hall of Fame. And if Mrs. Attell were still around, she would no doubt still whack anyone who disputed her son's extraordinary accomplishments. She honored her son as the hero who rescued the family from its crippling poverty until the day she died.

3

OWNEY MADDEN AND FIXING THE HEAVYWEIGHT CHAMPIONSHIP

It's no wonder that Abe Attell found his way to Owney Madden, for Owney was far more involved in boxing than Arnold Rothstein. For Rothstein, boxing was a minor subsidiary activity, just another outlet for his sure-thing gambling. It was not a primary undertaking.

Owney Madden, although a major player in the world of boxing, didn't start out as a corruptor of the pugilistic sport. Instead, he started out as a common hoodlum and killer. In fact, he was known as "The Killer," and that sobriquet was often inserted between his first and last names as if it were his true middle name.

Although regarded as an Irish American gangster, Owney was actually English, having been born in 1891, in Leeds, England. His poverty-stricken family moved from one poor neighborhood to another, either in the same city or in other cities, all of which offered anonymity from creditors to whom they owed money. The industrial cities in which the Maddens lived were depressing and offered few opportunities to rise out of poverty. Owney's father, Francis, was discouraged by his lack of economic opportunity and often drunk; he deserted his family, leaving Mrs. Madden to find ways of feeding and dressing herself and her children.

Desperate to improve her family's economic circumstances, while staying a few steps ahead of unpaid landlords and grocers, Owney's mother, Mary, decided the family should set sail for New York. She doubted the fables that she would find streets that had been paved with gold bricks, but anything was better than the mean existence the Madden family endured in bleak, rundown neighborhoods in their native country. Owney's father supported himself by committing petty thefts and often landed in jail. Prior to her solo departure to New York, Mary Madden told her children that their father had died and that she would send for them as soon as she could earn enough money. (This was a story often told years later by Owney Madden.) In her absence, she left her children with whatever money she had saved and hoped it would be enough for their needs until she was able to purchase tickets for their departure.

It was many years later that Owney learned from English arrest and prison records that his father survived until 1932. Francis neither saw nor heard from his offspring, and he made no attempt to contact them. More than an ocean separated them. One can assume Francis learned of his son's notorious reputation as one of New York's stone-cold killers and a premier bootlegger, for Owney's escapades, indictments, and trials were front-page tabloid news from the second decade of the twentieth century through the 1930s. Owney was considerably smarter, more devious, and cold-blooded than his father. He didn't follow in his father's footsteps: He created much larger ones that few men were able to match.

Mary Madden, saddened that she did not have enough money to fund the emigration of her children, set sail by herself for New York City in 1901; it was a rough passage on stormy North Atlantic seas, and she was glad to finally disembark down a runway onto streets paved with common cobblestones. She didn't have to find her own apartment, for her sister invited Mary to live with her. Mary settled into the Irish slum known as Hell's Kitchen, which in those days extended from 30th Street to 59th Street and from Eighth Avenue to the Hudson River. With no skills, she found work as a scrubwoman and spent many tedious hours either on her knees with a hard brush and a bucket of soapy water or standing at an angle as she pushed and pulled a mop.

The following year, having saved sufficient funds for the transportation of her children, Mary purchased tickets for Owney and Martin, her sons, and Mary, her daughter, to sail to New York. They booked steerage passage on the SS *Teutonic*, one of the recently built ships of the Star Ship Lines. The crossing was as rough as Mary's had been, and the three Madden children, confined to steerage like cattle, had to breathe in the putrid odors emanating from the vomit of sick passengers that sloshed around the floor of the lowest inhabited deck of the stormed-rocked ship. The Madden children eagerly awaited their escape into the fresh air of New York.

Eager for sunlight on their pale, pasty faces and dry land for their rubbery sea legs, the Madden kids arrived in Manhattan. According to Donald L. Miller in *Supreme City,*

> When the Maddens stepped off the streetcar that brought them to 10th Avenue, their new American home, they entered a place more dispiriting than the Liverpool slum they had fled. Identical brick tenements formed solid walls on both sides of the avenue for as far as the eye could see, and the streets and sidewalks were unspeakably filthy. Dead cats and bloated brown rats lay rotting in the gutters; the streets were littered with garbage and steaming piles of horse manure; and nearby were the freight yards of the New York Central Railroad, set in the midst of stock pens and fat rendering plants that gave off fumes "so intense at times to be almost suffocating."[1]

One may assume they were sorely disappointed, appalled, and disgusted by what they saw. Resentful resignation reigned, and the Maddens remained grim in the grime of their surroundings. They settled into a dark, dreary railroad apartment at the southernmost point of Hell's Kitchen at 352 10th Avenue.

Although English, the Maddens felt at home among the thousands of Irish immigrants of Hell's Kitchen, according to details in *The Gangs of New York* and *Paddy Whacked: The Untold Story of the American Irish Gangster.*[2] Their neighbors accepted them as just another poor immigrant family. There were also numerous German and Italian families there, so one English family simply added to the mix.

Poor immigrant neighborhoods have invariably been breeding grounds for ethnic gangs, and Hell's Kitchen was no different. It spawned some of the most violent gangs that terrorized New York neighborhoods, first the Gophers and then the Westies, in particular. And from Brownsville, Brooklyn, and the Lower East Side of Manhattan came gangs of Italian and Jewish gangsters whose notoriety is the subject of countless books and movies. While the Italian and Jewish gangs often blurred their ethnic differences (Murder, Inc., for example, comprised Italians and Jews), Hell's Kitchen was the stomping grounds for Irish gangsters right up through the demise of the notorious, wild Westies in the late 1980s. Since then, Hell's Kitchen has undergone extensive gentrification: Popular restaurants have replaced Irish bars, boutiques have replaced mom-and-pop stores, and tenements have been renovated into expensive co-ops and condominiums.

But when Owney Madden arrived in 1902, the neighborhood was a perfect incubator for boys and young men who believed crime could be a first-class ticket to a world of wealth, privilege, and power. The only other professions neighborhood young men gravitated toward were the priesthood and law enforcement, neither of which promised the power and wealth associated with top racketeers. Like most children of poor immigrants forced to live in grimy tenements, Owney disliked his neighborhood and the lack of legitimate upward economic mobility. Crime would be his means of escaping poverty. Years later, while a resident of Hot Springs, Arkansas, Owney told the following story:

> My mother, brother, and I didn't have a thing to eat in the house in New York City. Didn't know where the next dollar was going to come from. Mother was worried about how she was going to provide for us—about what we were going to do. I decided I was going to get money from somewhere, and I went out on the street . . . got myself a club . . . then waited in a darkened doorway until a certain individual came along. . . . As he passed the doorway, I hit him with that club and knocked him out. He had $500 on him. . . . That was the first crime I committed.[3]

Although only 11 years old, Owney joined a local gang of thugs known as the Gophers. He didn't have to be drafted, for he saw membership as an opportunity to enjoy the fruits of an expansive life his mother could not afford.

One night, he had entered a cold, dank, poorly lit basement where the Gophers were meeting. The boy was accepted and told that he was now part of a criminal enterprise to which he must pledge his loyalty. He enthusiastically embraced the opportunity to be a Gopher as other immigrants ambitiously embraced their roles as newly minted citizens. The Gophers were known for hatching their criminal plans in dank, cave-like basements, hence the name Gophers.

The Gophers comprised more than 500 members, making it one of the largest gangs in Manhattan. The gang specialized in burglaries, muggings, extortion, prostitution, murder-for-hire, and illegal gambling, among various other activities that opportunistically were available. One opportunity proved not only irresistible, but also highly profitable for the Gophers. It was the 11th Avenue railroad tracks and depots. When night fell and railroad workers had departed for their homes, leaving only a pair of easily intimidated guards, the Gophers would descend like wild and hungry packs of wolves and break into freight cars and steal whatever they could carry off. They saw themselves as modern-day train robbers, descendants of Jesse James and Cole Younger. They fenced their stolen merchandise and celebrated their affluence with gang girls and booze in local clubs.

Their days as railroad thieves, however, were numbered: The owners, unwilling to accept further losses, decided to hire squadrons of former cops, many of whom had been victimized by Gophers while still in uniform. Eager to get even, splitting heads and shooting their former antagonists, the ex-cops took to their new jobs like lions hunting small game. Many Gophers were stomped, clubbed, blackjacked, pummeled with brass knuckles, and shot. Those unable to escape to their basement hideouts were the wounded and unconscious; they were hauled to a local precinct, booked, indicted, tried, and sent to prison. Owney Madden was one of those who escaped to angry safety.

Herbert Asbury, in his definitive study *The Gangs of New York*, writes, "Within a few months the new [police] force had devastated Hell's Kitchen with blackjacks, and thereafter the Gophers avoided railroad property as they would a plague. To this day a New York Central watchman is regarded as the natural enemy of the Hell's Kitchen hoodlum."[4]

The Gopher gang reassembled and worked other illegal venues, and regardless of what crimes they committed, Owney felt he was in his element. For him, his fellow Gophers constituted not only a fraternity of criminals, but also his street-smart professors, each with an expertise in crime. And Owney was a quick learner. The Gophers loved crime the way other kids love baseball, football, or basketball. Criminal activity excited them and was the glue that bonded them and made them into an often unbeatable and terrifying force. Even other gangs tried to stay clear of the Gophers.

Beat someone, rob him, steal the contents of a car or store, run off with the loot. Owney learned the necessary skills for robbing and fighting in the Gophers. He was a fearless little thug, a vicious junkyard dog, who was willing to throw himself into any altercation. His special weapon was a metal pipe wrapped in newspaper; it proved effective for cracking skulls and breaking knees and elbows. At age 12, he had killed his first antagonist and was proud of his accomplishment, according to Asbury in *The Gangs of New York*. Although small and wiry, and determined as a terrier going after a rat, he was looked upon as a big little man, fearless and enthusiastic in any gang rumble; he would absorb any punishment and deliver ferocious blows that could easily kill or maim whomever he attacked. His ferocity and fearlessness garnered him the admiration of his fellow gang members and respect from opposing gangs. Killing, robbing, fighting, looting, and threatening were Owney's tried-and-true methods for getting what he wanted. By the time he was 18, he had killed five members of rival gangs. He was an unwounded warrior on his way to becoming a general leading his troops into battle. And when his ascension to a leadership position finally happened, it was approved by everyone. The notches on his reputation had ultimately made him a leader without challengers. While the Gophers had many talented thieves and remorseless killers, none had the prestige of Owney. And from 1910 onward, he would indeed be known as Owney "The Killer" Madden.

A short-lived challenge did occur sometime later when Owney was laid up in a hospital, recovering from multiple bullet wounds from a gang fight. But the challenge was resolved gangland style, and Owney returned to his throne, his position as leader secure. The usurper disappeared, his very name forgotten.

The Gopher gang was like a corporation for Owney, its chief executive. It paid him a salary, as well as tributes and dividends. He was earning hundreds of dollars a day from the gang's various illicit activities, plus he earned an additional $200 a day from his protection racket, which relied on forcing local shop owners and peddlers to pay insurance premiums that guaranteed their businesses would not be firebombed. Money seemed to flow to Owney; according to police and newspaper reports, Owney acted like a man who owned Hell's Kitchen. He was no longer a poor waif, worried about getting enough food. He and his family would no longer be chased by creditors. He had more money than his mother could possibly spend on food, clothing, and shelter. And so Owney spent his money lavishly; he was known as a big tipper, a sport. He loved spending his money on clothes and women; he regarded himself as a fashion plate and a highly desirable ladies' man. As such, he would fly into a rage if one of his girlfriends dated another man.

One day, following an argument about a girl whom he and William Henshaw (a clerk in a dry goods store) had dated, a fuming Owney followed the unsuspecting Henshaw onto a street car. There, in front of stunned passengers, Owney pulled out a pistol, aimed it at the back of Henshaw's head, and fired a single shot. It was midday, and the street car was crowded with passengers. Owney didn't seem to regard those passengers as possible threats who could identify him to the police, and so he nonchalantly departed the car, after ringing its bell. The police did manage to piece together enough information to identify Owney as the killer. When he was captured soon thereafter, he was booked, indicted, and brought to trial. None of the passengers who may have originally given information to the police about the shooting would testify against Owney. It became readily apparent to potential witnesses that the Gophers would murder anyone who agreed to identify and testify against their leader. Without the testimony of witnesses or a confession from Owney, the DA's office had no choice but to drop the case. Owney swaggered out of the court a free man. He knew that in Hell's Kitchen no one would testify against him. Cross Owney Madden and you would be buried with a cross marking your stupidity.

Owney's invincibility was sorely tested on November 6, 1912, when his rise in the underworld almost took a nosedive. He and his wife attended a dance on West 52nd Street. He danced several dances with his wife and was then approached by a woman who told him several friends wanted to speak with him. They awaited his arrival on a balcony that overlooked the dance hall. There, he was met and encircled by 11 Hudson Dusters, an Irish gang from Greenwich Village. They were known as Dusters for their love of cocaine. According to Herbert Asbury,

> He saw enemies on three sides of him, 11 men who stared at him out of cold eyes. He knew that hey intended to kill him, and would shoot before he could even so much as make a movement toward his pocket. Nevertheless, he slowly rose to his feet and faced them, for Owney the Killer was no coward.

"Come on, youse guys!" He cried. "Youse wouldn't shoot nobody! Who did you ever bump off?"

One of the 11 men cursed. That broke the tension. Guns blazed and Owney the Killer went down, and while he lay unconscious on the floor his enemies went calmly down the stairs and into the street; and no hand was raised to stop them.[5]

The sounds of gunfire had caused a stampede out of the dance hall and down 52nd Street. The Dusters joined the crowd of people running away and vanished before the police arrived on the scene. Having learned that a man was lying wounded and bleeding on the balcony of the dance hall, detectives rapidly ascended the stairs and found Owney, groaning in pain, his blood-soaked hands clutching at his stomach. The cops thought he was a goner but nevertheless called for an ambulance to rush Owney to New York Hospital. He refused to tell the detectives who had shot him but said he would take care of the matter himself. Owney not only survived, but also had apparently instructed his cohorts to take care of the Dusters. The Gophers would not let an attempt on the life of Owney go unanswered, and during the next few weeks, 11 Dusters were murdered. None of the Gophers were arrested for the murders. It was a well-established commandment throughout the West Side of Manhattan that no one should testify against the Gophers.

While Owney got away with the murder of William Henshaw and none of the Gophers were prosecuted for the murders of the Hudson Dusters, Owney was tempting fate and drawing too much police attention to himself. Henshaw was not the only man whom Owney killed in a fit of jealous rage. There would be two more, but it was only one of those killings that earned Owney a 20-year sentence in Sing Sing. He had gotten into a heated dispute with Patsy Doyle, a leader of the hated Hudson Dusters gang. The argument revolved around a young beauty named Freda Horner, whom both men had been dating. While she favored both men with her sexual favors, Owney thought Freda was solely devoted to him. He had been romancing her, spending money on her, buying her all sorts of gifts, and taking her to expensive nightclubs. He had invested a lot of time and money in the relationship, and he was furious that Freda would so discount his attentions as to date another man, especially the head of the gang that had drilled a dozen holes into his guts.

Not willing to further intensify their feud, knowing that it would lead to a shooting, Patsy decided to play it safe and so cunningly revealed details of Owney's criminal operations to the police. He hoped to put Owney on the spot and have the cops eliminate him as a rival. It could all be done without the firing of a gun; however, when Owney learned of Patsy's treachery, he lured Patsy to a meeting where they could supposedly settle their differences like gentlemen. But, in typical gangland fashion, Owney expressed himself with a gun, shooting and killing Patsy moments after greeting him. This time there were witnesses who did not live in Hell's Kitchen. Asbury notes,

> Owney the Killer was arrested two to three days later, and at his trial Freda Horner and Margaret Everdeane turned state's evidence. Crying and raving that he had been jobbed, Madden was sent to Sing Sing for 10 to 20 years. . . . And at police headquarters the detectives drew a breath of relief and scratched the name of Owney the Killer from their list of dangerous gangsters.[6]

Their relieved breathing would last for years, but it would ultimately be replaced by groans of anger, for they had naïvely indulged in wishful thinking. Owney would eventually reemerge as a more powerful gangster than before.

But at the time of his sentencing, the fate of Owney Madden seemed certain. And he may have thought so, too. He was certainly shocked that the DA had flipped Freda and gotten her to testify against her once-ardent lover; he was further angered and disappointed that the Gophers had been unable to get to Freda and have her recant her testimony. He had always beaten the raps, but now he was going to one of the most notorious prisons in New York. His fraternity of criminals, the Gophers, would not even be able to give him a proper send-off. No going away party for Owney, although a few of the Gophers could be seen outside the courthouse, where they waved their solemn good-byes. Although Owney was sentenced to a 20-year term, on his journey up the river, he must have contemplated schemes that would result in a possible early release—for he changed his persona, becoming an apparently remorseful and law-abiding individual who realized the errors of his ways. His new persona would attract and win over the warden of the prison.

So, Madden entered prison a humble and affable young man. He was obedient to the rules and respectful of the guards. He didn't frater-

nize with the other prisoners. He proved to be a model prisoner. He never got into fights, never disobeyed any orders issued by guards, and offered his help to the warden in helping other prisoners to see the value of going straight once they were released. Every word he uttered, every move he made, every thought he had were designed to convince the parole board he had been rehabilitated. And so it happened: With the help of a politically connected lawyer and the passing of large sums of money to influence doubtful politicians and win the unanimous approval of the parole board, Owney was released from Sing Sing prison after serving less than nine years of his 20-year sentence.

It was 1923. Much had changed while Owney was in prison. Prohibition was the law of the land, and many of the Gophers had either died of natural causes or in battles with other gangs. When former convict Owney Madden hit the streets of Hell's Kitchen, he found that the Gophers no longer existed as a gang. The bootleggers had taken over. Big money, millions of dollars, more than Owney had hoped to accumulate when a Gopher, was being made in the illegal liquor trade. Prohibition was the best opportunity offered to ambitious and opportunistic mobsters. Because the competition to control the illegal importation and distribution of liquor was so keen, there were many fierce battles between opposing gangs. They were willing to fight and kill to make their fortunes, to risk life and limb to expand their market share. The tommy gun became the weapon of choice, and it shot many an ambitious bootlegger. When a speakeasy refused to take liquor from one bootlegger instead of another, he was usually bombed out of business. Rarely has the violent violation of a law made so many people millionaires. In fact, Prohibition proved to be the foundation for numerous American fortunes. And Owney wanted in on the action.

While still in prison, he had read the newspaper articles about the bootleg wars for territory; he had heard tales, via prison gossip, about the fabulous wealth bootleggers were earning. He heard about Lucky Luciano; Meyer Lansky; Bugsy Siegel; Joe Adonis; and the financier of many of their operations, the estimable Arnold Rothstein. They made the Gophers look like pip-squeak hoods. Owney was determined to invade the world of big-time gangsters and shoot right to the top of their pyramid. He was not merely a man in a hurry, he was a rocket aimed at the top layers of gangsterdom. He would conquer the world of

New York City bootlegging and stash millions of dollars in foreign banks.

Back on 10th Avenue, Owney looked up an old friend and former Gopher, Larry Fay. Fay was devious and scheming, and as seemingly sincere as a parson delivering a Sunday morning sermon. The combination of those traits, plus a nose for sniffing out illegal business opportunities, led him into many profitable deals; however, he was not a strong-arm personality; he was not known as a man who relied on his muscles to reach his goals. He lacked Owney's ability to strike fear in opponents, although he did pack a gun and would use it as a last resort. Owney could make up for Fay's deficiencies as a mobster; he would be the ideal partner for Fay. Their combination of charm and muscle, plus their combined cunning, would be a passport to control whatever businesses they decided to dominate.

Owney began by helping Fay solidify his control of New York's taxis. He arranged to hire many ex-convicts as taxi drivers, men who would do what they were told to do, especially if there was more money coming to them than they were able to earn from fares and tips. Owney understood that once he and Fay controlled all of the taxis, they could control a large part of the trafficking of liquor to speakeasies. Their taxi drivers, in effect, were their delivery service. In addition, Owney made sure that their taxis had all the pickup spots at Grand Central Terminal and Penn Station. His drivers owned Broadway and the entire area of Hell's Kitchen. Owney decided he could maximize his profits if he owned and operated his own brewery. He began looking around the West Side for a building that could serve his purposes. He would also run his own fleet of boats for smuggling booze into New York from Canada. He would have his own fleet of trucks. Those trucks and his taxis would distribute liquor to the speakeasy owners he had convinced to buy from him. It was all falling into place.

In a little less than two years after emerging from Sing Sing, poor and without a gang, Owney Madden succeeded in opening the Phoenix Brewery on 10th Avenue, between 25th and 26th Streets. He pretended it was a cereal factory and paid beat cops to ignore its operations. In fact, when federal agents were planning to raid the brewery, they were told by local cops they would handle it. And handle it they did, receiving generous handouts from the brewery's CEO.

So confident was Owney in his ability to operate without being busted that he even brewed a beer that he named for himself, Madden's #1, which was sold to speakeasies throughout the city. He sold it to speakeasies owned by others and also sold beer and liquor to speakeasies he and Fay opened or took over from others.

He was a man reborn, and it was not surprising that he chose the name Phoenix for his brewery. He had risen from the ashes of his old life to a new one in the rackets: He had gone from teenage punk to destitute convict to millionaire bootlegger. His was the American Dream in spades.

As Donald Miller writes in *Supreme City*,

> After taking control of the Phoenix Brewery, Madden purchased a penthouse that had a balcony overlooking the brewery, the largest in New York City. Damon Runyon and other Broadway personalities were regular visitors. "It's really better than killing somebody," Madden supposedly told Runyon, pointing proudly to his massive red-brick plant.[7]

He had smartly figured he could get it all without the use of a gun. It was a gun that had earned him a 20-year sentence in Sing Sing, and he didn't want a gun to be a passport back to prison. Although perceived as a tough guy, Owney had learned from Fay how to accomplish his goals without the use of physical violence. Of course, his reputation as a killer served sufficiently to intimidate others so that a gun was not a necessary accoutrement to his wardrobe. For the rest of his life, he would be known as Owney "The Killer" Madden.

Writes Miller, "A feral brawler and hard-eyed killer in his younger days, he packed away his revolver and safecracking tools, curbed his wild drinking and carousing, and transformed himself into a gangland organization man with a Broadway office and a bulletproof car."[8]

He was well on his way to being the biggest bootlegger in New York. But just to make sure that DAs and cops were convinced of his postprison legitimacy, he maintained his partnership with Fay in the taxi business. It served as an ideal front for his illegal activities.

Moving from one success to another, Owney established himself as New York's premier crime czar, owning not only a brewery that supplied hundreds of speakeasies, but also a city-wide laundry that had a monopoly on linens for restaurants and buildings that housed his speakeasies. When necessary, he partnered with Italian and Jewish gangsters, and bought majority shares in such legendary nightclubs as the Stork Club and the Cotton Club (which had been owned by heavyweight boxing champion Jack Johnson). He even financed the careers of such stage and movie stars as Mae West, a sometime mistress, and his boyhood pal from Hell's Kitchen, George Raft. Like Arnold Rothstein, Owney's reputation became so inflated that he became the inspiration for one of Damon Runyon's fictional characters, Dave the Dude, a Broadway mobster.

While Owney met Mae West when they were both on the road to success, Owney's relationship with George Raft (né, Ranft) went back to his boyhood. Together they had climbed an often-shaky ladder to success. They had met as teenagers, and Raft rapidly became an Owney Madden acolyte and epigone, imitating his mannerisms and vocalizations, holding his gun, his burglary tools, his pipe wrapped in newspaper. When Owney and his gang of Gophers would be on the roof of a tenement, dropping bricks, flower pots, and garbage onto cops, the young Raft would join in the fun. For the rest of their lives, Owney and Raft remained friends in regular contact with one another. Years after Raft moved to Hollywood and established himself as a major movie star, often playing gangsters, he was called upon for help by James Cagney, who had also made a name for himself playing gangsters. According to Cagney, when some mobsters put out a contract on him, he turned to Raft for help. Raft phoned his boyhood pal and asked if he could arrange to have the contract shredded. Owney obliged, saving Cagney's life.

Owney believed that favors done would result in favors repaid. If he needed something from Cagney or Raft, he would get it. Owney had a jeweler's eye for spotting opportunities, and it was not just in those created by doing favors. Opportunities required creative thinking, and Owney was expert as a creative opportunist. One such opportunity appeared in the form of George "Big Frenchy" DeMange, a retired leader of the Hudson Dusters. Based on Owney's history, one would have thought that a former member of the Dusters would be anathema to Owney. Instead, Owney realized that Big Frenchy would be a better partner than adversary. Frenchy was as big as a linebacker and twice as tough. He and Owney made a curious pair together, for Owney was built like a wirehaired terrier, Big Frenchy like a Rottweiler. Big

Frenchy knew the nightclub business, and so Owney made him a part-ner in the Cotton Club and the Stork Club. Owney and Frenchy also purchased numerous other clubs. Each of their nightclubs was supplied by booze from the Phoenix Brewery, linens from Owney's laundry, and food from food delivery businesses Owney had an interest in.

Operating from his office in the Publicity Building on a corner of 47th Street and Broadway, Owney, the puppet master, pulled the strings of his many operations. It was odd that he chose the Publicity Building, for Owney always tried to stay out of the newspapers. Other than John Gotti and Al Capone, gangsters like to maintain a low profile. Yet, Owney enjoyed being recognized and honored in Broadway thea-ters and nightclubs. He expected a kind of obeisance to be paid to him. He quietly, deceptively, and crookedly continued making a fortune from Prohibition and its related businesses. His brewery was the most successful one in the city and did a brisk business, and the beer it turned out was considered to be of exceptionally good quality, which could not be said of many other brews sold to thirsty customers.

But Prohibition was coming to an end. Owney and many of the bootleggers knew it would be repealed. While he could have converted the Phoenix into a legal brewery upon Prohibition's demise, he chose not to. Things that were illicit were magical and exciting; things that were normal and legal were not. He never thought of importing high-quality liquor from Canada and England, as did Joseph Kennedy Sr. and Edgar Bronfman, both of whom built even greater fortunes than they had accumulated during Prohibition. Instead, Owney turned to a venue he had known well since boyhood.

He had admired many boxers and bet on them, especially if he knew the fights were fixed. He had hired washed-up palookas for Larry Fay's taxi company. He had invested in small-time amateur and journeyman boxers. It was like owning racehorses. It was not a big business, but he realized it could be. If you could own the heavyweight champion, you could take in millions of dollars. The heavyweight championship would not be hard to own. One only needed the right fighter in harness and the right connections with their hands out.

So, with the government about to bury Prohibition in a grave of good intentions, along with many other dead government misdeeds, Owney decided he would make another fortune from the lively art of pugilism. He would not have to deal with honest promoters and managers, for the sport invariably attracted quick-buck opportunists, in fact, waves of them, who were willing to evade rules and regulations to cash in on their fighters.

Owney wanted a boxer he could easily control, one who wasn't very bright and so could be trained like a circus animal. That boxer should look like a champion, act like a champion, and convince the public he was born to be a champion. He would be a puppet on a string.

If he could find an eager fool hungry for glory, Owney figured he could set him up and convince the public the guy was a genuine world-class pugilist. And if he were stupid enough, Owney could pluck every dollar from his hide. In addition, millions of dollars could be made from betting on all the fixed fights the champ would win. The perfect patsy arrived in the form of an Italian circus strongman, Primo Carnera.

Carnera arrived in New York with his European manager, Leon See, who was nearly as greedy as Owney but almost as naïve as Carnera. It would not be difficult for Owney to buy Carnera's contact from See, which he would do at the right time. When that time arrived, he would place a .38 pistol against See's temple and say "sign it." See would, of course, do as he was told. It was a standard gangster method of sealing a deal, after which Owney would encourage poor See to leave the country for reasons of health. So what if he was humiliated and humbled, and had little money to show as a return on his investment: He would be a little wiser about messing with professional gamblers.

Once he could take full possession of Carnera, Owney looked forward to promoting the 6-foot-7 strongman, a perfect image of a heavyweight champ. Meanwhile, unbeknownst to See, Owney proceeded to sell pieces of the heavyweight to three low-level gangster-investors: Louis Soreci, Walter Friedman, and Billy Duffy. Owney and his investors knew Carnera was no fighter, he just looked like one. For Carnera to put on convincing performances of pugilistic skill, he would need to be trained by someone who was not only a skillful boxer, but also knowledgeable about the underworld of gambling and fixed fights. He needed someone who would not reveal Owney's schemes to either Carnera or the public. Abe Attell, the "Little Hebrew," former world champion, was Owney's choice. He had met Attell through Arnold Rothstein, and he knew all about the 1919 World Series fix. He admired Attell's role in that scandal, as well as his ability to skate free of prison. He thought Attell would be an ideal trainer for the "Ambling Alp," as Carnera was known. Owney had complete confidence that he could rely on Attell, who would help to make the chump a champ.

Prior to his first big fight in Madison Square Garden, Carnera was sent by Owney on a national publicity tour to build interest in his fighter. Leon See had not yet been pushed out the door, because Owney thought it was a good idea to keep him until Carnera had grown to trust Owney's cohorts. At that time, See would prove superfluous and be pushed aside.

At one stop in California, a radio announcer wanted to interview the big heavyweight; however, Carnera could neither speak nor understand English. Leon See had served as his translator. They spoke to one another in either French or Italian. What should See do? Owney wanted to get as much publicity for Carnera as possible, and radio could serve as an excellent venue. But when a radio interviewer asked See if he could interview the big heavyweight, See thought such an interview would leave the impression that Carnera was a fool. Although See did not want to displease Owney, he declined the offer. Yet, the interviewer persisted. He said he would ask Carnera just three simple questions, each of which would be supplied beforehand. Carnera could memorize the few words of his responses, words that would never form more than a single a sentence. See finally agreed. The interviewer would ask Carnera his age (23 years old), his weight (275 pounds), and his height (6-foot-7).

After intensively coaching Carnera for more than an hour between training sessions, See accompanied his fighter to the 36th floor of the building that housed the radio station. See escorted Carnera into a studio and, in Italian, introduced him to the interviewer. Carnera extended a large hand, like a bear's paw, that swallowed the interviewer's small hand. The interviewer informed a nervous See that the interview would be live and that thousands of listeners would hear the voice of the next heavyweight champion. See offered a faint smile and nodded nervously. The interviewer held a microphone up to Carnera's large, rectangular head.

"Primo," the announcer began, "how old are you?"

"Two-hundred and seventy-five," the Alp beamed.[9]

See's Adam's apple jerked in nervous disappointment, and he rapidly escorted his fighter from the studio before any additional mistakes would lead listeners to think they had been listening to a vaudeville comedy routine.

Back in New York, Carnera was being trained to put on more convincing performances, none of which involved answering a reporter's questions. Instead, he would lumber about the ring in Stillman's Gym, throwing awkward punches at a sparring partner who had been warned not to hurt Carnera. For good measure, the sparring partner was told to fake a couple of falls just to impress the onlookers, of which there were many, especially middle-aged Italian ladies who called out greetings in their native tongue.

Carnera had already won a number of fights against journeymen and palookas, each of which had been fixed. Carnera was "likely unaware of these [fixed fights] arrangements."[10] Primo's children have said,

> Daddy told us that he never knew that [his fights had been fixed]. He told us that he never knew and that the decision only depended on the boxing ability of his opponents. He was too naïve. We are sorry to say so, but it is like that. His relation to arranged bouts is to be found in his naivete, which came from the goodness of his heart.[11]

He believed he had actually beaten his opponents and was sure he could beat his next opponent, "Big Boy" Eddie Peterson. Peterson was a good, although not superior, fighter, and he too thought he could win. He had sized up Carnera and knew he was more image than proficient boxer. His punches were like pats and slaps, hardly the means for knocking someone out. Peterson figured he could easily defeat the Ambling Alp. He thought so right up until he was paid a visit in his dressing room and offered a generous payday to take a dive. He happily accepted the money, but after a few days, he complained it wasn't enough. Owney was worried Peterson would keep on insisting on more and more money right up to the bell announcing round one. Owney didn't trust Peterson and was unwilling to shell out additional funds. He came up with a surefire solution: He called on his boyhood crony, George Raft, who owed many favors to Owney and was happy to be of assistance.

Raft, after getting his instructions from Owney, called on Peterson in his room at the Claridge Hotel. Glad-handing and exuding charm, Raft suggested they celebrate Peterson's likely win over Carnera later that night with a bottle of champagne. They emptied the bottle, although

Raft nursed only a single drink, while Peterson became inebriated and wobbled on rubbery legs when he walked across the room heading to the bathroom. Raft was satisfied Peterson would be in no condition to win the fight. And just to be sure, he had added a tranquilizing drug to the champagne.

That night Peterson was indeed woozy and wobbled like a drunk on soft, rubbery legs out of his corner. By contrast, Carnera came out of his corner on powerfully muscled legs that looked like Greek columns. Strong and straight, he was the image of power and strength. He brought the fight to Peterson and quickly knocked him out. Peterson flopped onto the canvas after suffering a powder-puff punch that just managed to find its target on Peterson's chin. The referee declared Carnera the winner, and Owney and Raft exchanged the grins of pleased conspirators.

It did not take long for the cognoscenti of boxing to estimate the true level of Carnera's skills and learn about the underworld's control of the Ambling Alp. Conspiracies invariably involve people who like to gossip, share their special knowledge, and brag about how clever they are, and so the news of the fix spread from person to person and to every sportswriter in New York City. Owney didn't like it, but the con could still be executed, and poor Carnera thought he was a genuine tough guy, an indomitable mountain of a man who could knock out anyone he faced, while never being felled.

On February 10, 1933, Carnera faced Ernie Schaaf, who just six months earlier had suffered a devastating defeat at the fists of Max Baer, who had one of the hardest-hitting right crosses of any boxer in the twentieth century. Schaaf had been unable to get to his feet for several minutes at the conclusion of the fight and complained of terrible headaches for weeks thereafter. Nevertheless, he and his manager agreed to a fight with Carnera.

In the 13th round of a 15-round fight, Carnera seemingly knocked out Schaaf with one of his typical soft punches. Schaaf fell to the canvas, unconscious. He could barely stagger and was sent into a coma. He was rushed to a hospital; underwent surgery, which could not revive him; and died four days later on Valentine's Day. No one believed Carnera's soft punch had been the cause of Schaaf's death, for Schaaf had exhibited signs of brain damage after his loss to Max Baer. Rather than blame the giant for the death of Schaaf, the media blamed Baer. They regarded him as a killer, for he had killed another boxer named Frankie Campbell years earlier in California.

On June 13, 1934, there would be a match to decide who was the one with the true killer punches, Primo Carnera, the heavyweight champion of the world, or Max Baer, his powerful challenger. The media went to town, ginning up excitement about the bout between the killer gladiators. Dempsey declared that Baer had the most powerful right fist of any fighter, and he expected him to pummel Carnera into a state of humiliated submission. Opponents who had been knocked out by Baer's right fist often compared the experience to being hit by a speeding locomotive. There was no way Primo Carnera could emerge victorious from his bout with Baer unless, of course, the fight was fixed. And that's just what was attempted: A pair of Owney's thugs entered Baer's dressing room before the fight and offered him and his manager, Ancil Hoffman, money to throw the fight. Hoffman yelled that the thugs should get the hell out and pound sand. There was no way his fighter would give up the chance to knock the crown off of Carnera's head. The thugs snarled a few threats, and Hoffman again told them to beat it. For reasons that remain unknown, they exited the dressing room, and neither Baer nor Hoffman suffered the wrath of Madden and his cohorts. One can assume the smart money was then bet on Baer.

Baer was known as the clown prince of boxing for his amusing antics in the ring; it was not unusual for him to laughingly taunt an opponent and turn to the spectators as if they were in on his jokes. It was no different in his bout with Carnera: Baer occasionally laughed at the Ambling Alp, sometimes calling him a sissy. It was not the kind of contest fans had expected. In round one, Baer knocked down the giant three times, although Carnera sprang up, only to be chased around the ring by Baer. When Carnera threw punches at Baer, he seemed to be pawing and slapping his jabs. Round two was no better for Carnera: He was knocked down three times, his large feet and legs getting intertwined with Baer's as they both tumbled to the canvas, seemingly wrestling rather than boxing.

By round three, Carnera finally realized this fight was different from those that had preceded it. His opponent was determined and fierce in his pursuit of victory. Carnera desperately fought back, using some of the skills Abe Attell had taught him. Although obviously outclassed by

Baer, Carnera not only fought back, but also pursued Baer, who easily danced away from Carnera's telegraphed punches. Baer seemed to lay back as if he wanted spectators to see they were getting a real battle of gladiators, not a one-sided massacre.

And so it went for the next few rounds. By round seven, Carnera was punching with confidence, but his punches had no effect on Baer, although a few landed. Baer was still laying back, not often throwing his powerful right. In round eight, Carnera, in his haste to land a defining punch, tripped over his large, awkwardly planted feet. Many in the audience laughed at the awkward giant. In round nine, Carnera seemed the aggressor, while Baer seemed to be little more than an observer. So impressive was Carnera for several rounds that the judges would later say he had won three of those rounds. But poor Carnera was not about to win any more. Baer had gotten his fill of fooling the spectators and his opponent. In round 10, he gave Carnera a terrible beating, knocking him down three times. Obviously, Baer was no longer playing with Carnera; the pantomime of equals was over. Baer was now determined to knock poor Carnera down into a netherworld of senselessness.

One of Baer's powerful right crosses struck Carnera behind his ear, and the big guy collapsed onto the canvas. Yet, he managed to go on. Many in the audience admired his courage and cheered him when he sprang to his feet. While they admired his courage, others said he was a fool to let himself be hammered over and over; he appeared to be a broken and bloody specimen of one who had been mistaken for a genuine boxer. In the 11th round, Carnera was like a dumb, hapless beast being led to slaughter. He was knocked down, got up, and was wobbly on rubbery legs, and the referee finally called a halt. No one wanted to see Max Baer kill a third fighter. After two minutes and sixteen seconds of the 11th round, Max Baer was declared the heavyweight champion of the world. It had been Baer's easiest fight, and it was utter humiliation for the defeated and broken Primo Carnera.

Deserted by his mob handlers, poor Carnera found himself alone in a hospital ward, suffering from a broken jaw, a fractured rib, and a broken nose. Owney and his cohorts, having bet on Baer and having earned millions off the hide of Carnera, vanished from the world of the Ambling Alp. They refused to spend a nickel on their defeated fighter's hospital bills.

In his biography of Primo Carnera, Joseph Page writes,

Most of Carnera's handlers were greedy at best and organized crime thugs at worst. Men such as Owney Madden, Billy Duffy, and Luigi Soresi leeched off Primo during his rise as a professional fighter and were nowhere to be found after he was broken down—they had bled him dry, and he was no longer of any value to them. [12]

Generous and kindhearted out of the ring, Baer not only regularly visited his erstwhile opponent, but also paid all of his hospital bills. He regarded Carnera as a man of courage. What Owney and his partners did not understand about many fighters is that they respected one another, admired one another for their courage to get in the ring and possibly suffer terrible injuries. Few fighters disliked their opponents.

For Owney, Carnera had been a piece of property, an annuity that paid off until that final defeat. Max Baer was no Owney Madden. He saw boxers and boxing from inside the ring. To him, all boxers were men who tested themselves in a manly competition and exposed themselves to either glory or defeat. As one who hit and got hit, he had a compassionate attitude toward other boxers. Of all the boxers whom he fought, the only one he disliked was "Two Ton Tough" Tony Galento, a fat, crude, vicious street fighter, who used every dirty trick available to defeat an opponent: eye gouging with his thumbs, hitting below the belt, rubbing the laces of his gloves on his opponents' eyes. Baer, in his onetime bout against Galento, took obvious pleasure in beating him and would later say Galento was the only fighter he profoundly disliked.

Baer's compassion and empathy manifested itself in not only paying Carnera's hospital bills, but also helping him get started in new a career. Following Carnera's recovery and release from the hospital, Bear arranged for him to have a career as a professional wrestler, a career that permitted Carnera to earn the money he should have earned as a pugilist.

Carnera was perfectly suited to be a wrestler. He looked the part and was widely and affectionately known by millions of people. Yes, he had proven himself to be a hapless pugilist, but he was admired for the courage he had demonstrated in his defeat. As a wrestler, he was a huge success. Audiences loved him and applauded his every win, no matter how obviously scripted his matches were. Even better for the veteran fighter, he was no longer being managed by the mob and so was not being cheated out of his earnings. He was able to bank a considerable amount of money and invest it in legitimate enterprises. With the money he earned from wrestling, Carnera bought a beautiful villa in Italy and opened a liquor and grocery store in Los Angeles. He had two children, one of whom became a successful doctor.

Years after his boxing career was over and the gangsters had cheated him of his earnings, Carnera was visiting his parents and aunts and uncles in Italy when he received the news that Baer had unexpectedly died of a heart attack at age 50. Carnera wanted to mourn his friend and benefactor, to be present at Baer's funeral, and so he rushed to get on the first plane to California; however, he arrived too late to attend the funeral. He had wanted to be one of Baer's pallbearers, all of whom were heavyweight boxers Baer had defeated, as well as Joe Louis, who had defeated Baer.

Late the night of his arrival in Los Angeles, Carnera had his driver take him to the cemetery where Baer had been buried. The gates were locked, so Carnera and his driver climbed over the cemetery fence and wandered around in the dark with a flashlight, searching for Baer's grave. When Carnera found it, he knelt down, bowed his head, whispered a prayer, crossed himself, and said good-bye to his friend and departed.

In 1998, Carnera's children, devoted to the memory of their once-disgraced father, established the Primo Carnera Foundation, which provides financial and emotional support to neglected and abused children, helping them complete their educations and lead productive lives. It is a legacy Carnera would have been proud to endorse. He was a good-hearted giant who empathized with those who he felt had been given little. He was a man who realized that there is always someone who is worse off: You may not have shoes, but what of a person who has no feet? Carnera deserved, like all boxers, a manager who would not have robbed him. But that's how Owney Madden operated. He was not known for his kindness, compassion, or empathy. He was one of the mobsters who almost brought boxing to its knees. There would be others who would follow in his footsteps. And one in particular, Frankie Carbo, would be a far more ruthless mobster than the former Gopher.

Owney still had a few moves left in him. Carbo would have to wait. Shortly after Carnera's defeat, Owney continued to own several other boxers, none of whom were as famous or as profitable as Carnera had been. Yet, each one turned a profit for Owney and his cohorts. Prohibition and boxing had left Owney with a fortune estimated in the tens of millions of dollars. All that money did not prevent Owney from suffering a parole violation and being sentenced to a year in prison at Sing Sing. Not wanting any publicity, he had himself driven to the gates of the prison, where he had to convince the guards that he was, indeed, the notorious gangster, Owney "The Killer" Madden. He asked to see the warden, who welcomed Owney back to his home away from home and even escorted him to his old cell.

Upon his release, Owney decided he had made enough money and had no intention of serving more time in prison. He retired to Hot Springs, Arkansas, divorced his wife, and married the postmaster's daughter. He became an eminent citizen, contributed to local charities, and was cordial to his neighbors. Yet, he would neither disassociate himself from his past nor remove himself from the *Guys and Dolls* characters who had inhabited his New York rackets world. He turned Hot Springs into a refuge for gangsters on the lam from the law, as well as for gangsters who were merely on the lam from their identities and wanted to reinvent themselves. For others in need of a change of scenery or for recuperation from gunshot wounds or police beatings, he turned Hot Springs into Owney Madden's Restful Haven for Wanted and Unwanted Criminals. He welcomed them with open arms and the hospitality of a Southern gentleman.

As Owney aged, his reputation with old-time New York mobsters remained as a pillar of their community. For true crime buffs, he was regarded as a tourist attraction, and for historians, screenwriters, and novelists, he was a much sought-after resource; however, he neither gave interviews nor posed for cameras. He was an unopened encyclopedia of crime. And local reporters, whose publishers were friendly with Owney, were smart enough to leave him alone. In the world of organized crime, discretion and silence have always been necessary virtues, and Owney had learned long ago to keep his own counsel.

Whenever a reporter asked Primo Carnera about Owney Madden, he would turn away and say nothing. He had his own file of memories, too painful to visit. He did know that numerous boxing historians and sportswriters regarded Owney as one of boxing's preeminent villains. When they made such statements, Carnera would nod and say nothing, neither in Italian, nor in broken English. His suffering was part of his history, and there was no reason to scratch open the scabs of those old wounds.

Owney suffered from his own maladies, and in his 70s he was frequently a guest in a local hospital or nursing home. The nurse who devoted years to taking care of him, and whose ministrations Owney often requested, was the mother of President Bill Clinton. Owney died in 1965, two years before Primo Carnera, his former annuity, who died in Sequals, Italy.

4

THE MACHIAVELLI OF PROMOTERS

Mike Jacobs may have been one of the most disliked men in boxing, a distinction he shared with numerous others, for boxing is a sport in which there have been villains aplenty, although Jacobs held a unique position and was disliked for the coldhearted leverage he used to manipulate boxers and managers. Jacobs did not value having friends, and few people even attempted to offer him friendship. If they naïvely did, they were met by indifference. He did, however, have numerous partners and several lackeys. To say Jacobs was a hard man is a polite understatement, for he was cold-blooded and remorseless. One of Jacob's relatives told the author that not even his relatives liked him. Yet, Jacobs managed to smooth-talk many boxers and managers into accepting his deals, and if smooth-talking didn't grease the wheels of a deal, various forms of leverage made the wheels turn; in particular, a threat to end a career was one that boxers and their managers took seriously.

As boxing's ultimate gatekeeper, Jacobs was able to issue such threats. He held the keys to matchmaking, and those keys could either unlock the gate to future wealth or lock the gate, thus dooming a boxer to fight in second- and third-rate venues for the run of his career. If you wanted to play in the big time, you had to play by Jacobs's rules or not play at all. As boxing's king and king-maker, he made millions of dollars. He did so by not only promoting matches, but also secretly owning percentages of fighters' contracts. How did Jacobs obtain his power and where did he learn to be a consummate hustler? It all began in the deprivations of his childhood.

Jacobs was born into poverty in 1880. By the time he was 12 years old, he was out on street corners, a newsie, hawking morning and evening editions of newspapers to commuters who were rushing to and from work in Brooklyn. It was a typical occupation for poor boys, many of whom were tough and fought one another for the best spots. Close to transportation hubs or in front of factories and office buildings were the most desirable locations. Not willing to fight other newsies for territorial advantage, Jacobs subcontracted the corners he claimed to own to other boys who were big and tough enough to defeat their ambitious challengers. Being a franchiser of sorts gave Jacobs the opportunity to extend his entrepreneurship to other activities.

Coney Island was a hot summer attraction. Crowds surged over the boardwalk and around the food concessions, rides, and games. It was advertised as Brooklyn's very own Rivera, albeit a proletarian version of one. For Jacobs, however, it presented a commercial opportunity; he perceived it to be more like an open-air Middle Eastern market than a summer resort. He bought cheap gadgets and souvenirs, which he subsequently sold at inflated prices to those seeking a day of sun and fun. When he earned enough money to invest in more profitable enterprises, he bought concessions and hired others to run them. Not being landlocked, Coney Island was home to many excursion boats, so the young Jacobs bought concessions on those boats. Following a pattern, he hired others to run the oceangoing concession for him. His employees sold candy, ice cream, soft drinks, artificial flowers, whatever customers wanted. Jacobs was becoming known with some awe as Young Mr. Jacobs. People kidded him that one day he would own all of Coney Island. Jacobs neither smiled nor disagreed with them. He simply went about accumulating money, overcoming his poverty.

While many boat passengers patronized his concessions, a number did not, and Jacobs wanted their business—and their money. He realized that the items they could not avoid purchasing were the tickets to board the excursion boats. The passengers were a ready-made customer base, so Jacobs bought up large quantities of tickets at discounts. With those tickets in hand, he offered them at scalpers' rates to tourists eager to sail the seas off the coast of Brooklyn. Scalping tickets seemed like an easy way to make a quick buck, and so Jacobs decided to scalp tickets for train rides, too. Since most of his customers were immigrants with a limited command of English, Jacobs was easily able to overcharge them for their tickets, and he invariably did so with a smile that was as ingratiating as it was cynical.

Jacobs was all business. Legendary sports journalist Jimmy Cannon said Jacobs was the "stingiest man in the world."[1] And no matter how much wealth he accumulated, it would never be enough. Coney Island was a good start for his ambitions, but it provided seasonal work only. Jacobs was on the lookout for new business deals, ones that could be perpetuated year-round. He would ask people about what businesses they were in; he would attempt to eavesdrop on the conversations of businessmen. He was an investigator, checking out the latest quick-buck opportunities. He shied away from anything that was illegal. Jail would be an unwelcome interruption to his ambitions. He was racing in a mad dash to get his hands on the next deal before anyone else could compete with him. Although he would not do anything that would result in his being arrested, he would not hesitate to outmaneuver an unsuspecting fool. If he had to pretend to suckers and fools that the rewards of a deal would be greater than he knew they would be, then his pretensions were offered as a sure thing. He posed as a hardheaded realist. Jacobs was a man without a conscience. He couldn't escape the poverty into which he had been born fast enough. He never looked back. He always had his eyes set on the future.

Enough was never enough for Jacobs, and after taking over the concessions on boats, he decided there would be even more money in owning some of the boats. His boats were not part of the Star Ship or Cunard lines, but he acted as if he were commodore of the harbor. And he relished his position.

Like many successful entrepreneurs before and after him, Jacobs cleverly never used his own money when buying boats: He always went to the banks, all of which were eager to lend him money at attractive rates of interest. He showed them his books, which were so detailed and thorough that the bankers were always impressed. One would have thought that the books had been issued by the Treasury Department. Jacobs was no fool, and in addition to providing the bankers with impressive books, he would not stiff them, not be delinquent making repayments. As long as the banks financed his operations, he would pay off his loans. His credit with the banks was exceptional. The bankers and Jacobs developed mutually profitable relationships that endured for years. As far as the bankers were concerned, Jacobs had a Midas touch.

He regularly turned a profit, and he presented one set of books to the banks and kept another for his private review.

Not satisfied with the money he was squeezing out of his boats, Jacobs decided Broadway offered an even more lucrative arena for his ambitions. Broadway was not only the street of broken dreams, but also the street of hustlers and those to be hustled and fleeced. He had learned to base the art and practice of scalping tickets at Coney Island; now he would bring his expertise as a scalper to the sale of tickets for such sporting events as wrestling matches, bicycle races, operatic concerts, dance competitions, and so on. Whatever could be staged on Broadway, Jacobs was ready to sell tickets to it. The business of tickets proved more remunerative than Jacobs had anticipated, and he saw that business as one that could naturally lead into another. The name Mike Jacobs had become synonymous with ticket brokerage. He was known to play producers, boxing promoters, matchmakers, and special events producers.

Having made a name for himself as a ticket broker, he decided to move on to the next level: He would own shows to which he had sold tickets. And so Mike Jacobs Productions was born, and its birth announcement appeared in the Broadway trade publications. Up and down Broadway and its side streets, marquees were hauled up above stage entrances with bold bright announcements: A Mike Jacobs Production. There was one for a bicycle race, another for an opera, a circus, a charity event, a wrestling match. Whatever performance could be staged in a theater, an auditorium, or an arena was being produced by Mike Jacobs. If one had an idea for a show or an event, Mike Jacobs was the man to see. Of course, he drove hard bargains. He was a tough negotiator who used all the leverage available to him. No one ever got the better of Mike Jacobs, and some got by with what they considered miniscule profits.

Jacobs earned a reputation as an energetic and corner-cutting hustler, but that is not the image he wanted—which is why he supported a number of charities aimed at helping poor children. "Outwardly [Jacobs and his partners] appeared to be motivated by an inexorable philanthropic compulsion to help Mrs. Hearst's Free Milk Fund. In reality, they were an avid cabal of self-seekers. . . . They cloaked themselves in the garb of charitable men."[2]

He may not have aspired to be another Flo Ziegfeld, but he certainly wanted the kind of respect afforded to the city's elite businessmen. Jacobs never forgot the importance of his relations with the Brooklyn bankers: Never stiff those who control the flow of money. Now Jacobs needed to attract a better breed of banker than those who had lent him money for his Brooklyn ventures; he needed bankers who could attest to Jacobs's creditworthiness. He was hailed and well met when he entered a bank or brokerage house on Wall Street or Broad Street. He had figured, like so many others, that the best way to earn the respect and admiration he sought from the city's blue bloods was not to attempt to ingratiate himself at their social gatherings, but to support their charities. He set about doing so with the kind of single-mindedness that brought him success as a Broadway producer. He would opportunistically donate his considerable producing and publicity skills to benefiting the charity events that his would-be audience of admirers supported. After reimbursing himself for his expenses, there would be plenty of money to support the mission of whatever charity he was promoting.

Serendipitously, Jacobs met and befriended a man who could help him climb to the top of a promoter's pyramid of wealth and power. He was Tex Rickard, one of America's most successful boxing promoters and a man who knew how to add commerce to charity to produce profits that would satisfy the greed of a pillaging army. He had begun his professional career as a marshal in Texas but soon tired of arresting people for little or no financial reward, while incurring injuries, some of which were serious. Tex bought a railroad ticket and boarded a train to the Klondike Gold Fields in 1897. He figured the life of a prospector held out more promise of riches than one as a poorly paid marshal. Rickard was no more cut out to be a prospector than he had been as lawman. He had no luck in finding gold but showed a considerable gift for incurring debt. He was not yet ready to give up the dream of finding gold; it was the kind of dream that can drive gold prospectors into following mirages. Rickard had left one golden dream for another and headed to the Nome goldfield. There, too, gold strikes eluded him; however, he made friends with a man who would open doors to a new career. The man was another former marshal and prospector, a true western legend, the sui generis Wyatt Earp. The two became fast friends, sharing tall tales about outlaws and badlands. They drank together, gambled what little money they had, and patronized the prostitutes who followed the gold prospectors, and who—it should be noted—often retired from the goldfields with enough money to open small businesses, some respectable, some not.

After all the tall tales and after all the gambling and whoring, Earp's presence served a valuable purpose in the life of Tex Rickard, for Earp introduced him to the world of boxing. Earp had earned money refereeing fights and often betting on the outcomes, especially if he could get boxers to throw their fights. He explained what was involved in refereeing a fight and the different ways you could guarantee the outcome: You could bribe a fighter, you could let him know you had bet on his opponent and would be willing to share your winnings, you could slow down a fighter by drugging him, you could manipulate fighters in the ring so a strong fighter might be prevented from landing knockout blows. Regardless of how you managed it, boxing could be a surefire way of earning good money. And since he too had failed as a gold prospector, he decided boxing was the better choice, for it offered steady, remunerative work. Earp was another one of those gamblers, like Rothstein, Madden, and Attell, who didn't like true gambling but preferred betting on sure things. The goldfields were for dreaming optimists. Boxing would be their ticket to new wealth. Earp and Rickard sold off their prospecting tools and headed for the big time, a place where large sums could be made in boxing. They were on their way to New York, the Mecca of boxing years before Las Vegas began to draw hordes of eager gamblers.

Rickard found an investor who was prepared to finance his new racket; it was none other than Arnold Rothstein, who, during the prior year, had earned a small fortune from the Black Sox Scandal.

Jacobs was drawn to Rickard, as he was to any new profitable opportunity he espied; he quickly befriended Rickard, impressing him with his ability to put together deals and cut and dispatch the smokescreen of obstacles that hindered many other men. Jacobs became, in effect, Rickard's aide-de-camp.

Jacobs did not have to betray his mentor, for Rickard unexpectedly died from a botched appendectomy operation. Jacobs did not attend the funeral, but he did attend to the schemes and plots Rickard had laid bare for him.

Some Broadway cynics said that because Jacobs had stood so close to Rickard, he was able to walk in the dead man's shoes. With Rickard gone, Jacobs crowned himself boxing's king of promoters.

To solidify his image, Jacobs told tall tales about how he was responsible for the rise of Jack Dempsey, the "Manassa Mauler," although Rickard had been the one who promoted the fearsome heavyweight.

Although Jacobs profited from Rickard's death in 1929, he was worried at the onset of the Great Depression that the sick economy might infect the world of boxing. Perhaps more extravagant promotions would ignite the enthusiasm of potential customers. Jacobs was not one to back down in the face of adversity. He would do not only what was necessary to maintain his level of success, but also everything in his power to increase his success.

Owney Madden was far more sanguine than Jacobs and told him that economic hard times would only serve to increase the public's appetites for more diverse attractions. There would always be customers willing to pay for a well-promoted event, especially a highly touted boxing match. Such events would help to relieve people of their worries as they cheered for their favorite pugilist to pummel an opponent. Jacobs accepted Madden's view and also accepted the fact that he would have to deal with him. Madden was too powerful to go up against, and it was good to have him on one's side, even if that meant sharing profits with the killer.

As the bleak years of the 1930s settled like a dark cloud on America, Jacobs thrived, just as Madden had predicted. Jacobs did not have to inflate his reputation with tall tales, for he was solidly regarded as boxing's premier promoter. He was not just the Machiavelli of promoters, he was also its Caesar. One could imagine him giving a thumbs up or down to any fighter who wanted to have a bout in New York's Madison Square Garden, the twentieth century's answer to the Roman Coliseum, where gladiators fought a different kind of combat. Boxing in the 1930s, minus Mike Jacobs, would be a story without an author. While never having thrown a punch, he was the man who determined which boxers would get to throw punches and at whom. He also had a hand in deciding who would lose and who would win. He helped managers become rich by making himself rich. Jacobs gave nothing away. If he was generous to a manager or boxer, he knew his generosity would result in a sizeable profit, one certainly greater than his initial costs of doing business. He had become the only game in town, and anyone who wanted to box had to play by Jacob's rules.

Jacobs did not operate from a palatial office. His place of business was commonly known as Jacobs Beach (without an apostrophe). It was a hangout for bookies, managers, promoters, hustlers, and, of course, boxers eager for a match in Madison Square Garden. Jacobs Beach was located at 49th Street between Broadway and Eighth Avenue, opportunistically located between the Garden and Jack Dempsey's Restaurant, which was seen briefly in the first *Godfather* movie. Across the street from Jacobs Beach was the notorious Forrest Hotel, where rats ate the leftovers from room service. Sometimes the rats were known not to wait for leftovers, but to attack a plate of food when a diner's back was turned. According to a 2005 article in the *New York Times*, "By 1950, the Forrest sued Bob Hope for saying that its maids changed the rats daily."[3]

Jacobs did not reside at the hotel, but many fighters and managers spent nights there while getting ready for a fight at Madison Square Garden. The Garden was Jacobs's staging ground, as was the Hippodrome. And in both places he promoted hundreds of fights, resulting in millions of dollars for himself, Madden, and various cohorts.

Because Jacobs felt his reputation was besmirched due to his association with Madden and other gangsters, he leaped at the opportunity to associate himself with a socially prominent strata of society by promoting himself as a benefactor to the city's poor. As with so many people, he believed if you were seen as doing good, then you were, ipso facto, a good person. The ideal opportunity arose, and he took advantage of it with the same drive he used to pursue his other ventures. To wit: He organized a boxing extravaganza for William Randolph Hearst's Milk Fund Boxing Benefit at the Bronx Coliseum in 1933. Hearst and Jacobs had been motivated by the same impulse: proving to the public that they had hearts of gold. Some cynics, however, said that the acquisition of gold alone was their true ambition. Kevin Mitchell writes, "In boxing, it's all about the numbers. Mike Jacobs, who had the heart of an accountant, was the number-one Numbers Man, and Garden was his bank."[4]

Because Jacobs's efforts resulted in far more money than had been anticipated, he was lauded in the press as a great benefactor of the poor. Although he had risen to economic heights, Jacobs often commented to reporters that he had not forgotten the people who had been his friends and neighbors when he was a poor boy growing up in Brooklyn. In the papers owned by Hearst, the stories about Jacobs were so laudatory as to think he had saved the human race from an imminent disaster. Even Damon Runyon, whose cynicism extended to the entire world of boxers and mangers, and who had popularized fictional versions of Rothstein and Madden, proceeded to pour lavish praise on the edifice of Mike Jacobs. By the end of the superlatives, one would have thought that a statue of Jacobs would be erected in Times Square. For Runyon and other cynical celebrants of the demimonde, there was nothing wrong with making a profit from good deeds, even if one's motivations were entirely self-serving.

In fact, so impressed was Runyon by Jacobs's ability to turn dross into gold that he ventured to form a partnership with the master promoter. He also invited two other journalists to join him in founding the Twentieth Century Sporting Club, which would dominate boxing promotions for more than a decade. The first fighter that the club promoted was future lightweight champion Barney Ross in 1934. The following year, Jacobs became the manager of one of the greatest heavyweights of all time, Joe Louis. And once he got his hooks into Louis, he would never let go. Louis was the biggest catch of Jacobs's career, and Louis became one of Jacobs's most reliable annuities, one that lasted for years. The name of Joe Louis on a Madison Square Garden marquee was a guarantee that every seat in the arena would be sold out. With an eye to creating a million-dollar gate, Jacobs promoted a bout between Joe Louis and Max Baer. Jacobs used every available technique to promote the bout: newspapers, radio, magazines, wire services, posters plastered all over New York. Huge numbers of fans turned out to witness the "Brown Bomber" face the man who had killed two boxers with what Jack Dempsey said was the most powerful right fist of any boxer in the last hundred years. For Baer's fans, the fight was a disheartening disappointment. Baer had a broken right hand; a doctor injected it with novocaine. The fight at Yankee Stadium was postponed for several hours due to rain. By the time the rain ceased and the bout was scheduled to commence, the novocaine in Baer's right fist had worn off. Baer was not only in pain, but also helpless without the use of his powerful right fist. He lost the bout, the most humiliating loss in his career.

Baer's hand healed slowly as he nursed it back to health. After six months, his right fist felt as good as it ever had been. It was solid and as powerful as a brick, a weapon that could shatter an opponent, leaving him with broken bones and unconscious. It was Baer's only effective weapon. He was not a great pugilistic stylist; he didn't have the technique of a Joe Louis or a Sugar Ray Robinson. Instead, he relied almost exclusively on his right fist. Baer told his manager, Ancil Hoffman, to get in touch with Jacobs and arrange for a rematch with Louis. Jacobs nixed the idea, regardless of how much money Hoffman was willing to give up, for if Louis succumbed to Baer's powerful right punch, Jacobs might lose his ability to cash in on each of Louis's successful matches. The fight that might have changed the history of the heavyweight division never took place. Louis went on to fight many top-rated opponents, each of whom was mischaracterized as a member of the "bum of the month club," and Jacobs got a hefty percentage of each of those fights. From January 1939 to May 1941, Louis blazingly defended his title 13 times. And 13 times, Jacobs made large deposits in his growing bank accounts.

Since Jacobs controlled Louis as if he were little more than an indentured servant, and as long as Louis maintained his championship status, Jacobs controlled the heavyweight division. Although the press didn't report it as such, the heavyweight division, in effect, belonged to Jacobs and Louis. It was an unequal but mutually advantageous partnership that was born of greed and sustained by a shared goal that Louis should wear his crown for as long as possible.

When Louis was discharged from the army following the end of World War II, he had significant debts. Before the IRS threw a net around Louis and hauled away his savings, Louis owed various lenders more than $100,000. In addition, Jacobs claimed Louis owed him $250,000. Louis had earned more than $4.5 million for himself and his managers during his career. Yet, he got to keep only $800,000. And that was before taxes.

While Jacobs made money from each of Louis's bouts, he didn't like sharing his profits with partners in the Twentieth Century Sporting Club. So, he decided the partnership had served its purpose and run its course, and the journey had reached its destination. It was time to take the club private and push out his partners. With the assistance of Owney Madden, Jacobs made his move, giving his partners an offer they dared not refuse. The Twentieth Century Sporting Club was now Jacobs's plaything. And he played it like a virtuoso. Every manager, trainer, boxer, champ, and contender knew that any important fight in New York would need the imprimatur of Jacobs. From the featherweight division to the heavyweight division, it was all ruled by the Caesar of New York boxing, Mike Jacobs, a man to be feared and a man to be flattered with money. And as a living, breathing monopoly, he was able to charge as much as he liked. He knew the market and the market knew and respected him. After all, there was nothing managers could do but accept Jacobs's terms. Pay as you go or don't go at all.

Sensing new opportunities with the instincts of a bloodhound, Jacobs smelled heretofore untapped opportunities in radio. In 1938, he produced the first fight on radio, and fans were drawn to the broadcast as if hypnotized. Not only did fans love it, but also sportswriters and advertising agencies. For the latter, it opened an entirely new arena for clients who wanted to expand the market for men's products. *Friday Night Fights* became one of the most popular radio programs right up until America's entry into World War II. It also proved a bonanza for local bars, each a predecessor to today's popular sports bars. Bartenders not only sold beer and liquor (and sometimes food) to fight fans, but also placed bets for them. As go-betweens for fans and bookies, the bartenders found an extra cash dividend. One Third Avenue bar had a chalkboard sign above its long bar that read, "Bettors, Beer, & Boxing Served Here."

As the years rolled on and Jacobs's power and income grew, he wanted more. After radio, television offered another opportunity. If radio had been a bonanza, then television would offer even more gigantic rewards. Now you could not only hear a fight, but also see it. And the audience would be so much larger than the ones who attended fights at the Garden or in Yankee Stadium. Jacobs knew advertisers would love to cash in on the expanded audience, and he was ready to turn their greed into dollars. The money to be made would be dazzling. Boxing, with its three-minute rounds, was made for TV advertising. Between each round, advertisers could insert their product messages, and those messages came fast and furious.

As with all of Jacobs's new ventures, boxing on television was given a full-court press promotional blast. Viewers would gather in front of their small black-and-white screens, beer in hand, and be enthralled by the sight of two men fighting to attain the championship of the world. Jacobs's first staged boxing match was for the championship of the featherweight division. The bout he staged was between Chalky Wright and lightning-fast puncher Willie Pep. Advertisers sold every break between rounds, and it was whispered that advertisers had encouraged the fighters to make the fight last as long as possible. There were implicit promises of rewards to the fighter if the bout accommodated all of the time the advertisers had paid for. There would be extra money in it for them. The fight lasted the full 15 rounds, and Pep won the decision and the title. Fans loved Pep, and his subsequent fights on television attracted large audiences. He was a magnificent boxer, and he would end his career after a total of 241 fights, including 229 wins, 65 of which were by knockout.

As his reputation as lord and master of boxing continued to grow, so did the perception among journalists and others that Jacobs's associates were shady characters, some of whom were hardened criminals who would resort to violence to accomplish their ends. As before, Jacobs intended to erase such impressions and chose another charitable event as an opportunity to present himself as a civic-minded do-gooder who supported his country. World War II was raging, and celebrities (including surreptitious draft dodgers) got on the patriotic bandwagon to support "our boys in uniform." Here would be an opportunity for Jacobs to surpass the role he had played when he promoted the William Randolph Hearst milk charity.

The United States had provided Jacobs with economic opportunities that few, if any, other countries could have delivered. Support for the American cause in World War II was not only an opportunity to burnish his somewhat tarnished reputation, but also it could add a new dimension. He would prove to the world that he loved the country that had made him a rich man. He would let the media proclaim him as more than just a philanthropist, but also a patriot. He staged an enormous boxing event to support U.S. war bonds. The event generated $36 million. That amount of money drew ooohs and aaahs from the media and politicians alike. As a result, Jacobs was honored by local politicos; he received a congratulatory telegram from the White House. His picture appeared in newspapers throughout the country. Even Owney Madden congratulated him. It was a magnificent PR coup. Common opinion was that Mike Jacobs may have had shady associations, but that was impossible to avoid in the world of boxing. He was, at heart, a generous patriot, who raised a substantial sum of money that would help the country win the war. He deserved the plaudits he received.

Unfortunately, good news doesn't last long; in the case of Mike Jacobs, the good news was followed by bad news. Jacobs's health had been faltering. He had untreated high blood pressure. His heartbeat, at times, felt irregular. First came a splitting headache as sudden as an unexpected hammer blow. Then came a momentary blinding flash of light, followed by a sharp scream of pain. Jacobs was the victim of a cerebral hemorrhage. He collapsed onto the floor as if receiving a powerful right cross to his temple. His role as boxing's ruler was over. It was 1946, and Jacobs's run for the big money, which had lasted through the Great Depression and World War II, was over. He sold his company to Madison Square Garden. He lingered on until 1953 and died peacefully in his mansion in New Jersey. Few people missed Jacobs.

Budd Schulberg writes, "People played up to him. But I don't think I remember any of us who could say he was a real friend. He was strictly business all the way. Totally unsentimental. And he had all the power."[5]

In his book *Ringside*, Schulberg quotes legendary trainer-manager Ray Arcel, saying,

> Mike may be a hard man to love. Somehow I don't think he even wanted people to like him. He was a lone operator. He played all his cards close to his chest. I don't think he ever let anybody get close to him. After all, he's been operating in this town all his life. . . . Some of the biggest people in this city call him Mike, and yet he hasn't got a single close friend.[6]

Schulberg continues his appraisal by writing,

> The tallest Horatio Alger tale is mild stuff alongside Mike's upward climb from the seamiest slums of Manhattan to the palatial home in New Jersey, and only the Lord (and probably not even the Treasury Department) knows how many millions. Whether Mike's been good for the fight game is what might be called along 49th Street a "mute pernt."[7]

By 1982, grievances about Mike Jacobs had either evaporated or been viewed through a soft-focus lens. He had been an integral part of boxing, and whether you liked him or disliked him, it didn't matter. He was a presence to which no one could be indifferent. As the prime minister of boxing, he was a legend to all those with whom he had dealings. He was elected to the Boxing Hall of Fame with barely a demur.

When he suffered his cerebral hemorrhage, he unintentionally opened a door to ambitious criminals who would be far more vicious and ruthless than Jacobs ever could have been. The leader of that insurrection was more brutal than any professional boxer. His takeover of boxing would corrupt the sports for decades to come. Frankie Carbo, a man with as many aliases as he had suits, was a man without a conscience, who believed that all disputes could be settled via the barrel of a gun. It is said that sharks must keep on moving or they die, and so it was with Carbo: He was always on the move, whether it was being several steps ahead of the law or several steps ahead of other boxing managers as he took over the contracts of their boxers. Carbo had formed his own organization, not quite in the mold of the Twentieth Century Sporting Club; Carbo formed the International Boxing Club (IBC), which sounded as benign as a health club or gym. Its name left no hint that its director had previously used his talents and temper for volatile violence and intense intimidation, for Carbo had been a member in good standing with Murder, Inc., the most notorious army of hired killers ever employed and deployed by organized crime in the United States.

The IBC had a board of directors that resembled a rogue's gallery more so than the back office of a sports team. Along with gambler and gangster Blinky Palermo and sometime furrier and boxing manager Hymie "The Mink" Wallman, and a pair of white-collar executives, the club controlled the welterweight and middleweight divisions of boxing. It also owned shares, large and small, of individual boxers in other divisions, for example, heavyweight boxer Sonny Liston.

In *Jacobs Beach*, Kevin Mitchell writes that Frankie Carbo "muscled in on the operations of Uncle Mike with sledgehammer subtlety. Perceiving no resistance, he went on to formalize the relationship" (forming the IBC).[8]

The life and career of Frankie Carbo is a seedy mansion with many rooms, each one with enough misery and crime to incarcerate him for years. He almost destroyed professional boxing.

5

THE GRAY CZAR OF BOXING

He had the hard, cold eyes of a killer, the eyes of a gray wolf before it lunges at a wounded deer. He was Frankie Carbo (commonly referred to as "Mr. Gray" or "The Gray"), the man who would invade, conquer, and corrupt the world of boxing.

He was born Paolo Giovanni Carbo on the Lower East Side of Manhattan. His parents were poor immigrants from Sicily, and young Carbo endured the deprivations that are congruent with dire poverty. He took out his anger on those he could bully, and there were many victims. As a public-school boy, who attended classes infrequently, he would pick on kids who wouldn't stand up to him and steal whatever small change they possessed. Day after day, even when not attending classes, Carbo would stake out a position in the schoolyard and demand of some hapless kid that he turn over his luncheon sandwich or be prepared for a pair of black eyes and a bloody nose. On his way out of the schoolyard, he would occasionally beat up some kid whose appearance or manner offended him.

By age 11, Carbo, who was now called Frankie, had such a fearsome reputation among his schoolmates and was in trouble so often that he was sent to reform school. But like so many other delinquents who entered the world of boxing (e.g., Jake LaMotta and Rocky Graziano), Carbo was not reformed in reform school. If anything, reform schools were schools that taught budding criminals the techniques of successful criminality in the world beyond confinement. Inside, young Carbo learned to channel his antisocial behavior into learning small-time criminal skills and schemes that would yield a few dollars here, a few dollars there. Upon his release, he saw the legitimate world with new eyes: It was a place where he could pounce on victims and probably not get caught for the crimes he would regularly commit. He had a new image of himself: a successful young hoodlum who could intimidate or—if necessary—shoot his way to success.

As an entrepreneur of crime, he looked around for various career opportunities and stumbled upon the protection racket. Instead of beating up kids for their lunches and small change, he would demand protection from those who had more than a few dimes and nickels in their pockets. Although he was promoting himself to a higher level of criminality than he had enjoyed as a schoolyard tough guy, he used the same sales slogan: If you didn't want to be beaten up, then you better pay up. Without the finesse of Owney Madden, who organized taxi drivers, Carbo attempted to strong-arm taxi drivers into subscribing to his protection racket. The protection amounted to not having Carbo bludgeon them with a metal pipe or shoot them. Staring into the eyes of a skeptical or intimidated taxi driver, Carbo's message, menacingly hissed, was pay up or else. "The terror he imposed was subtle and meaningful. His hair was gray and contrasted with the deep blackness of his eyes, which were piercingly alert and challenging."[1] He was a master of the Mafia hard look.

However, when that menacing look didn't produce the desired result and a driver proved recalcitrant, Carbo used his muscle and the barrel of a gun to persuade the driver that he better join Carbo's ad hoc taxi union or the consequences would be grave indeed.

Carbo's methods didn't always succeed. He had expected that there might be a few guys who thought they were tough enough to avoid their obligations to him. The brazen lack of fear of one taxi driver proved to be an insult to Carbo's machismo. That taxi driver posed a direct challenge to Carbo's self-image as a tough guy, and so the driver had to pay the ultimate price. Carbo pulled out a snub-nosed .38 and fired a bullet into the heart of the once recalcitrant driver, who collapsed next to his cab. Carbo's explosive temper didn't end by pulling a trigger: He kicked the life-leaking body lying on the pavement, then tucked the pistol into a jacket pocket and disappeared into the hazy moonlit night. His freedom was short-lived. Two cops nabbed him, and Carbo went off quietly, without a struggle.

Although a number of witnesses had seen the murder, no one stepped forward to offer testimony. Yet, someone must have identified him, otherwise why would he have been arrested? Carbo knew that only a fool with a death wish would volunteer or agree to testify against him. People regularly read in newspapers about witnesses turning up dead, a bullet in the back of the head, an ice pick jammed into a spinal cord, a body burnt beyond recognition in a weed-strewn vacant lot. Still, Carbo was concerned that some witness might be so asinine that he wanted to show the world he was a good, conscientious citizen and offer to testify against him. Or the cops might be holding a witness incognito, keeping him on ice until there was a trial. And, indeed, the cops claimed they had such a witness and that Carbo or his associates would not be able to get to him. Carbo figured he would be better off if he copped a plea. He had his lawyer negotiate a plea deal for a reduced sentence based on Carbo agreeing to plead out to self-defense. For this plea, Carbo was rewarded with a guilty verdict for manslaughter. The judge handed down a sentence of two to four years. Many mobsters, facing jail time, voice a cliché of their trade that they can do their time "standing on their heads." Carbo seemed the incarnation of that expression, for he left the court with a smile on his face.

In prison, he craftily demonstrated neither bravado nor arrogance; he played it smart: He was a peaceable prison inmate who knew the value of good behavior. He didn't talk back to guards, didn't attack other inmates, didn't instigate fights. His good behavior was rewarded, and he was out of the joint in 20 months. Freedom presented him with new opportunities to seek other criminal activities not involving taxi drivers, who he now felt were too diverse and independent to be easily organized into a union. Carbo also realized that he should operate in the shadows, avoiding moonlit nights (no matter how hazy), as well as bright, sunny days. He had enough of prisons. A smart gangster was one who just didn't get caught, and Carbo had no intention of ever being caught again. He became known as Mr. Gray and even took to wearing dull, gray business suits topped by a gray fedora. He no longer needed to strut brazenly like a tough young hood showing off his manhood. In his dull, corporate uniform, he could blend into a passing parade of urban executives in any big city in the United States. His grayness would become his camouflage. Darkened rooms and alleys suited his surreptitious style. And although he was often referred to as Mr. Gray, some referred to him (but always behind his back) as "Jimmy the Wop," a tough Sicilian gangster.

His street reputation as a calm, unemotional killer was a circulating and admired résumé, and Murder, Inc., a feared company of more than 100 hired killers and knee breakers, offered Carbo an attractive position. It wouldn't be a contract hit here and another hit there. Instead, the management offered him full-time employment as a hired hit man. He would be on call seven days a week, 24 hours a day. For his services, there would be a monthly retainer, plus a fixed price for each murder. The price depended on the difficulty of carrying out the hit and its geographic location, as well as the prominence of the victim.

Murder, Inc., comprised squads of depraved killers, mostly Italians and Jews, who operated out of a candy store in the Brownsville section of Brooklyn. They were the storm troopers for labor racketeers Louis "Lepke" Buchalter, Albert Anastasia, and Jacob "Gurrah" Shapiro. (Shapiro was given the nickname Gurrah because he seemed to growl out the word *Gurrah* when confronted with unpleasant questions. It was a growl of disgust, interpreted to mean "get out of here.") The Murder, Inc., hierarchy also had an alliance with Thomas Lucchese (aka "Three Fingers Brown"), head of the Lucchese crime family, which controlled much of New York's garment industry. The thugs of Murder, Inc., and their bosses worked for those who paid the highest prices. One day, they could break heads and knees for a union, the next day they could do it on behalf of companies. There was no loyalty, no ideology. It was all business. Murder, Inc., was also hired to silence stool pigeons, competitors, interlopers, and witnesses: anyone who could pose a threat.

The killers of Murder, Inc., each had their own set of skills, whether it was the garrote, the lead pipe, the ice pick, the switchblade, the blackjack, brass knuckles, or a snub-nosed .38. For Frankie Carbo, the .38 pistol was his weapon of choice. It was easy to conceal, and it never failed him. He wore gloves when loading the bullets into the chambers, and he wore gloves when firing the pistol: No fingerprints. If picked up by the cops, he could always claim he had wrestled the gun out of the hands of the murdered man who had tried to kill him. His prints weren't on the gun because it wasn't his gun. If pinched, he would claim he had been trying to go straight and some wiseguy had attempted to rob him. He simply acted in self-defense. Carbo was sleek and sly, and for him the .38 was the source of a clean hit. If he didn't get too close to his victim, there wouldn't even be the splash of the victim's blood on his well-tailored gray suit and white shirt. Although Carbo had his hits well planned, he also had his departures well orchestrated. He did not want to sit for a police grilling, did not want to see prison doors openly inviting him to serve another sentence. Murder, if it couldn't be plea bargained, could result in a long prison term, and if his prison terms piled up, he could wind up spending his life in a damp little cell. It was better to never get caught.

However, as for future murder convictions, he was less than Velcro but not quite Teflon: indicted but not tried. Jimmy Breslin, in *A Life of Damon Runyon*, writes the following about when Carbo heard a knock on his hotel room door:

> "Yeah, what do you want?"
>
> "Western Union. Telegram for Mr. John Paul Frankie Carbo."
>
> "Put it under the door."
>
> "I'm sorry mister, but I need you to sign."
>
> "Don't open the door, Frankie. Are you crazy?" [warned his girlfriend]
>
> "Forget about it. I know what this is. They got a fighter, Freddie Steele, coming in for me on the train. That's the one going to win a title. You're telling me don't answer the door."
>
> "Frankie don't," the young woman shrieks.
>
> There is the sound and grumbling of at least a quartet of detectives.
>
> "What's your problem?" Frankie says.
>
> "You mean you don't know?" the detective says.
>
> "Frankie make them show you a warrant."
>
> "Here," the detective said.
>
> "Let me see that!" the girl said.
>
> There is a crackle of fresh paper and then at least a gasp. "Frankie, this says you murdered somebody! Who is this guy they say you murdered?"
>
> "It never took place," Frankie said.
>
> "You're under arrest for the shooting of Mickey Duffy," the detective said.[2]

For this arrest and a brief time in jail, there would be no witnesses to justify neither an indictment nor a murder conviction, and so Frankie Carbo walked out a free man.

The 1931 murder of bootlegger Mickey Duffy was only one of several murders attributed to Carbo. In 1933, on behalf of Murder, Inc., Carbo killed Max Greenberg and Max Haskel, members of Waxey Gordon's mob of bootleggers. He had shot each of them in the Carteret Hotel in Elizabeth, New Jersey. In 1936, the law caught up with Carbo for those two hits, and cops arrested him outside Madison Square Garden, where he had been sniffing out the possible opportunities of the fight game. He was jailed for six months; but again when no witnesses would agree to testify, Carbo was released. He exited the jail dressed in his trademark gray suit and fedora, a sly smile on his face.

Carbo must have felt he was untouchable. He had committed murder after murder and was rarely arrested. But he was not like fly paper: Nothing stuck to him. Three years later, he teamed with fellow Murder, Inc., thug Allie "Tick Tock" Tannenbaum; notorious gangster and glamour boy of the mob Bugsy Siegel; and Siegel's brother-in-law, Whitey Krakower. Together, they carried out a hit against Harry "Big Greenie" Greenberg, who was singing a song of accusations against his former mob cohorts. There was nothing more dangerous than a rat, who could send a passel of hoods to the electric chair or gas chamber. Big Greenie had to be silenced, and he trusted his old pal Bugsy to protect him. He should have known better; when the mob wants to kill you, they often send one of your friends to do the job, or at least to set you up. While Bugsy and Krakower departed the scene in a fancy car, and Tannenbaum in a car driven by Harry "Champ" Segal, Carbo departed by other means.

Shortly after five bullets had invaded Big Greenie's head and torso, Carbo was seen trotting down a street in Hollywood, California. As he trotted, he puffed on a big cigar and was understandably out of breath. He jumped into a waiting car and would soon be on his way out of Los Angeles.

Big Greenie was not the only one singing to the cops: Abe "Kid Twist" Reles had been arrested and offered a deal. And Allie "Tick Tock" Tannenbaum, stricken by his conscience, was also singing a similar song to the DA in New York. The duo claimed Carbo, Siegel, and Krakower had killed Big Greenie on orders issued by Murder, Inc., which, in turn, had been carrying out the orders of Buchalter and Anastasia. If someone didn't silence the songbirds, a few people would fry in what was known as "Old Sparky," more commonly known as the electric chair. Worried that Krakower might also be inspired to confess and testify, Murder, Inc., arranged for his demise. With one gone, there were still two to worry about. First on the list of Murder, Inc., was Reles.

He was put under police guard at the Half Moon Hotel in Coney Island. He would be kept there until called to testify. His end came as no surprise to the mob. According to the five cops who were supposedly guarding him, Reles tied sheets together to descend six stories out of his hotel window and escape the cops who were standing watch. Unfortunately, there was not a sufficient length of sheeting, and so Reles plunged to his death. None of the cops looked as if they were about to break into gales of laughter as this unlikely story was told. Instead, they were stone-faced in their seriousness. It was later revealed that Frank Costello, the "Prime Minister of the Underworld," had arranged for the cops to split $100,000 among themselves for flinging Reles out of the window. None of the cops was prosecuted, although each of them was demoted. For the $20,000 each of the cops received, a demotion was worth it. At the tail end of the Depression, $20,000 was a great deal of money.

Now there was only one witness who could cause trouble, and Tannenbaum was better guarded than his erstwhile partner. At trial, a jury of 12 men wrangled about Tannenbaum's testimony and then agreed that without corroboration, his testimony couldn't be accepted. Some reporters speculated that members of the jury had been paid to ensure the proper verdict. Others whispered that payoffs went as high as the mayor's office. Siegel was delighted with the verdict but furious that he was referred to as Bugsy in the newspapers that covered the trial. He preferred being called Mr. Siegel. For Carbo, all that mattered was an acquittal. Once again, he proved that nothing the law could throw at him would stick. Neither cops nor mobsters expressed sympathy for Reles. In fact, in mob circles, it was joked that Reles was the "canary who could sing but couldn't fly."[3]

Carbo's elusiveness had become his nonsignature trait for many years. He was like T. S. Eliot's Macavity the cat: "He always has an alibi, and one or two to spare: At whatever time the deed took place—MA-CAVITY WASN'T THERE!"[4]

Carbo's most successful disappearing act would occur years later. It involved one of the most stunning unsolved mob murders of the twentieth century. It took out Carbo's associate, the Mafia's handsome ladies' man, Hollywood man-about-town, aspiring actor, and Las Vegas visionary Bugsy Siegel. He had been reading a newspaper on the couch of a palatial home on Linden Drive in Beverly Hills, California. The anonymous killer, after firing bullet after bullet into Siegel, faded into the night and was never caught. But years later, Ralph Natale, former boss of the Philadelphia mob and a Mafia historian, claimed that Frankie Carbo, Siegel's onetime pal and partner in killings, had fired the fatal rifle shots into the cranium and body of Bugsy. Years earlier, when asked about mob ethics regarding murder, Siegel had given an answer that could have applied to his pal Frankie Carbo: "We only kill each other." And it came as no surprise that no one was ever indicted for the murder.

Like most mobsters, Frankie had no loyalty to any of the men with whom he did business. His loyalty was to his schemes and scams. If you had mentioned honor to him it would have been as far-fetched as if you had asked him if he had a conscience. It didn't matter to Carbo that he had once helped Bugsy, along with Krakower and Tannenbaum, kill Harry "Big Greenie" Greenberg, the snitching songbird who could have ended their careers by giving each of them a one-way ticket to death houses in either Sing Sing or San Quentin State Prison. Greenie had known that as a member of a gang, he had been expected to keep his mouth shut; to pull a trigger when so ordered; to come when called, no matter the day or the hour; and to never let his conscience interfere with his job. The two worst sins of a mobster are stealing from the boss (e.g., Bugsy Siegel had paid the price for skimming money from the Flamingo Hotel and Casino's investors) and becoming a rat. There were less serious sins, but those two could lead to death. Paranoia was the carapace that kept a mobster vigilant. Don't trust anyone was as much a motto for the mob as semper fi is for the Marines.

But Carbo would never be doubted by those who employed him. His life was not marked by any sort of conscience, large or small. His life was fueled by his rapacious need for self-satisfaction, and he protected himself from any loss of favor via his own well-developed paranoia. He trusted no one and suspected everyone with whom he did business. His sole object was making money, and he did so easily but spent it sparingly, if not painfully. In the movie *Prizzi's Honor*, Kathleen Turner's character, Irene Walker, states, "The Sicilians would rather eat their children than part with money." Carbo seemed to value money in that tradition. Money was not only a sign of his success and cleverness, but also, at times, a necessary means for paying off cops, judges, and prosecutors. It came as no surprise that rumor had it that Carbo may have been required by his Murder, Inc., bosses to contribute some money to paying off the cops who flung Abe "Kid Twist" Reles out of the window at the Half Moon Hotel. After all, Carbo was a primary beneficiary of the defenestration of Reles, and so he was required to make a financial contribution to ensure his own freedom. It was an investment that provided positive returns, for Carbo was able to go on, unhindered, making money.

Of all the murders Carbo committed, he was only convicted of the murder of the taxi driver. He had so mastered the techniques of intimidation that there were never any witnesses to testify against him for the murders of Mickey Duffy, Max Greenberg, Max Haskell, Bugsy Siegel, and his other victims. Carbo could slip away quickly, and he could terrify potential witnesses with a series of threatening phone calls or late-night personal visits. There were also his emissaries, whose skills at intimidation were second to none. The lengths to which Carbo would go to silence a witness were without limit.

The techniques of intimidation, along with a fearsome reputation as a cold-blooded killer, would later contribute to Carbo's success in gaining control of many boxers. Boxing offered Carbo a profession that seemed more profitable and less attractive to the gaze of law enforcement than being a hired gun. By the time almost all of the members of Murder, Inc., had been tried and found guilty, Carbo had entered the world of boxing. He had stealthily avoided the fate of his comrades in arms and was a new man.

He had seen the profits that accrued to Owney Madden and Mike Jacobs, and he wanted those profits for himself. Owney, too, had given up the life of a killer, first to become a bootlegger and then the owner of boxers' contracts. His role in the career of Primo Carnera was well known in the world of boxing. Carbo figured he could easily follow in the footsteps of Madden. Rather than threatening witnesses to his crimes to remain silent, he could threaten boxers and their managers to cut him in for large percentages. Once he owned boxers, the next step was to let promoters know that if they wanted one of his boxers, they, too, would have to cut him in for large percentages. The threats, some implied, others overt, intimidated boxers and their managers to accede to Carbo's demands. But it wasn't only the threats, for through his ownership of various contracts, Carbo had sufficient leverage to determine if boxers got fights or didn't.

When offering terms to boxers, trainers, and managers that they could rarely refuse, Carbo would often put on the mask of one of his fictitious identities; the most commonly used was Mr. Gray. Some boxers, managers, and trainers knew him by other names; he was known as Frank Russo or Frank Tucker or Frank Gray, or Frank Fury. The names really didn't matter because by whatever name Carbo was known, he had the power to make or break a fighter's career.

He would initially come on as a nice guy who could offer a boxer newfound opportunities to make a lot of money. It would not become apparent to the boxer and his manager what they would have to give up until it became time to sign a contract. At that point, there would be considerable resistance, even outrage, at being conned, but whatever form the resistance took, it was demolished as easily as a bulldozer demolishes cement walls. The force of threats was sufficiently intimidating. Boxers and their managers learned too late that they could not back out. The deals were inked, and no one would complain. Thereafter, Carbo would seemingly fade away and blend into the background of a fighter's life, only making sure to collect on each fight. No one dared withhold Carbo's cut.

And so the doors to the world of boxing seemed to swing open for Carbo and his entourage. It seemed so easy he could have asked Blinky Palermo why he hadn't muscled his way in earlier. Boxing would earn Carbo and his cohorts millions of dollars. Once managers and Carbo's repertory company of boxers had been signed (for they would all have to act the parts assigned them, either as winners or losers), Carbo or one of his emissaries would tell them what was expected of them. They did what they were told to do and were rewarded to the extent that Carbo, as czar, saw fit. Many of them were shortchanged but increased their earnings by betting on the predetermined outcomes of their bouts. Exercising dictatorial control, Carbo rarely had to resort to his old methods. It did not take boxers and their managers long to learn the obedience Carbo expected of them, and so they played their parts with consummate skill, with the exception of Jake LaMotta, whose case is examined in the next chapter.

With boxers and managers signed to unbreakable contracts, Carbo moved to take full control of the world of boxing. He would have to push Mike Jacobs off his throne, but he would permit him to wear the tin crown of a figurehead ruler. Carbo would be the true czar of boxing.

Before Jacobs was pushed off his throne, he had owned boxers the way kids own baseball cards. He owned contracts and treated his plantation of boxers as if they were annuities. Joe Louis, one of the greatest heavyweight boxers of the twentieth century, was tied to Jacobs for years. Every time Louis fought, Jacobs made a deposit into his own bank account.

As Jacobs was aging, his tightfisted grip on the reins of boxing matches at Madison Square Garden began to loosen and the shadowy figure of Mr. Gray became more distinct. Following a TKO from a pair of disabling strokes, Jacobs was counted out and in no shape to ward off the encroachments of Frankie Carbo. Carbo, ever persuasive, was able to get Jacobs to sell his Twentieth Century Boxing Club to Madison Square Garden for $100,000. Thereafter, Carbo's International Boxing Club (IBC) of New York was given the right to promote fights at the Garden. The IBC developed a stranglehold on championship boxing, especially in the welterweight and lightweight divisions, promoting 47 out of 51 championship bouts in the United States from 1949 to 1955. While the IBC earned millions from fixed fights, it earned even greater sums from television's twice weekly bouts from the Garden. The advertising dollars poured down into the hands of the IBC.

The welterweight and lightweight divisions of boxing were now in the hands of men who treated their boxers as money-generating chattels. The IBC was monopolistic, and Carbo was the de facto ruler, supported by his tribe of henchmen: Frank "Blinky" Palermo, Hymie "the Mink" Wallman, Ettore "Eddie" Coco, James (aka Jimmy Doyle) Plumeri, and Harry "Champ" Segal. Under the aegis of the IBC, they would make sure orders were obeyed and no outside group would be able to interfere with their operations. They were aided in their ambitions by the socially prominent and exceedingly wealthy James Norris, who was propped up as president of the IBC. His prestige added an illusion of luster and legitimacy to the IBC's rough tactics. Their enterprise was represented in legal matters by Truman Gibson, a fascinating example of a progressive and socially conscientious lawyer, who was later convicted of promoting the illegal activities of the IBC and the shady characters who controlled it.

As Kevin Mitchell writes in *Jacobs Beach*,

> Together with purblind acquiescence of other timid types, Carbo, Palermo, and their friends would turn Madison Square Garden into a sordid hall of deceit. Or rather, they made sure it would remain that way. Because in truth, it had had rarely been anything else. Frankie and Blinky, along with their sharp-suited cohort, Jim Norris, and the smooth-talking lawyer, Truman Gibson, robbed boxers remorselessly within its walls and from the East Coast to the West, they froze out good fighters who wouldn't do as they were told, arranged results, and controlled titles—perhaps not so brazenly as some before them, maybe not so subtly as some that followed, but with no less enthusiasm.[5]

Of these nefarious characters, three stand out as representing entirely different backgrounds and ways of doing business. First, there was James Norris. He was scion of a super-rich family. He and his father owned the Detroit Red Wings hockey team and a string of racehorses. He was chairman of the board of the Norris Grain Company; a partner in a Chicago stock brokerage firm, Norris & Kenly; director of the American Furniture Mart in Chicago; director of the Upper Lakes Transportation Company; director of the West Indies Sugar Company; a coowner of the Chicago Black Hawks; and owner of Spring Hill Farm, a successful Kentucky horse breeding farm. Yet, this well-educated, well-tailored man with an upper-class accent and impressive pedigree loved the company of mobsters and the boxers they controlled. He fulfilled an early ambition of being in charge of a major boxing organization by becoming president of the IBC, where he reigned from 1949 to 1958. Yet, as powerful as he appeared to be, there was always the shadowy figure of Mr. Gray, whispering in his ear. One would have thought that all the wealth possessed by Norris would have insulated him from the power of Carbo, but Norris was as bendable as a newborn shoot in spring. He was worth $250 million, but he didn't use a dime of it to build a wall between himself and Carbo.

Second was Frank "Blinky" Palermo, a short and short-tempered man, not much more than five feet tall, who always seemed to operate on the edge of anger. He reminded some people of an angry bulldog. He was a Philadelphia mobster who had an arrest record that included auto theft, assault, and violation of state liquor laws. He was known among police, mobsters, and reporters as the "numbers king" of Philadelphia. Ultimately, in addition to owning boxers and promoting matches, he was Carbo's muscleman, the guy who threatened recalcitrant boxers and devious managers that they had better accept Carbo's deals, no matter how unfair and onerous they were. Few had the courage or the foolishness not to go along.

Third was Truman Gibson. Every business, whether legal or illegal, requires superior legal services, and the IBC found their legal eagle in the person of Gibson. As a lawyer and a man of probity, he had a sterling reputation. In 1940, President Franklin Roosevelt appointed Gibson as an assistant advisor to the secretary of war, Henry L. Stimson, and as a spokesperson and advisor on behalf of black soldiers. In 1943, he was appointed chief civilian advisor to Stimson. Gibson had previously negotiated a contract for Joe Louis and organized the American Negro Exposition in Chicago. For his work on behalf of black soldiers, he was awarded the Legion of Merit in 1945. As an advisor to President Truman, Gibson was instrumental in getting the president to issue an executive order ending segregation in all branches of the military. By 1949, he had become director of Joe Louis Enterprises and then secretary of the IBC. When legal issues forced Norris to resign his position with the IBC, Gibson became its president. In 1961, Gibson was convicted of extortion and conspiracy, along with Carbo and Palermo, and two of their thugs, Joe Sica and Louis Dragna. Gibson's reputation was shattered when he was sentenced to five years' probation and fined for his deeds on behalf of the IBC. His life in professional boxing had come to an ignominious end, but more on that later.

These were the men who helped Carbo corrupt boxing, and two of whom seemed the least likely pair to participate in such doings. But the excitement of being around boxers, hanging out at their gyms and training camps, and earning vast sums of money proved to be irresistible temptations. They were an odd collection of men who supported one another's schemes and conspiracies right up until they were found guilty in courts of law.

There were many fighters and managers who wanted to participate in championship bouts at Madison Square Garden. They came from Canada, Central America, Europe, and throughout the United States. They were willing to make deals with the devil to gain entry to their golden dreams of success. Managers and boxers had to deal with the IBC, obey its orders, and accept being shortchanged, while agreeing to deals that generously lined the pockets of the men of the IBC. Many of those boxers and managers must have felt humiliated, for they were no more than actors in dramas in which the IBC wrote the closing lines. If a boxer was instructed to take a dive, he better do so, for the consequences of not obeying could be grave indeed. Sometimes, just to be on the safe side, it was also necessary to guarantee an outcome by paying off judges and referees who would deliver expected verdicts.

Great trainer Ray Arcel was one of those who didn't feel he had to go along to get along. He and two others had started the *Saturday Night Fights* on television. For the privilege of doing so, he had to pay the IBC. When he was called to testify about this relationship, he revealed details that angered Norris and Carbo, not the most forgiving of men. It didn't matter to them that Arcel was one of boxing's most talented and esteemed trainers; 20 of those he trained went on to become world championship boxers, including such notables as Benny Leonard, Barney Ross, and Tony Zale. Years later, he would be honored as the trainer of Roberto Duran and Larry Holmes, among various others. Standing outside a Boston arena in September 1953, while awaiting the first bell of one of his *Saturday Night Fights*, he was hit on the head with a lead pipe wrapped in a brown paper bag. He suffered a severe concussion and spent time in a hospital. Upon his recovery, he briefly retired from boxing. His assailant was never caught, but the word was that he received street justice for standing up against the IBC, according to testimony at the 1961 trial of Carbo and his cohorts. Arcel's televised *Saturday Night Fights* were subsequently canceled. No one could televise a professional boxing match without the permission of the IBC.

Such acts, along with stories of fixed fights and managers who were cheated and threatened, eventually led to law enforcement focusing a beam of light onto the dark doings of the IBC. Trials and tribulations would soon follow, and punishments would be handed out. Carbo, who had avoided being nailed by law enforcement for the murders he had committed, except the one of the taxi driver, had operated in the shadowy darkness of the boxing world. He was safer than someone who commits murders, safer than a mobster who seeks the spotlight, safer than a mobster who exults in his fame. He operated under a cloak of near-anonymity, and his crimes were far less serious than murder. All he did was fix boxing matches, muscle his way into management positions, and take inordinately large percentages of the money his fighters earned. Such behavior could not compare with the crimes he had committed as a member of Murder, Inc. Yet, the law was not making comparisons: For them Carbo was first and last a criminal. Everything he touched was a result of his criminal greed and nefarious tactics. He didn't see it coming, but he was about to feel the law's hot breath on the back of his neck.

On July 24, 1958, Frankie Carbo, under the name Paul John Carbo, was indicted on 10 charges of illegal operations in the sport of boxing. He was charged with one count of conspiracy, seven counts of undercover management of boxers, and two counts of unlicensed matchmaking, although the IBC—not Carbo—was listed as the official matchmaker in the cited cases. Each count was listed as a misdemeanor, and states where Carbo might have been operating or hiding were obligated to extradite him. If convicted of the charges, Carbo could have been sent to prison for 10 years and fined $2,500. The indictments were announced by New York district attorney Frank S. Hogan. He did not know where Carbo was hiding, but the mobster had last been spotted at a racetrack in Tijuana, Mexico. Border agents were on heightened patrol, looking out for Carbo. Thinking that he could be arrested at a lightweight championship bout in Houston, detectives were sent to nab Carbo, but he did not appear. Detectives had also visited Carbo's home in Hollywood, Florida. Again, Carbo was not there. Carbo had no intention of doing time.

Hogan, speaking to reporters, said the police would eventually catch Carbo: He could not run and hide forever. Hogan also noted, in response to a reporter's question, that because of Carbo's 1928 conviction for manslaughter, he was not eligible for a license either as a boxer's manager or a matchmaker. Since he could not legally manage a boxer, Carbo had conspired with Hymie "the Mink" Wallman, a furrier and manager of boxers, to secretly manage a number of boxers during the period from September 1, 1957, to March 31, 1958.

Wallman, having been granted immunity, testified to a grand jury that in exchange for appearing to be the manager of numerous of Carbo's boxers, he had gotten his own boxers matches in Madison Square Garden and various other venues. Those matches would not have taken place without the connivance of Carbo. Evidence had been presented to the grand jury by the head of the DA's rackets bureau, assistant DA Alfred J. Scotti, and another assistant DA, John C. Bonomi. They laid out evidence that Carbo had operated as a manager without a license and a matchmaker for a welterweight bout between Virgil Akins and Isaac Logart at Madison Square Garden. Other fights for which Carbo was charged with unlicensed management included the following:

A featherweight match on March 7 between Ike Chestnut and Harold Gomes, which took place at the Garden.

A heavyweight bout between Clarence Hinnant and Yvon Durelle at the Garden, for which Carbo was charged with "undercover" management.

A middleweight bout at the Garden between Jimmy Peters and George Chimenti, for which Carbo was charged with undercover management. Wallman had been listed as Peters's manager.

A heavyweight bout between Alex Miteff and Nino Valdez, for which Carbo was charged with undercover management. Wallman had been listed as Miteff's manager.

A heavyweight bout between Don McAteer and Burke Emery at the Garden. Carbo was charged with undercover management of McAteer, whose listed manager was William Plunkett.

A fight at St. Nicholas Arena between middleweights Jimmy Peters and Rudy Sawyer resulted in another charge against Carbo. Wallman was listed as Peters's manager.

Another member of the IBC, Harry "Champ" Segal, was indicted as the undercover manager of Sawyer.

The police received an anonymous tip that Carbo was hiding in a house in New Jersey. He had been there for 10 months, going out only at night. After hiding out for 10 months, Carbo was arrested at 357 Crystal Lake Terrace in Haddon Township, New Jersey. When New York detectives and New Jersey state cops, guns drawn, banged on the front door, Carbo ran down a flight of stairs, down a hallway, through a kitchen, and out of the back door of the house. He ran for about 25 feet.

Detectives shouted that Carbo should halt. If not, he might have been shot. He was grabbed by two detectives. Carbo claimed he only ran because he thought the detectives were Mafioso who had been sent to kill him. Having blurted out that excuse, he smiled and did not put up any resistance. When asked to empty his pockets, Carbo handed over to detectives a large roll of bills secured by a rubber band. The detectives counted $2,800 in hundreds, fifties, twenties, and tens. Carbo did not respond when a detective inquired if that was going-away money. Carbo claimed he would have surrendered in a couple of days, he was just organizing his belongings; however, DA Hogan strongly disagreed and asserted he had evidence that Carbo was about to flee the United States.

In addition to the 10 indictments brought by Hogan, the federal government charged that Carbo owed $750,000 in back taxes, penalties, and interest. The government claimed Carbo had not paid taxes for the periods from 1944 to 1946 and 1949 to 1951. When all else fails, the government has learned that a tax case may be its only option when nailing a racketeer. It had learned that lesson from its prosecution of Al Capone.

Carbo was being held in the Camden County Jail, awaiting extradition to New York. But his lawyers were working feverishly to frustrate an extradition order. And they succeeded, when the extradition was suddenly halted. Carbo's lawyers had been granted a stay pending the outcome of an appeal. His lawyers immediately filed a petition for a writ of habeas corpus. A judge reviewed the writ but then denied Carbo bail, pending an appeal. Carbo's lawyers were ultimately successful, as Carbo was released on $100,000 bail. His release was not without consequences, for he had to plead guilty to all charges. To obtain such a large bail for misdemeanor charges, assistant DA John Bonomi had made a strong case against Carbo. He told the judge that "Carbo is not merely a racketeer and underworld figure, but he is more powerful than any boxing promoter or manager. He is high commissioner of the whole boxing industry where racketeers predominate and control."[6]

Bonomi concluded his remarks by noting that Carbo had a record of 15 arrests, four for homicide and one conviction for manslaughter.

Carbo, after being arrested, had refused to be photographed or fingerprinted, claiming that because he had been charged with misdemeanors, he did not have to be printed or photographed. He was correct: Only felons were photographed and fingerprinted.

At trial, the chief assistant DA, Alfred Scotti, stated that Carbo had held a meeting with James Norris, president of the IBC, during which Carbo dictated terms of deals. He also stated that Hymie "the Mink" Wallman was a Carbo puppet. When Carbo pulled his strings, Wallman pretended to be the manager of Carbo's boxers.

DA Scotti stood at the prosecution table, on which was a tape recorder. He was about to press the play button, revealing to the courtroom, which was crowded with spectators and reporters, hours of wiretapped conversations of Carbo talking with members of the IBC and managers with whom Carbo had been making crooked deals. Suddenly Carbo's lawyer, Abraham Brodsky, jumped up like a jack-in-a-box and, in a loud voice, in fact, almost yelling, claimed that his client wanted to change his plea from not guilty to guilty of three of the charges. He would plead guilty to the first, second, and seventh count of the indictment. The counts were for undercover management, undercover matchmaking, and conspiracy. None of the spectators and none of the jurors had known that a plea bargain had been going on. Each of those counts carried a one-year jail sentence. Scotti announced to the judge that he agreed to the plea, whereupon Carbo proceeded to admit guilt to the following charges:

1. Conspiring with Herman (Hymie "the Mink") Wallman to act as an undercover manager for numerous of Wallman's boxers and arranging matches for those boxers, most of which had taken place at Madison Square Garden.
2. Participated as a manager without having been licensed to do so regarding the bout between Jimmy Peters and George Chimenti on February 21, 1958.
3. Participating as an unlicensed matchmaker in the bout between Virgil Akins and Isaac Logart on March 21, 1958.

Following his admission of guilt, Carbo was sent to the Rikers Island Hospital jail, located in the East River. He was reported to have been suffering from diabetes and heart disease. He was to remain there until his sentencing.

Back in court, on November 31, Carbo heard his attorney, Brodsky, ask the judge for mercy for his client. That may have been too much for prosecutor Scotti, who asked the judge if he could address the court. Permission was granted, and Scotti read the following statement:

> The evil influence of this man has, for many years, permeated virtually the entire professional sport of boxing. I believe it is fair to say that the name of Frankie Carbo today symbolizes the degeneration of professional boxing into a racket. This man is beyond redemption. He is completely impervious to public opinion.

Judge Mullen added his own thoughts:

> In boxing your wish was tantamount to a command performance. You had terrific, improper, and illegal influence in the fight game. You enriched yourself to a degree I can't contemplate.
>
> You had a long, long, and merry dance in the pursuit of power in the boxing game, but the time has now come when the piper must be paid.[7]

Taking into account Carbo's health, Judge John A. Mullen sentenced him to two years in jail, instead of the three years he could have imposed.

As he was being led away, Carbo smiled and thanked the judge. There goes Mr. Gray, commented one boxing fan. Good riddance.

Although Carbo may have thought that after two years of imprisonment, he would be free, law enforcement agents had no such intention. To them, Carbo had gotten off easy. There would be more to come.

On May 30, 1960, Carbo and five other defendants, after a 13-week trial, were found guilty in federal court of trying to take over the management of a welterweight champion named Don Jordan. Carbo and his associates had threatened Jordan's manager, Don Nesseth, and boxing promoter Jackie Leonard. The defendants included Carbo, Blinky Palermo, Truman Gibson, Joe Sica, and Louis Dragna, the latter two were notorious Los Angeles mobsters.

According to journalist Barney Nagler in his book *James Norris and the Decline of Boxing*, these are the events that led to the trial: In 1959, Jackie Leonard, a former boxer, was a 42-year-old matchmaker in Los Angeles. Jackie Leonard was the name he adopted while boxing; his original name was Leonard Blakely. He was the matchmaker for the Hollywood Legion Stadium. Leonard was friendly with Nesseth, who—in addition to being a used car dealer—managed the excellent welterweight boxer Don Jordan. Nesseth was having difficulty getting Jordan's matches televised, so he turned to Leonard, who, in turn, contacted Truman Gibson in Chicago. They had met in 1958, when Gibson told Leonard that Carbo wanted his boxers to get matches in the Hollywood Legion Stadium. Gibson was able to accommodate Leonard and arrange for three of Jordan's bouts to be televised. Nesseth and Leonard were pleased because not only had the bouts been televised, but also Jordan had won the three bouts.

Now, Leonard and Nesseth were in debt to Gibson, when, in fact, the debt was really owed to Carbo, and he wanted prompt repayment. Leonard and Nesseth were called to a meeting with Gibson at the Bismark Hotel. During the meeting, Gibson received a phone call. He handed the phone to Leonard, telling him Blinky Palermo wanted to speak to him. For Jordan's upcoming championship bout against Virgil Akins, Blinky brusquely informed Leonard that he and Carbo wanted 50 percent of Jordan's earnings from the bout. In addition, they wanted a 50 percent ownership of Jordan's management contract. The call ended without Leonard's compliance and with loud expressions of Palermo's anger. He wanted an answer right away, and it had better be the answer Palermo and Carbo wanted to hear. Gibson told Nesseth and Leonard that Palermo and Carbo controlled Akins, and that by refusing to share Jordan's profits with them, there would be no fight. Nesseth indignantly refused to go along with the request, for it was extortionate. Leonard attempted to straddle ambiguity and resort to equivocal vagueness. To Carbo and Palermo, Leonard seemed to neither reject the deal outright nor accept it. His fence-sitting led to additional phone calls from Palermo, each of which concluded with a threat, some murderous.

Leonard kept trying to put off Palermo, but each conversation left Leonard feeling that he was being pushed into a corner from where there was no escape. Finally frustrated by Leonard's dithering, Palermo demanded that he meet with him and Carbo in Florida. When Leonard hesitated and made excuses about why he couldn't attend the meeting, Palermo sent him a thousand dollars and a plane ticket to Miami. He warned Leonard that he better arrive in Miami, otherwise he could expect men of few words and hard intentions to visit him in California.

A nervous Leonard boarded a plane to Miami. He headed for his meeting not knowing if he would walk out of the meeting or be carried out by Miami cops. Once he sat down with Carbo in a Miami motel, he hoped all outstanding matters would be settled. Leonard was a nervous wreck. He knew he had no choice but to meet with Carbo. If he hadn't taken that flight, he might be dead. Pleasantries were brief, and Carbo got right to the point: He insisted that Jordan fight one of his boxers. Leonard, while not caving to Carbo's demand, said Nesseth wouldn't agree to such a bout. Nesseth wanted to choose who Jordan would fight. That response almost ended Leonard's life. He was told to go back to California and convince Nesseth that it was in his best interest to cooperate.

Back in Los Angeles, Leonard failed to persuade Nesseth to acquiesce to the demands made by Palermo and Carbo. So, instead of fighting one of Carbo's boxers, Jordan fought and easily defeated Alvaro Gutierrez on January 22, 1959. Jordan earned $12,500 for the match. Shortly thereafter, Palermo phoned Leonard and demanded his share of the money that Jordan had earned in that fight. He then handed the phone to Carbo, who screamed a string of threats at Leonard, letting him know he had associates in Los Angeles who could take care of him. Leonard could no longer be evasive, so he sent some of the money to Carbo, but it wasn't enough. Palermo and Carbo again phoned Leonard and told him that if he didn't send additional funds to them he would have to arrange for Jordan to fight boxers whom they controlled. Leonard would also have to guarantee the outcomes of those bouts and pay what they demanded.

Leonard attempted to stall until he could work something out with Nesseth. He was being both recalcitrant and obedient. He seemed to acknowledge Palermo's threats, while trying to placate him. Palermo, however, was not a cat to be toyed with; he was becoming increasingly frustrated by Leonard's less than fully cooperative behavior. Palermo decided to fly to Los Angeles and personally confront Leonard. Shortly after his arrival, Palermo met with mobster Louis Dragna at Puccini's Restaurant. There, Palermo explained that he wanted Dragna to persuade Leonard to be more cooperative. Dragna, however, was busy with his own problems and suggested that Joe Sica, another mobster and friend of Bugsy Siegel, smash like a sledgehammer through Leonard's wall of resistance.

The following night, Joe Sica, Palermo, and Leonard met in a room at the Beverly Hilton Hotel. Leonard was greeted with icy, stone-faced greetings, followed by a few threats. Either out of fear or feckless courage, Leonard turned his back on the two tough guys and left the room. Palermo was now boiling mad. The following day, Leonard received an angry phone call from Palermo, in which the mobster punctuated his demands with a series of explosive expletives. He told Leonard he had no choice but to come to another meeting, this one in a nearby restaurant. Palermo warned Leonard that he better not walk out of this rendezvous, for if he did there would be no more talking. In addition to Palermo, Sica would be there, along with actor George Raft. Once again, Leonard was met with icy glares and a series of demands. Leonard explained there was nothing he could do. He was powerless to persuade Nesseth to cooperate.

The next day, Palermo and Sica showed up unannounced at Leonard's office, where Don Nesseth was also in attendance. Nesseth uneasily listened to Palermo's demands, then told everyone there he would not let his boxer fight anyone picked by Carbo and Palermo. He was not beholden to either man and could operate freely. He had always done so and would continue to do so. Leonard looked around at the faces clenched with anger and turned up his palms as if silently saying there was nothing he could do. Nesseth merely shrugged off the ensuing threats. Palermo could hardly contain his anger; he warned both men that reasoning was no longer possible. They had no choice but to cooperate. Their lives were in jeopardy.

Prior to his meetings in Los Angeles with Sica and Palermo, Leonard had gone to the police and explained how he was being harassed. The threats were eating him up: He was unable to sleep and could barely hold down food. The cops outfitted Leonard with a wire. Leonard had recorded a stream of threats made against him and Nesseth. There was sufficient recorded information now to begin an investigation.

The following day at the Los Angeles airport, after purchasing a ticket for a flight back to Philadelphia, Palermo shopped in a newsstand, where he purchased a package of peanut butter crackers; however, he had failed to pay for two magazines and a package of gum. He hadn't noticed the cops in plainclothes who had been surveilling him and was rattled when they arrested him for shoplifting merchandise valued at 80 cents. He subsequently paid his bail of $500 and angrily flew back to Philadelphia. After all, he was not some common criminal: He was Blinky Palermo, a power in the world of boxing, the numbers king of Philadelphia.

Meanwhile, having listened to Leonard's tapes, the cops told Leonard that to avoid danger to himself and his family, he should cooperate with the IBC. They reiterated that such a move would guarantee his own safety. Frustrated and angered by the police reaction and advice, Leonard went to the California State Athletic Commission, where he testified that Carbo had told him to make sure Jordan's manager would turn over half of Jordan's future earnings to the IBC. Leonard said he and Nesseth had refused to cooperate, and so Carbo then threatened to gouge out Leonard's eyes and, if necessary, leave him for dead.

Unbeknownst to Carbo and Palermo, the California State Athletic Commission began an investigation into their activities in May 1959. The commission was particularly interested in how Carbo and Palermo threatened their way into the attempted management and promotion of Don Jordan. On the witness stand, Leonard vividly chronicled what had happened to him and Nesseth. He related how he had been harassed and threatened by the two mobsters and some of their associates. Leonard's evidence was turned over to Captain James Hamilton, chief of intelligence for the Los Angeles Police Department. Hamilton then turned over the evidence to the FBI and the U.S. attorney, Francis Whelan, who presented it to a grand jury. Leonard was praised in the press as one of the few fight promoters who had the courage to stand up to threats from Frankie Carbo and his ilk. This was getting to be too much for Palermo and Carbo. They were furious. Leonard's mouth would have to be permanently shut, although Leonard felt they could no longer threaten him. He had done the right thing and won the plaudits of those who wanted to rid boxing of its corrupting elements. His life had undergone a significant change. He was honored for his testimony.

And now,

> Leonard felt secure because Captain Hamilton had assigned him police protection, but on June 3, 1959, just two weeks after he told his story before the boxing board, his name hit the headlines.
>
> That evening Leonard drove up to the garage of his home in Los Angeles, turned off the ignition, and emerged from his car. Just as he

reached up to pull down the garage door, he felt a blow on the back of his head. [8]

Leonard collapsed on the ground, where he was repeatedly kicked by his two assailants. Leonard suffered from a concussion to the brain; a pair of blackened eyes; and numerous bruises on his chest, legs, and groin. The local police chief confirmed that Leonard had been attacked by two mobsters. The following week, the chief, with a straight face, changed his original opinion, stating, "It now appears that Mr. Leonard suffered some acute physical incapacitation of a stunning nature that produced an illusion of assault."[9]

Perhaps the chief did not want to suffer an acute physical incapacitation himself and so accommodated himself to his own need for self-preservation; his once-vaunted valor and virtue had vanished.

In Los Angeles, Philadelphia, Miami, and Chicago, a fearless, uncompromised, and well-coordinated group of FBI agents descended almost simultaneously on the homes and offices of Carbo, Palermo, Gibson, Sica, and Dragna. Within minutes, the surprised quintet was in custody, handcuffed and grim and furious. Carbo, the perceived kingpin of the group, was held on $100,000 bail, while his frustrated, anger-snorting crony Palermo was deemed less important and held on $25,000 bail.

Carbo had already been found guilty of managing fighters without a license and sentenced to two years in Riker's Island, the New York City prison in the East River. Shortly after his release in 1960, he was subpoenaed by a Senate investigations committee about his involvement in boxing. He took the Fifth Amendment against self-incrimination 25 times. His nontestimony opened a can of worms, and he was no longer able to hide under a rock of anonymity. From his sentence in New York, plus the government's charge that he owed them $750,000, Carbo's room to maneuver was getting claustrophobically smaller and smaller. He and his cohorts went on trial in Los Angeles on February 21, 1961. Only Gibson was granted bail, for Judge Ernest Tolin believed the others might try to influence the prosecution witnesses. Leonard and Nesseth provided the testimony the prosecution required to win guilty verdicts: Carbo received a sentence of 25 years, plus a $10,000 fine; Palermo received a sentence of 15 years and a $10,000 fine; Gibson got off lightly with a 5-year suspended sentence and a $10,000 fine;

THE GRAY CZAR OF BOXING

Sica received a 20-year sentence and a $10,000 fine; and Dragna received a 5-year sentence and no fine. While awaiting their appeals, only Carbo was kept in prison. Not satisfied with his quarters at the Los Angeles County Jail, he requested to be sent to the infamous Alcatraz prison, for he claimed it was a lot cleaner than his Los Angeles jail cell. He was granted his wish and shipped off to Alcatraz; meanwhile, Palermo, Sica, and Dragna were granted bail.

The Court of Appeals in San Francisco announced its decision in a 75-page opinion on February 13, 1963: While it reversed the conviction of Dragna, it upheld the convictions of Carbo, Palermo, and Gibson. It threw out one of the counts against Sica, but that didn't alter his prison sentence. When Alcatraz was later closed, Carbo was relocated to the McNeil Island Federal Penitentiary.

The elusive Mr. Gray was no longer the elusive criminal of years past. Carbo's criminal career was over. He shuffled in and out of his cell, looking every bit like a man without a purpose. His aliases were translated into a series of prison numbers. Yet, he would attempt to still exert influence on boxers and managers from behind bars.

Although the prosecutors and judges were pleased that Carbo would be serving a long prison sentence, the federal government was not so satisfied. A further torment was imposed on Carbo by the IRS, which obtained a judgment against him for $1,100,940. The amount represented unpaid income taxes, interest, and penalties that covered seven years during which Carbo was delinquent in his tax obligations. The largest amount of income on which Carbo was delinquent occurred in 1945. He had reported a gross income of $30,000 and paid taxes on $21,000. Yet, Carbo had deposited $300,000 in his personal bank account that year. For one as crafty as Carbo, it seemed remarkably foolish of him to have deposited such a large, undeclared amount of income into a bank account that would surely come under scrutiny by the government. The judgment against Carbo infuriated him, and he fulminated to his lawyers. He insisted that they appeal and try to get the amount reduced.

Shortly after his release from prison, he died of a heart attack in Miami Beach, Florida, in 1976. He was 72 years old. The IRS judgment did not die with his death. And had the government known that Carbo had continued to have a powerful influence on boxing while incarcerated, it surely would have piled on even greater penalties. It was not until years later that the government learned that Carbo had been involved in fixing some of Sonny Liston's matches. Liston would become known as a merciless thug who was controlled by thugs and finally killed by those thugs. Law enforcement speculated that Liston had been cheated out of much of his earnings by Carbo and others, and when he said he would testify against them, his life was ended by a hot shot of heroin.

Of Carbo, a New York boxing commissioner commented, "In many places, you have a haunted house. But when you press an investigation, you find no one who has actually come into contact with the haunt. You have pretty much the same thing with this phantom of boxing."[10]

6

THE BIG FIX

Imagine a six-year-old boy out on the street boxing another boy for pennies, nickels, and dimes that a group of men toss at his feet. Imagine that group of men yelling encouragement and laughing at the sight of two pint-sized gladiators, arms flailing, throwing wild punches at one another. One boy is a determined little fighter; he will neither give up nor cry. He will just keep swinging his arms, hammering with his tiny fists until the other boy quits. The boy's father will pick up the scattered change, which he will use to buy food for his family and himself. He will also buy alcohol for himself. That man, when drunk, often becomes an angry, mean persecutor of his wife and sons, frequently slapping his wife for imagined wrongs and beating his boys for being failures, for being blurred mirror images of himself. He frequently ties one of his boys to a bed post and beats him with a broomstick. When released, that boy is like an attack-trained, snarling pit bull terrier, sometimes kept on a short leash, sometimes left to wander the streets.

Rather than fighting other boys on the street, he should have hammered his father, but that would have been impossible. Instead, a red-hot rage burned inside of him, and when he couldn't stand it any longer, he would erupt with devastating results. His rage would come to define him.

Such was the childhood cauldron of Giacobbe LaMotta, who was born on July 10, 1922, on the Lower East Side of New York City. His indigent family, always one or two steps ahead of their various landlords, would move to Philadelphia and then to the Bronx. While the tough, angry young boy would grow up to have a stocky, muscular body and a hard head, he had surprisingly small fists, almost delicate and feminine. Yet, those fists would prove to be devastating weapons against boxing opponents, and his hard-as-cement chin and head made him the man who could not be knocked out. He was one of the most intense and relentlessly ferocious boxers of the twentieth century. He was fortunate to find boxing as an outlet for his rage; otherwise, he surely would have killed someone in a bar, on the street, in a pool hall, or in a brothel, or even one of his numerous wives.

Jake LaMotta, the "Raging Bull," came out of the same mold as his boyhood pal, Rocky Graziano: Anger, poverty, and abusive fathers combined to make them into vicious teenage hoodlums. While Rocky was eventually saved by a loving wife and a paternalistic manager, LaMotta was not so fortunate. He had to find his own way, and that way was the way of his rage. Fueled by rage, he was always ready to erupt, suspect the worst of others, and hit at the slightest provocation. He was also ready to rob and beat someone he envied. According to his autobiography, *Raging Bull*, LaMotta was just itching to rob a local bookie one night. Cloaked by the darkness of a moonless night, LaMotta snuck up behind the neighborhood bookie, a gentle, good-humored man named Harry Gordon. LaMotta hit him repeatedly with a lead pipe. Because Gordon didn't immediately fall to the ground, LaMotta hit him over and over again. LaMotta could not control himself. Rage coursed through his body. Even after Gordon finally lay unconscious on the ground, LaMotta hit him again and again, believing he had killed the bookie. LaMotta searched the man's pockets, looking for the $200 he was supposed to be carrying. LaMotta found the man's wallet, but it contained no money. It had a couple of photos and an identification card.

LaMotta was eventually arrested, but it was not for killing the bookie. He had been taken into custody for a less serious crime. He was arraigned, tried, and found guilty, and because he was an incorrigible and remorseless delinquent, he was sent to a reform school. He was an angry, resentful inmate of the Coxsackie Reform School. He would have been happy to beat up the guards, but instead they beat him, often tossing him into solitary.

LaMotta's lifelong pal, Rocky Graziano, was also doing time there, and he recommended that LaMotta redirect has anger at opponents in the school's boxing ring. There, he would be able to hone his skills as a pugilist and perhaps take up boxing as a profession upon his release. And so the two boys channeled their anger into boxing and developed the skills that would eventually make each of them a middleweight champ.

Of the facilities at Coxsackie, LaMotta writes in his autobiography,

> The gym there wasn't too bad in my day. It was a real, full-size gym, with polished hardwood floors, a regulation ring set up in the middle, a whole series of punching bags down at one end, plenty of weights and barbells and dumbbells, and those pulley weight systems all along one wall, and even a row of rowing machines. In other words, the whole works.
>
> Maybe in a way, Coxsackie did reform me, because if I hadn't been sent up there, I doubt now that I ever would have really learned boxing bumming around the Bronx the way I was. I might have, but knowing me I doubt it. I would have been much more likely to stop a slug from some cop's gun before I learned anything. So maybe Coxsackie was a good thing, not that I'd really recommend it as a way to get started in life.[1]

Released from reform school, LaMotta indeed decided to devote himself to becoming a professional boxer. He believed it was the only thing he was good at, the only thing for which he seemed to have an instinctive talent. It really did provide an outlet for his rage. As he became known as a hard-hitting slugger, he attracted the attention of a number of guys connected with the mob. Those were the guys who hung out at boxing gyms, always on the lookout for up-and-coming talent they could manage, manipulate, and bet on or against, depending on the odds. They, of course, wanted to manage LaMotta's career, attempting to entice him with grandiose promises of great riches and fame, but LaMotta rebuffed them. His anger would not permit him to be placed in harness by guys who would take 30 percent or more of his earnings. He wanted to manage himself and not give up one dime of his earnings to guys he couldn't trust. If he needed a manager, he would choose his brother, Joey.

Not having succeeded with their original offer, the mob guys next tried to bribe LaMotta into throwing fights, but he refused to go along with that, too. His defiance of mob wishes and suggestions resulted in threats and warnings but no repercussions, no beatings in dark alleys. The mob's anger seemed to sputter out with a few dismissive curses. Maybe the mob guys were simply biding their time until LaMotta realized he wouldn't get far without them. Their wishes had not turned into nonnegotiable demands. Not yet anyway. And LaMotta, at that time in his career, was not important enough to warrant being killed for not acceding to what the mob wanted.

LaMotta told his brother he had no intention of giving up half of his earnings to some mobsters who wanted to manage and train him. LaMotta figured he could scale the steep cliffs up the mountainous terrain of boxing and go right up to its summit. One day, he would be a world champion, he told his brother. And when that happened, LaMotta figured no one could touch him.

But when he told a mob guy he would make it to the top on his own, he was told he could expect to get nowhere, especially without the mob's help. He was told he was a fool for thinking he could make it on his own. No one, he was told, makes it on his own.

Although LaMotta didn't agree to the mob's overtures, there was nothing he could do about the mob guys who regularly hung out at the boxing gym where he trained. They were part of the scenery, always measuring his skills and those of the men he sparred with. They figured the time would come when LaMotta finally realized he needed them to make his dream into a reality.

LaMotta notes,

> Managers, by and large, were a collection of thieves and almost to a man tied in with the mob, but they were always on the lookout for a promising kid, because even if the kid was destined to become a champ, still if you're taking a third or a half of his purses, besides what you can steal, you can make money out of even a second-rate fighter.[2]

And because the fights also attract bettors, there are always bookies hanging around and the mob guys who let those bookies operate. Boxing attracted not only the mob, hangers on, and wannabe gangsters, but also professional and amateur gamblers, and even sportswriters, who for an envelope of money would tout some boxer in their newspaper columns. Even when the mob's suggestions became entreaties, tied to implicit threats, LaMotta refused to give in. He had no qualms about socializing with many mobsters, drinking and dining with them, partying with them, and going to brothels with them. He was a divided man, but in time the divisions would briefly be soldered together. And although the mob personally liked LaMotta, they continued to place obstacles in his path. It's one thing to have drinks together and patronize the same prostitutes, but it's another to do business together, and LaMotta was not yet prepared to enter into a business relationship with those guys. Once they have their hooks in you, they never let you go, and LaMotta still wanted to be hook free.

The mob-connected boxing promoters assured LaMotta that he was a great fighter. They told him they personally liked him, but they would still block him from getting the kinds of bouts he wanted. Having no alternative, LaMotta sought fights outside of New York. He fought in Cleveland, Detroit, Cincinnati, Pittsburgh, and Boston, where he became well known and enlisted thousands of fans who would turn up regularly to see the Raging Bull defeat opponent and after opponent. Sometimes, however, he lost fights on disputed decisions, where the referees and judges had been paid by local gamblers to make sure LaMotta lost.

As a result of his formidable ring performances for years, LaMotta had been referred to as the uncrowned middleweight champ. He was uncrowned, of course, because the mob wouldn't give him a shot at the title. The crown would be worn, although not in every case, by fighters who succumbed to the threats and irresistible offers of the mob. LaMotta took out his frustrations by pummeling one opponent after another. From May 3, 1941, to September 3, 1947, LaMotta had 78 fights, winning 64 and losing 11, with the rest ending in draws. In all of his fights, he had never been knocked out. Sportswriters, whether or not flacking for promoters, all conceded that LaMotta had a cement chin and head, and no one without a sledgehammer could knock him out. They would watch LaMotta get hit by some of the hardest punches thrown in the ring, and those punches never seemed to faze him. Although not a champ, he was making good money winning fight after fight, so when the mob offered him $100,000 to take a dive against Tony Janiro, he refused.

While he continued to win in the ring and win the plaudits of sportswriters and fans, he couldn't defeat judges who had been paid to give a winning decision to a LaMotta opponent. And a streak of wins certainly would not induce the mob to offer LaMotta a title fight. His frustration grew and fermented into anger, as he was getting no closer to a title shot. Then it all changed. He had fought Cecil Hudson in Comiskey Park in Illinois on September 3, 1947. He lost the bout on points but figured he had surely won. Fans and sportswriters thought so, too. LaMotta was sufficiently angry that he decided to make the deal that was being offered to him by the mob. The mob had figured all along that it would happen eventually, and its patience and steady placing of obstacles in LaMotta's path finally paid off.

Yes, he had been offered money before, but never with the promise that he would get a shot at the title. Now, an offer came that he did not want to refuse, for it lifted the only obstacle on the road to a shot at the title: All he had to do was take a dive against Blackjack Billy Fox and he would not only get a shot at the title, but also be paid $100,000.

It didn't matter that Blackjack Billy Fox was a paper tiger whose wins had been reportedly bought by the mob. He was thought by many to be in the same class of phony boxers—all image, little talent—as Primo Carnera in the 1930s. It was not the way LaMotta had wanted to get his chance to be champ, but it was the only toll road open to him. If he had refused to accept the deal, he would have continued as the uncrowned middleweight champion until he retired from boxing. So LaMotta signed a contract for a fight to be held in Madison Square Garden on November 14, 1947. Fox's manager was notorious Philadelphia promoter Frank "Blinky" Palermo. Although Fox was to receive 20 percent of the net receipts from the fight, the bulk of that money went into Palermo's safe deposit box. LaMotta was to receive 30 percent of the net receipts. The odds going into the fight favored LaMotta 8 to 5; however, as mob money poured out of Philadelphia and was rapidly being bet on Fox to win, the odds changed to 3 to 1, favoring Fox.

Before the fight took place, LaMotta collected his payoff and thoughtfully invested his money in two enterprises that would prove to be highly profitable business ventures: He bought two boxing arenas, both in the Bronx: Jerome Stadium and Park Arena. But because a licensed boxer was not permitted to own such establishments, LaMotta's relatives fronted as the owners; however, LaMotta was often there on fight nights. He seemed like a combination maître d', host, boxing promoter, and stand-up comedian and raconteur. He welcomed everyone who entered his establishments; in fact, four days before his bout with Fox, he was seen shaking hands with Frankie Carbo and Blinky Palermo in the lobby of Park Arena.

Unbeknownst to the public, the fight's promoters, and Fox, LaMotta had visited his doctor, who diagnosed him as having a ruptured spleen. The doctor told LaMotta he shouldn't fight. Now LaMotta had the excuse he wanted if he needed to explain why he lost the fight. He could testify that he received such a hard blow to his body that it caused excruciating pain, limiting his ability to wage a successful defense.

It would be an excuse few people would accept but one no one could successfully challenge: His doctor said he had a ruptured spleen, a serious injury. And when it was revealed that LaMotta had fought with such an injury, there was an outcry. How could a doctor, a manager, or anyone else permit a boxer to get in the ring with that kind of injury? And why hadn't LaMotta reported it to the New York State Athletic Commission? The only reason, of course, was that LaMotta needed an excuse for not mounting a formidable defense against Fox.

There were, however, reasons why Fox might prove to be the more successful combatant, said some sportswriters. First of all, he had a terrific record going into the fight: He had won 36 consecutive bouts by knockout before being knocked out by Gus Lesnevich. Second, he was taller than LaMotta and had a longer reach. Fox was more than six feet tall, while LaMotta was 5-foot-8. LaMotta would have to get in under Fox's longer arms and punch up, bullying his way past Fox's defenses and delivering powerful uppercuts. In the first round, LaMotta was his usual aggressive self, driving Fox to the ropes, landing punch after punch. The judges and referees would award LaMotta that round; however, LaMotta was not about to renege on his deal with Carbo and Palermo, for such an outcome might have left LaMotta bleeding to death in the trunk of a stolen and abandoned car in the swamps of New Jersey.

So, in the second round, LaMotta held back. Fox flailed away with both fists, driving LaMotta against the ropes. LaMotta didn't so much as throw a single punch in his defense. The crowd of fans booed loudly, and some began shouting, "Fix, fix, fix." The third round was a repetition of the second round. By the fourth round, LaMotta was ready for the curtain to come down on his unconvincing performance. He fired a few ineffectual punches at Fox, then let Fox do his imitation of a skillful pugilist. LaMotta pretended to stagger as if he had been dazed by one of Fox's punches. The referee stopped the fight after two minutes and twenty-six seconds in the fourth round, declaring Fox the winner by a technical knockout.

No one believed the legitimacy of the outcome, including the New York State Athletic Commission, which called the referee, Frank Fullam, to testify. Fullam, with a straight face, said,

> As a referee of many contests, I thought that LaMotta showed great durability to survive the punishment that he took. If I didn't stop the fight, it would have been a tragedy, and perhaps the fellow might have been killed. As a representative of the Commission, I am there to see that it is an honest and fair fight, and to see that the boys are not hurt. [3]

When his words were reported in the daily newspapers, there was a collective guffaw from bookies, boxers, and bettors. One reporter, Dan Parker of the *Daily Mirror*, said, "[LaMotta's] performance was so bad he was surprised that Actors' Equity didn't picket the joint."[4]

When LaMotta was called to testify at the New York State Athletic Commission, he reported on his spleen injury and offered to get a note from his doctor to support his claim. (The doctor would later confirm to the commission that LaMotta did indeed have a ruptured spleen.) When asked where he got $10,000 to invest in Park Arena, LaMotta said he earned it from boxing and took the money from his safe deposit box. Feeling as if he had successfully buffaloed the members of the commission, LaMotta swaggered out of the hearing. Nevertheless, he was suspended from boxing for seven months and fined a thousand dollars for not reporting his spleen injury to the commission. In addition, his purse was withheld pending further investigation. LaMotta, therefore, sued the commission, claiming it had not acted in good faith; he further claimed that he knew nothing of a fix in the fight between Fox and himself. His share of the net profits, about $23,000, was eventually turned over to him, and the case against him died, as did his reputation as the Raging Bull.

Palermo and Carbo were separately questioned, but neither one of them offered any information that would have indicated the fight had been fixed. Carbo was also called into the DA's office at 155 Leonard Street, where he denied ever meeting with LaMotta at Park Arena. He insisted that such reports to the contrary were mistaken. Not taking any chances of being indicted, neither Carbo nor Palermo would sign waivers of immunity in exchange for their grand jury testimony. How much money Palermo and Carbo won on the fight has never been revealed, although bookies claimed that hundreds of thousands of dollars had been bet on Fox to win. The 18,340 fans who felt cheated of a legitimate boxing match had paid the Garden $102,528 for their tickets to see a performance that would not have been convincing if performed by clowns in a rural circus.

Poor Fox. When the mob finished with him, they disposed of him as if he were nothing more than used tissue. He got a job setting up pins in a bowling alley. From there, as his life spiraled ever downward, he found a home of sorts in a men's shelter on the Bowery. He finally wound up in a mental institution, a poor, misused man whose athletic prowess was stolen by the greedy hands of the mob. The mob had made millions of dollars from fixing his fights, as it had from fixing those of Primo Carnera, and then it moved on, taking advantage of other boxers who dreamed of championship belts and fat bank accounts and fame.

LaMotta paid a different price than his erstwhile opponent: He not only lost the public esteem for the Raging Bull, but also failed to live up to his promise that he would never deal with the mob to advance his career. The public regarded him as a phony, a sellout, a man without a conscience, who would take the public's money much as a con artist would.

People's opinions mattered to LaMotta, but not as much as an opportunity to win the middleweight championship of the world. The opportunity to win the championship did not come about quickly. LaMotta had to wait two years and battle his way through nine fights. He wondered if he had been lied to, if the opportunity would ever come his way. He kept on fighting, racking up wins, and still attracted thousands of fans who enjoyed watching the Bull. Many had forgiven him for his lackluster defense against Fox, but LaMotta knew he wouldn't gain the recognition he sought until he won the championship.

And, finally, the promise made two years earlier was about to come true. He got what he had been dreaming about: his opportunity to prove to the world that he was no longer just the uncrowned champ, not the patsy in a fixed fight, but the one who would wear the hard-won middleweight crown.

He would fight Marcel Cerdan for the National Boxing Association middleweight boxing championship. But before the fight could take place on June 16, 1949, at Briggs Stadium in Detroit, LaMotta had to pay Cerdan's people $20,000 for the privilege of fighting their man. LaMotta's share of the proceeds from the fight came to $19,000, or 15 percent of the net proceeds, which was considerably less than his standard 35 percent. For the opportunity to fight for the championship, he would lose $1,000. It didn't take LaMotta long to figure out how to make up for the loss. To make a profit on his $20,000 investment, LaMotta bet on himself to win. He knew he had to win. He would never get another chance, and he wanted that golden championship belt even more than the money his bet would deliver. The odds favored Cerdan 8 to 5. LaMotta bet $10,000 on himself. He would walk away not only as middleweight champion of the world, but also with $16,000 in hand. Cerdan, as champion, was able to demand 40 percent.

When Cerdan (aka the "Casablanca Clouter," "Marocan Bombardier," and "Moroccan Bomber"), a popular French boxer in both Europe and the United States, entered the ring, he was welcomed with round after round of cheers, whistles, and applause. He had, on September 21, 1948, knocked out an American favorite, Tony Zale, at the end of the 11th round and won the middleweight championship of the world. Zale had been the favorite going into that fight, especially after taking back the middleweight championship title from Rocky Graziano just three months earlier. Zale had knocked out Graziano in the third round. But it was Zale's loss to Cerdan that captured the attention of sportswriters, who had praised his style, courage, and aggressively dominant boxing skills. And fans admired Cerdan's ring presence, fast and aggressive openings, and indefatigable determination and bravery in taking on and defeating the tough "Man of Steel." So Cerdan had become a celebrity in both Europe and the United States. He was particularly admired in France for bringing the title to Europe. No boxer had done that for 15 years, not since Primo Carnera, in an allegedly fixed fight, had beaten Jack Sharkey in 1933.

When LaMotta entered the ring, he received a mixed greeting: Many of his stalwart fans applauded and cheered, yelling jingoistic calls for him to defeat the Frenchman and bring the title back to the United States; however, many others who had not forgiven him for his pathetically unconvincing defense in the Fox match booed and called out that he was a fraud. Although the New York State Athletic Commission had cleared LaMotta of intentionally losing the fight, boxing fans, sportswriters, and bookies believed otherwise. To them, LaMotta was a fake, a phony, a pawn of the mob.

Midway through the first round, each boxer was aggressively pouring it on, punching and punching, landing blow after blow, when suddenly Cerdan went down, landing on his left shoulder. LaMotta wasn't sure if he had punched Cerdan or pushed him, or if Cerdan had simply tripped. LaMotta retreated to a neutral corner, and Cerdan leaped to his feet as the referee started his count. But when Cerdan regained his footing, it was apparent that he had injured his left shoulder when it hit the canvas. As a result, he could barely use his left arm. He used it primarily to block and absorb LaMotta's hard-hitting punches. Yet, he continued to fight bravely, using his right fist to inflict as much damage as possible.

In the second round, both fighters continued to land punch after punch. LaMotta was more aggressive than Cerdan, but Cerdan continued delivering powerful punches with his right fist. LaMotta seemed unfazed by the punches and kept after Cerdan, driving him around the ring. Cerdan's right fist pounded LaMotta again and again, but the punches seemed to have no effect on LaMotta's cement jaw. Both men demonstrated a barrage of aggressive punching, each fighter slugging the other, attempting to do the necessary damage for a knockout. Although injured and unable to strike effectively with his left, Cerdan won the second round, according to the judges' scorecards.

From the third round onward, however, it was LaMotta's fight: He was outboxing Cerdan, scoring winning punch after winning punch. As the fight went on, LaMotta came more and more to dominate the injured Cerdan, who was now fighting defensively, covering up more frequently than launching an attack. After the eighth and ninth rounds, Cerdan's cornermen wanted him to quit. There was no point in going on: He couldn't win, and he risked serious injury, but Cerdan, ever proud, emphatically refused to quit. He shook his head no. Finally, after the ninth round, Cerdan sat in his corner, a tired and beaten man; he knew he couldn't go on. He was exhausted, and without his left arm, his ability to win by points was impossible.

The referee, Johnny Weber, approached Cerdan and his cornermen. A few questions were quickly posed, then a few whispers hesitantly were given in response. Weber walked to LaMotta's corner, grabbed one of his wrists, and led him to the center of the ring. There, he raised LaMotta's hand, declaring him the new middleweight champion of the world. (It was a mirror image of Cerdan's defeat of Zale, when in the beginning of the 12th round, Zale could not come out of his corner.) Shortly thereafter, Joe Louis presented LaMotta with the gold and bejeweled championship belt LaMotta had fought so hard to earn. It was his; he was proud of his accomplishment. He had realized his life's dream, but he would have to pay a price for it—a price that that would haunt him years later.

At a party celebrating his win, LaMotta had a happy surprise about another kind of haunting, one that had troubled him for years. He had never revealed to anyone the story of what had happened back in the Bronx during his teenage years, when he had mugged the sweet-tempered local bookmaker, Harry Gordon. For years, LaMotta had lived with not only the burden of what he had done, but also the fear of being caught, tried, and convicted. It would make his boxing career a hollow victory. When he was sent to Coxsackie Reform School for a less serious crime, he was sure the cops would eventually learn that he was the murderer, and he would then be sent to Sing Sing either for life or to fry in old Sparky. But on the night of his celebration as middleweight champion, those fears and anxieties suddenly vanished: Gordon, the man he thought he had killed so many years ago, appeared as if out of a dream.

There he was with a big toothy grin as he approached LaMotta. He grabbed LaMotta's right hand and shook it vigorously. He would not let go. He called LaMotta "Jakela." LaMotta could barely believe his eyes. Gordon was not dead. What the hell was he doing here? Had his ghost come to ruin LaMotta's triumph over Cerdan? But, there he was. LaMotta couldn't deny the reality. There was Gordon, grinning, laughing, and congratulating his former neighbor. He said he had always liked LaMotta, had been following his career for years and couldn't resist coming up from Florida to be ringside when LaMotta won the championship. He knew he would. LaMotta was speechless, amazed he hadn't killed Gordon. He was not a murderer. Gordon, who had always regarded LaMotta as a friend from their old neighborhood, never knew that it was LaMotta who sent him to hospital for six weeks to recover from a severe concussion. On the night of LaMotta's championship victory, a double burden had finally been lifted. The Raging Bull was almost lighthearted. LaMotta drank to his victory over Cerdan and toasted his good fortune.

Cerdan and LaMotta, as expected, signed for a rematch, and promoters felt confident that a sellout crowd would pay top dollar to see the two gladiators go at one another. Once Cerdan's shoulder was repaired, he would be hard to beat. Back in Paris, he prepared for the fight and resumed his love affair with popular chanson and torch singer Edith Piaf. Although Cerdan was married and had three children, he became a celebrated romantic figure and was the subject of numerous newspaper and magazine articles. He and Piaf were the talk of Paris; they were the couple of the year. They could be seen in nightclubs, dancing through the night, taking late-night walks along the Seine. It was inevitable that a movie of Piaf and Cerdan would be made, which was seen by tens of thousands of Parisians. The movie was called *Edith et Marcel*, and it starred Cerdan's son, Marcel Cerdan Jr.

While Piaf was singing in New York, Cerdan decided to join her before his rematch with LaMotta. He canceled his passage on an ocean liner, for it would take days to arrive. He didn't want to waste those days away from his lover, so he booked passage on an Air France Lockheed L749 Constellation. But it was not to be: His plane crashed into Monte Redondo on Sao Miguel Island in the Azores, killing everyone on board, 37 passengers and 11 crew members. Piaf memorialized her despair and lost love by composing and recording one of her most popular songs; it is called *Hymne a L'amour*.

Cerdan, with his shoulder in good operating order, would have been a formidable opponent for LaMotta, for Cerdan was rated as the number-one middleweight by *Ring Magazine*. Sportswriters and boxing historians estimated that if Cerdan hadn't dislocated his shoulder during his bout with LaMotta, he probably would have retained the title. There may not have been a rematch.

The following year, an investigative committee would begin looking into the activities of the mob, and while it would take some time before LaMotta would be called to testify, he knew that day would eventually arrive. When it did, an old wound in LaMotta's psyche would be torn open. He would become the target of unwelcome publicity, not just for him, but for Frankie Carbo and Blinky Palermo. As time passed, LaMotta had hoped his loss to Fox would fade from the minds of fans, and it would have, except that certain authorities were intent on revisiting it. LaMotta's ensuing notoriety would not only tarnish his reputation all over again, but also embarrass the mob guys to whom LaMotta had owed the chance to fight for the championship. LaMotta would be a star witness, and by the end of his testimony, he would be called a courageous rat.

Boxing, as if it were a contagious virus, would come under an investigative microscope. The investigators, by exposing the mob, hoped to vaccinate the sport against any further corruption.

It all began with a seemingly awkward senator from Tennessee who would popularize the raccoon hat, with its long, fuzzy tail. He was Estes Kefauver, who was born in 1903, serving in the House of Representatives from 1939 to 1949, and then the Senate from 1949 to 1963. He was a progressive legislator, who championed civil rights, consumer rights, and antitrust legislation. He projected honesty and decency, and could have been played by Jimmy Stewart. He was also a prig and a prude, and tried to suppress soft-core porn publications and pinup photos of scantily clad bathing beauties. One of his targets was the beautifully alluring Bettie Page, also from Tennessee and one of the most popular pinups during the 1950s, who remains a cult figure and whose many photos are collected by avid fans.

In 1950, Kefauver was made chairman of the Senate Special Committee to Investigate Crime in Interstate Commerce. In 14 cities throughout the country, the committee held hearings that were televised and riveted public attention. At the time, few Americans owned television sets, so crowds of people would gather in department stores to watch the hearings in the stores' electronics departments, where numerous sets were simultaneously tuned to the hearings. While more than 600 mob or mob-associated witnesses provided testimony or took the Fifth Amendment so as not to incriminate themselves, the witnesses who garnered most of the attention were senior members of the Mafia. Some of the best-known witnesses were Willie Moretti, Frank Costello, and Joe Adonis.

Costello refused to let television cameras broadcast his face, so the cameras focused on his hands, which nervously twitched and twisted. Costello finally refused to be further baited by provocative questions and left the hearings. He was cited for contempt. Willie Moretti, by other means, decided to entertain the committee. He told jokes;

laughed about not carrying a Mafia membership card; and claimed that if he were interested in politics, he would be sitting with the men who had been questioning him. This was too much for the mob. Moretti had talked too much and so had violated the code of Omerta. He was also suffering from an advanced case of syphilis, and the disease was affecting his mind. The mob decided it was time to get rid of him, and so while having lunch at a restaurant with several mob associates in Cliffside Park, New Jersey, he was shot in the face and head. His luncheon companions rapidly exited the restaurant and were never caught. It was unclear whether they paid the check, but it was reported that they left a generous tip. Years later, mob boss Vito Genovese said the hit had been a mercy killing.

For LaMotta and many in boxing, the hundreds of mob witnesses who had been interrogated by committee had been a preview of things to come. By 1960, LaMotta had finally received the summons he had been expecting. He decided not to rely on the Fifth Amendment but to tell the committee what it wanted to hear. Those who may have disdained LaMotta for his performance in the Billy Fox match would see a man of elemental courage, speaking his mind, regardless of the consequences.

Boxing may not have been an issue for the committee if Governor Edmund Brown of California hadn't said that if Congress didn't investigate how the mob controlled boxing, he might have to ban boxing matches in his state. He further stated that there would have to be new federal laws to control the sport.

LaMotta would be the committee's star witness, a man alone, facing his accusers and ignoring his accomplices. He had no organization to protect, and no organization would protect him. Would the mob get rid of him, if he confessed to what he knew? They, along with television viewers, waited. The mob would not be happy with the outcome. Some compared LaMotta's testimony to that of the character of Terry Malloy, an ex-boxer played by Marlon Brando in the movie *On the Waterfront*. In that film, Malloy testifies about how the mob controlled the New York waterfront and silenced rebellious members of the Longshoreman's Union. LaMotta's testimony, because it referred to real life rather than cinematic reality, proved more riveting and dangerous. It was certainly more revealing and compelling than the testimony of the mob witness who had gone before him.

LaMotta was escorted to a long, rectangular table, festooned with microphones. He faced a firing squad of TV cameras, and above the cameras were the faces of LaMotta's inquisitors, robed in moral superiority and indignant self-righteousness. LaMotta looked small and resentful, almost like a cornered wild animal. He would not resort to taking the Fifth, as so many of the other witnesses had.

LaMotta writes in *Raging Bull II*,

> I didn't mind admitting to my part in the deal [of the fixed fight with Fox]. I wanted to come clean. I wasn't exactly proud of it, but I did what I had to do to get the championship. I'd do it again. The statute of limitations was up on the whole goddam mess by now anyway. The DA couldn't touch me. They'd already put Frankie Carbo away.[5]

Questioning of LaMotta was led by former New York assistant DA John Bonomi, who was serving as chief counsel for the Senate Antitrust and Monopoly Subcommittee.

He had previously won a conviction against Frankie Carbo for undercover management. He had also investigated Anthony "Fat Tony" Salerno, who had financed the promotion of the Ingemar Johansson versus Floyd Patterson heavyweight championship bout.

LaMotta confirmed that he was 37 years old and resided at 345 East 52nd Street in New York City. Bonomi then wanted to know about not only LaMotta's bout with Billy Fox, but also his bouts with Tony Janiro and Marcel Cerdan. LaMotta told him he had been offered $100,000 to throw his fight with Janiro, but he refused to do so because he didn't need the money at that time, and because the offer didn't come with the promise of a shot at the title. The Cerdan fight was on the level. He beat Cerdan without any help from the mob. Bonomi also wanted to know how LaMotta's fights were tied to the IBC. LaMotta said the IBC had been controlled by Frankie Carbo, and that was the man who, along with Blinky Palermo, had paid him a visit at Park Arena. When asked how much money he had earned from 1941 to 1954, LaMotta said about $1 million. It wasn't long before Bonomi forced LaMotta to admit what everyone had suspected about his bout with Billy Fox. Bonomi asked if LaMotta was really knocked out by Billy Fox in the fourth round. LaMotta answered no. And had the fight been fixed? Yes, he said.

LaMotta went on to add,

When I signed for the Fox fight, after a couple of weeks, I received an offer of $100,000 to lose to Billy Fox, which I refused. I said I was only interested in the championship fight. It was said it could be arranged, a championship fight could be arranged. That is all I heard for a couple of weeks, and while in training I hurt myself and I went to a doctor and the doctor examined me and took X-rays and found I had a ruptured spleen. He said I couldn't possibly fight, but I thought I could, and I started training again, and I instructed my sparring partners to concentrate their punches on my face, which they did. But as the fight kept getting closer, I found out—I realized that I had no strength in my arms. So, therefore, when I was told again if I would lose the Fox fight, I kept stalling them off because I still felt I could win. But as the fight kept getting closer, I realized that it was going to be kind of difficult. But toward the end, when I realized that I couldn't possibly win, I said I would lose to Billy Fox, if I was guaranteed a championship fight.[6]

LaMotta offered further testimony that Carbo and Palermo arrived at his Park Arena four days before his fight with Fox. They all walked downstairs into the basement of the arena, where LaMotta was offered the $100,000 to lose to Fox. At first, he rejected the offer, saying all he wanted was a shot at the title. If Carbo and Palermo could guarantee LaMotta a title fight, then he would lose to Fox and take the $100,000. He didn't bother to tell them that because of his ruptured spleen he would inevitably lose. Why tell them that when he could pocket $100,000 by keeping quiet about his malady and agree to their condition? LaMotta said he felt like a cockroach, but it was the only way he could get what he wanted.

Bonomi wanted to know why years earlier he had denied to DA Scotti that the Fox fight had been fixed. LaMotta candidly explained that he lied the first time to avoid legal jeopardy but was telling the truth now because his lawyer told him that the truth would no longer get him trouble. The statute of limitations had run its course.

Bonomi also got LaMotta to concede that he originally lied not only because he wanted to avoid legal sanctions, but also because the mob might hurt him. Without prompting, LaMotta reiterated a third reason for lying: He wanted to become the middleweight champion of the world.

Following that, LaMotta admitted that he had to pay $20,000 to get his fight with Marcel Cerdan. He thought the money went to Cerdan's handlers, but he couldn't be certain about it. He also said that he had to sign an exclusive three-year contract with the IBC, and since the IBC meant Carbo and Palermo, they would profit from his fights.

LaMotta did not let the committee or Bonomi know that he had an anonymous note in his pocket, warning him to keep his mouth shut. Every once in a while, he would stick his hand in his jacket pocket and finger the note. But after a few minutes of testimony, after admitting to the fix and the payoff and the three-year contract he had to sign with the IBC, he crumpled the note.

When asked if he was able to name names of people who might threaten or hurt him, LaMotta said he knew of no names. When asked if he, his family, or his brother might be threatened or hurt as a result of his testimony, he said he knew no names. When it was suggested that the people in the boxing business were a rough group of individuals, the kind of people who would break someone's legs or take revenge by murdering someone, LaMotta responded, "I ain't afraid of none of them rats!"[7]

LaMotta came across as a genuine tough guy, not just a tough boxer, but the kind of guy who would stand up to any mobster who would threaten him or his family. About his career, LaMotta said he was pleased he had been his own manager: He was able to make his own deals with the help of his brother, Joey. He acknowledged that he had made numerous mistakes in his career, but they were his own to make. He thought even the wiseguys, the mobsters, the guys who controlled the IBC would respect him for that. He also admitted rather ruefully that because of the mob, fighters were treated like whores who sold their bodies. Regardless of mistakes and regrets, he said he did what he had to do, and he would do it again. You can't go back into the past and change history. Regrets are a waste of time. Where do they get you?

In the *New York Times*, Arthur Daley writes of the men who bribed Jake LaMotta:

> They are forever on the prowl, searching for the extra edge and dishonest dollar. They have no scruples, morals, or decency. They manipulate fighters and discard them coldbloddedly [sic] when their usefulness is over. Not until LaMotta blew the whistle did the fact emerge, for instance, that Fox is now a patient in a mental hospital.

> Boxing is the slum area of sports, and the forces of evil have thus far been able to prevent any attempts at clearance or rehabilitation. It is ruled by the gangsters' code of silence. Evidence at a municipal or state level has been too elusive. Perhaps Congress can sweep clear the debris and order the garbage jettisoned.
>
> LaMotta's whistle-blowing is a start, and strange doings of recent years in some of the lighter weight divisions may yet be laid bare. [8]

The result of the hearings and Carbo's incarceration was the demise of the IBC and its various associates. Boxing was still a profitable enterprise for the mob, and when a vacuum occurred, others filled it. A group of investors led by attorney Roy Cohn, who had been Joseph McCarthy's counsel, and which included businessman William Fugazy and Cohn's law partner, Thomas Bolan, formed a corporation called Feature Sports, Inc. In addition, former boxing promoter and uncle of William Fugazy, Humberto Fugazy, was brought into the corporation, no doubt for his boxing know-how. The corporation had bought the assets of Rosensohn Enterprises, Inc., which had been an offshoot of the IBC, and which included a contract for a rematch between Ingemar Johansson and Floyd Patterson for the heavyweight championship of the world. The match took place at the Polo Grounds on June 20, 1960. Patterson knocked out Johansson in the fifth round and regained the heavyweight title, a title he would later lose to Sonny Liston. Mob boss Tony Salerno paid for the promotion of that bout and so continued the mob's participation in the business of boxing. Jake LaMotta had moved on.

7

UP FROM THE MUCKLANDS

In upstate New York, there are acres and acres of onion fields. In Canastota, New York, those onion fields are known as the mucklands; it is where the young Carmen Basilio labored as his dreams of a better life withered but did not die. Often muddied and rain soaked, his hands were left raw and red.

Years later, after he had achieved success as a boxer, Basilio told interviewers that if he had continued in the mucklands he would have been heading, without any detours, to an anonymous grave. He said he had wanted recognition, not anonymity. "I did what I wanted to do. Not many people can say that their boyhood dreams came true. My boyhood dream was to be a professional fighter, be the world champion, and fight in Yankee Stadium."[1]

As one of 10 siblings, the children of poor parents with little to look forward to, Basilio refused to resign himself to a life of tedious hard labor that paid insultingly low wages. Getting up at five o'clock every morning to dig onions out of the ground did not portend a life of success, honor, or money in the bank. The poor Italian immigrants of Canastota worked the onion fields to put food on their kitchen tables and keep well-shingled roofs over their heads. Either work in the fields or starve. It was that simple. It was what many people had to do, but it was not what Basilio would do.

By the time young Basilio was in high school, he had gotten his fill. No more mucklands for him. No more digging in the mud, then going home with sore hands, wrists, and back. No more small pay packages.

He had dreamed of being a boxer since he was a small boy. He told an interviewer, "I can remember in the fourth grade, the teacher was asking all of us kids what we wanted to be when we grew up. I stood up and said, 'I'm going to be a boxer and be champion of the world.' She said, 'That was the most disgusting thing I ever heard.' I was embarrassed."[2]

As Basilio sat down, the class laughed at him. He didn't shrink down in his chair; instead, he muttered that he would show them all. He would become a world champion and, in doing so, an honored celebrity of Canastota—and not only of Canastota, but also the world. Was such a dream too grandiose? It didn't matter to Basilio. One day, those kids who had laughed at him would respect and admire him as a hometown hero, and so would every person who was a boxing fan.

Although his father was one of those devoted boxing fans, Mr. Basilio was not altogether happy when his son quit high school and decided to devote himself to pursing a boxing career. He warned his son that he would get hurt along the way and should be prepared to accept it. Otherwise, he should steer clear of boxing and try something else. Mr. Basilio was a decent man, a good father and a good man, who was known to friends and neighbors as the honest onion farmer, an appellation that would also accrue to his son years later. Young Basilio thanked his father for the advice and said he was committed to being a boxer and sure he would succeed at it. His father smiled and wished him success. Mrs. Basilio, however, was not so sanguine; for her, boxing was a brutal sport in which her son could get badly hurt. Years later, as her son rose up the ladder toward contending for a championship bout, she would become one of his most ardent fans, occasionally cheering him on at ringside.

Young Basilio went to a local boxing gym to learn the skills that could carry him to the top of his class. He tied on the gloves, hit the speed bag and the heavy bag, shadowboxed, and sparred with local talent. When he wasn't in the gym, he arose early in the morning and ran for miles. His was a tightly wound, sinewy muscled body of ambition, determination, and talent, but without contacts, those qualities would not garner him the kinds of bouts that would lead to a shot at a title. Basilio was advised to find a trainer and manager who could open doors for him. He asked around, saying he wanted to sign on with a manager who could advance his career. He needed someone who was a member of the fraternity of professional boxing managers.

However, before Basilio could advance in his career, he had to serve his country. It was not a long interruption, and it served him well. The U.S. Marines suited his temperament and sense of masculinity. The disciplined life of a Marine was entirely agreeable to him, and the Marines used his boxing skills as a morale booster. He was soon entered in a series of matches. He boxed with determination and skill. His fellow Marines were impressed by his ability to take a punch and then deliver a series of devastating combinations to his opponents. He was developing a following. Marines of all ranks looked forward to his bouts, and soon he was signed up for several important tournaments, where he scored a series of impressive wins. His skills continued to sharpen, adding more fuel to his ambition. Upon his discharge, he emerged as a highly confident and determined young boxer, who knew his fists would earn him the esteem and money he sought. He was set on his feet to embark on a successful ring career.

Basilio found the contacts that he needed: He met two men who would guide his career and to whom he remained loyal well after his retirement from boxing. They were John DeJohn and Joe Netro. Basilio signed on with them with the understanding that they would navigate his journey to pugilistic stardom. DeJohn, whose original surname was Di Gianni, was well known in upstate New York. He was one of the five boxing DeJohn brothers: John, Carmen, Ralph, Joey, and Mike. Of all the brothers, Joey was the spectacular one, the one who had the most promise of becoming a champion; he was a celebrity known throughout upstate New York as the "Golden Boy." He acted as if he were a rock star, expecting admiration, even adulation, not only from boxing fans, but also from young women, who were taken by his good looks and athletic bearing. Joey knew he was charismatic and expected waves of admiration whenever he entered a bar, a bowling alley, and the parties he attended. So impressed was he by his own sense of importance that he swaggered through his celebrity instead of seriously training for fights. Although he preferred drinking, carousing, and partying to train-ing, he nevertheless compiled an impressive record of 74 wins (52 by knockout), 14 losses, and 2 draws. His explosive style of fighting at-tracted legions of fans, and Carmen Basilio was one of his most ardent students, learning through careful observation. In fact, when Basilio fought on a DeJohn undercard, he would not return to his dressing room to shower after the fight. Although tired, sweaty, bruised, and sometimes bloody, he would sit at ringside and study the way DeJohn's propulsive punches pounded opponents into submission. Basilio would learn from Joey's example in the ring, not his example at local bars.

In contrast to Joey DeJohn, Basilio religiously devoted himself to training. In fact, he was so disciplined in adhering to his training regimen that other boxers said he was leading the life of a monk. He would be what Joey DeJohn failed to be; and so John DeJohn, the disappointed brother of Joey, who wanted to manage a champion, was the perfect choice for Basilio. He would help mold Basilio into the champ his brother should have been. Basilio worked hard at being the best he could be, and he adhered to the advice of DeJohn and Netro. He made his professional debut on November 24, 1948, in a bout against Jimmy Evans. The fight took place in Binghamton, New York. Basilio was the hard-punching aggressor, fighting as if his entire career depended on the outcome. He knocked out Evans in the fourth round. Five days later, he knocked out Bruce Walters in the first round. By the end of the year, Basilio had successfully fought in four bouts. He knew he was on his way.

Frankie Carbo and Blinky Palermo took notice of the up-and-coming ring gladiator. They would wait for their opportunity and then attempt to bite off the lion's share of Basilio's contract. They were the predators, and if DeJohn and Netro wanted their fighter to contend for a championship bout, they would have to feed the lions their share of the rewards. Basilio, an innocent at that point, was unaware of the control the IBC had on professional boxing. His focus was on winning and turning his dream into a reality. Although developing a local reputation as a tough, unbeatable boxer, the upstate newspapers nicknamed him the "Upstate Onion Farmer." He would have to show them, along with his former classmates and teacher, that he was no farmer. If tears came to his eyes, it would not be caused by onions, but by having decisions in the ring stolen from him.

Week after week, month after month, Basilio's star shone ever more brightly. By 1953, his was one of the brightest stars in the world of boxing. He was a major draw at the *Saturday Night Fights*, televised out of Boston by Ray Arcel. Basilio had also become known as an articulate, decent, and unpretentious fighter, much admired by sportswriters. He had boxed in 50 bouts and was considered a contender for the welter-weight title. One summer afternoon of that year, DeJohn was invited to have lunch with Frankie Carbo in the dining room of the Warwick Hotel on Sixth Avenue in New York City; the hotel and its barbershop were once a popular hangout with show business celebrities. Joining them for lunch were Hymie "The Mink" Wallman, a managerial front man for Carbo, and Angel Lopez, nightclub owner and manager of the welterweight champion, Kid Gavilan. Carbo was intent on maneuvering Basilio away from Arcel and feeding him into the vise-like jaws of the IBC. Carbo offered Basilio, through DeJohn, the opportunity to fight Gavilan for the welterweight title. While Basilio had been earning the respect and admiration of boxing fans and sportswriters, he was not yet sufficiently experienced to take on a fighter as skillful as Gavilan, so DeJohn said maybe in the near future, but not now. Undeterred, Carbo wrote down a series of numbers on the tablecloth, explaining that Basilio would get 20 percent and Gavilan 40 percent of the proceeds. He emphasized that DeJohn would make a lot of money.

DeJohn went to see Basilio and presented him with the offer; Basilio was doubtful. He had fought Chuck Davey, an IBC boxer, a year earlier, in Chicago. To everyone who saw the fight, the decision should have gone to Basilio, but the judges and referee awarded the win to Davey. It was obvious to Basilio that the IBC would control the outcome of any fight in which it owned one or both of the participating fighters. As if that incident hadn't been sufficiently discouraging, DeJohn told Basilio that he would have to give up part of his earnings to get a match with Gavilan. Basilio adamantly refused, telling his manager he should give up part of his share. Basilio was not about to feed the ravenous appetite of the IBC. In fact, throughout his career Basilio refused to negotiate with Carbo. If necessary, he would be cordial with the man, but he resisted getting entangled in Carbo's web of deceit and manipulation. If his manager had to deal with the gray fox that was his decision, but Basilio remained determined to be out of the range of Carbo's claws and clutches. Once DeJohn agreed to his boxer's stipulation, he went ahead and made a deal with the IBC. DeJohn and Netro would pay the IBC out of their own pockets.

The 15-round bout was scheduled to take place on September 15, 1953, at War Memorial Auditorium in Syracuse, New York. Up to that point, Basilio had fought in 50 matches that comprised 35 wins, 10 loses, and 5 draws. For his match with Basilio, Gavilan had to lose seven pounds to meet the weight criteria for a welterweight; he entered the ring weighing 146¾ pounds. Basilio entered the ring weighing 147 pounds. As the fight progressed, Gavilan's manager complained that his fighter's rapid loss of weight seemed to diminish his stamina. But it wasn't only the rapid loss of weight that made Gavilan appear less than his usual self; he was up against a man who was focused like a guided missile on a target.

In the first few rounds, Basilio was obviously the more aggressive fighter, pushing and pounding his opponent. His punches were as propulsive as those of Joey DeJohn. It was apparent to everyone that Basilio was driven by the most intense determination. He knew he had more riding on the outcome of this bout than any previous bout in which he had fought. He was a sensational crowd-pleaser as he threw devastating punches with both fists. This was his chance to take the title, and he had invested years of well-honed skills into his strategy for outboxing the man known as the "Cuban Hawk," for Gavilan's predatory ability to swoop in on an opponent with a brilliant flurry of combinations and win. Yet, Basilio proved more skillful than DeJohn had expected. Although Basilio was less experienced than Gavilan, he was surprisingly effective, landing numerous perfectly aimed punches that Gavilan surprisingly failed to block. And when Gavilan landed powerful punches, Basilio seemed to shake off each one. Once during the second round, Basilio knocked down Gavilan. In fact, during a number of the early rounds, he was the winner, driving Gavilan to the ropes, where the combatants had to be separated by the referee.

Although Basilio won the early rounds, Gavilan was developing his own aggressive attacks. As determined as Basilio was, he seemed to tire as the rounds went on. Gavilan, the clever strategist and tactician, was wearing down his opponent. It was now Gavilan who was landing the blows that would decide the outcome; he pounded Basilio's left eye until it was almost swollen shut. Basilio had to hold his head at an angle to target his punches. By doing so, his head became an easy target for Gavilan, whose punches landed exactly where he aimed each one. Yet, Basilio put up a magnificent defense. By the ninth round, Gavilan was winning and continued doing so through the 11th. Basilio, through sheer determination and undiminished aggressiveness, won the 12th round; he managed to make the 13th round an even contest. Those were Basilio's best later rounds. In the last two rounds of the fight, Gavilan was the more energetic and aggressive fighter. The fight ended with a split decision. Basilio won according to one judge, and Gavilan won according to the referee and one judge.

Even though Basilio and his fans thought he had won the fight at War Memorial, those close to Carbo figured Gavilan would win. After all, Gavilan had been a 4-to-1 favorite. The bookies knew on whom the smart money was being bet, and although local fans bet heavily on Basilio, people in New York and Philadelphia poured in big bucks for Gavilan to outpoint Basilio and maintain his ownership of the welterweight title. The smart money had a history of betting on sure things. Sportswriters wrote admiringly of Basilio's crowd-pleasing ring performances and ability to take a punch and keep fighting. They predicted that with some more experience, Basilio would be a formidable contender for the welterweight title. Some of them even predicted that one day, Basilio would be the champion. Although Basilio, DeJohn, and Netro, along with Basilio's fans, wanted a rematch with Gavilan, it was denied. The IBC figured Basilio had his chance and lost. If his managers wanted a rematch, they would have to negotiate a new deal at a later time, a time to be decided by the IBC. And at a price also to be decided by the IBC.

Perhaps Basilio had been too dispirited and dejected by his loss to Gavilan, for in his next fight, just two months later, he was knocked out by Johnny Cunningham in Toledo, Ohio. Four years earlier, he had lost to Cunningham in a split decision, and then 15 days later, he won against him in a unanimous decision. After his bouts with Cunningham, Basilio had 10 more fights, and he won each one. Then, on June 10, 1955, Basilio's opportunity for a second shot at the welterweight title arrived. It was delivered as a fait accompli by DeJohn and Netro, following their dealings with a shady character named Gabe Genovese, who was ostensibly just a barber, but unbeknownst to his clipper-and-comb customers, he was also a close business associate of Carbo. He was also linked to a number of boxers. To get Basilio a shot at the title, DeJohn and Netro had to pay Genovese $5,000.

The newspapers in upstate New York generated a great deal of excitement about the upcoming 15-round fight between welterweight champion Tony DeMarco and Basilio. The fight would take place at

War Memorial Auditorium in Syracuse, where Basilio's local fans would fill most of the seats.

Unlike his fight with Gavilan, who had to lose weight to qualify as a welterweight, Basilio now had to work off his extra pounds. After days of strenuous road work and ample sweating, he entered the ring weighing in at 145½ pounds to DeMarco's 144¾ pounds. Rocky Marciano provided exciting ring commentary, describing in detail what each fighter was doing right and wrong. DeMarco had a powerful right cross, but it kept missing Basilio's chin, for Basilio was able to throw DeMarco off balance by using his rapidly pumping jab against DeMarco's left shoulder, causing a slight turn in DeMarco's stance. As a result, one right cross after another missed Basilio. DeMarco aggressively drove Basilio against the ropes, but Basilio fiercely fought back, delivering a series of hard body blows, forcing DeMarco to back away from him. Basilio then went after DeMarco, getting inside of his punches, where DeMarco could not deliver his powerful right cross. When DeMarco finally saw an opening and threw a right cross, Basilio backed away from it and only the swish of air brushed his face.

Throughout the fight, DeMarco appeared to be the stronger fighter. He was winning on points even though many of his right crosses missed Basilio. Marciano commented that DeMarco was outboxing Basilio. Yet, DeMarco was wearing himself down, throwing a series of hard punches that left his arms tired and heavy. By the 10th round, it was apparent to everyone that DeMarco was tired; he wasn't holding his right fist high enough, and his left was just above his waist. He was the perfect target for Basilio, who knocked him down twice in the 10th round. DeMarco came back strong and aggressive in the 11th round, during which Basilio could not finish him off. The round was evenly scored. In the 12th round, however, Basilio hit DeMarco with a barrage of punches, hooks, and uppercuts, and the referee mercifully stopped the fight. Basilio had won the welterweight championship by a TKO. His mother, the woman who had loathed the idea of her son becoming a professional boxer, climbed into the ring and gave him a big maternal kiss, eliciting cheers and boos from fans.

Five months and two fights later, on November 30, 1955, in Boston Garden, Basilio met DeMarco for a 15-round title rematch. The crowd in the Garden was loudly in DeMarco's corner, cheering his entrance, while booing Basilio. DeMarco was the initial aggressor, landing a series of hard punches to Basilio's head and chin. The punches seemed to barely faze Basilio, who came back strong in the second round. He landed his own series of punches, bloodying Demarco's left eye. It was fascinating watching the two fighters, who were natural lefties, fight as righties. Although their right crosses and uppercuts were powerful shots, one wonders what they could have accomplished fighting as lefties.

By the third round, DeMarco was bleeding from his nose, and Basilio was landing more punches than his opponent. In the fourth round, DeMarco landed a powerful right that caused Basilio to stagger on rubbery legs. He did it again, this time opening a cut above Basilio's right eye. In the fifth round, DeMarco staggered Basilio again, almost knocking him down. DeMarco was dominant in the sixth round, and then in the seventh, DeMarco pounded Basilio, who wobbled like a drunk about to hit the canvas. Fortunately for him, DeMarco was unable to land a knockout blow, which would have ended the fight. DeMarco continued to dominate the fight in the eighth and ninth rounds. In addition to the cut over his right eye, Basilio now sported a reddish-purple bruise just below his left eye. His face was beginning to resemble raw hamburger.

The bout dramatically altered in the 11th round: Basilio was fighting like a desperate, cornered animal to save his very life. He landed hard punch after hard punch on DeMarco's cranium, which must have been rumbling with the flow of blood and the roar of the crowd. Basilio staggered DeMarco, then knocked him down. DeMarco looked like a wounded soldier, lost and confused on a bloody battlefield. Yet, he emerged from his corner ready to do battle in the 12th round; but the blows he had suffered left him too unsteady on his legs, and his tired arms were unable to deliver defensive counterpunches. The referee finally called an end to the fight and awarded the win to Basilio. Basilio, exhausted, his energy drained, retained the title at a painful cost. The two bouts between DeMarco and Basilio were fought brilliantly, and each of the combatants respected the other. In fact, they became good friends. When one of DeMarco's relatives died, Basilio boarded a plane to Boston so that he could console his former opponent. Years later, DeMarco told a reporter he could not have lost his title to a better man.

While there was no point in a third fight, Carbo proposed that there should be a third match. After all, the IBC had cleaned up on the first two, and the fans of each boxer would pay again to see if Basilio could repeat what he had done in two matches. Basilio said he wasn't going to sign for a third fight. He refused to be bossed around by the mob. Even if DeJohn and Netro had begged him to fight DeMarco again, Basilio would have refused. He also knew his managers would have to give up a share of their earnings to the IBC, but that was their business.

When Carbo and Palermo were later tried in court, prosecutor John Bonomi stated,

> Joe Netro and John DeJohn, the licensed comanagers of . . . Carmen Basilio stated to me that they paid $7,000 from the managers' share of Basilio's purses in 1956. In 1957, Netro and DeJohn shelled out $20,000 to Genovese from Basilio's earnings.
>
> In the past year . . . Basilio's comanagers, according to their own statements, gave Genovese $24,000.[3]

During a period of three years, Genovese had collected a total of $67,196 from Basilio's comanagers. Genovese, unable to cover his tracks, was sentenced to two years of imprisonment at Rikers Island, served one year, and died shortly after his release.

Basilio was focused on his career, not the machinations of the criminals demanding payments in the shadows of boxing arenas. He was proud to have retained his welterweight championship title; he felt he was on top of the world. He was certainly at the top of his game, seemingly unbeatable, as he stood at the head of his division. DeJohn and Netro also agreed that after Basilio's two matches with DeMarco, he seemed unbeatable and would probably remain so for years to come.

When Basilio signed for his next fight, against Johnny Saxton, he believed he would easily win. Basilio thought Saxton was not as tough as DeMarco; however, it wasn't toughness alone that Basilio should have considered. Into the equation of his estimation of Saxton should have been a warning that Saxton was managed, controlled, and owned by Palermo. Basilio wasn't the only one who failed to consider the influence of Palermo, for sportswriters also thought Saxton would be an easy opponent for Basilio. Neither Basilio nor his managers knew that Carbo and his associates had bet heavily on Saxton to win. Since the odds favored Basilio, those who bet on Saxton figured on having a cornucopia of money spilled into their bank accounts and safe deposit boxes.

It didn't matter to Basilio that he was two inches shorter than Saxton; Basilio, at 5-foot-7, had tangled with larger men and beat them. And because Basilio had a shorter reach than Saxton, he would have to fight in close. Indeed, throughout the fight Basilio tried to crowd Saxton, attempting to stay close enough to land uppercuts and right crosses. Saxton's strategy, by contrast, was to keep away from Basilio, as he hoped to land long knockout punches. Although Basilio was the aggressor, Saxton kept dancing away from him. In the 12th round, Basilio caught Saxton and pounded him, almost pushing him through the ropes. At the end of 15 rounds, both judges and the referee, to the outrage of the Basilio camp and sportswriters, awarded the decision to Saxton.

Fans booed and sportswriters shook their heads in disbelief and complained to one another. Their subsequent stories were filled with their doubts and mockery for the judges' decisions. The almost-unanimous decision by sportswriters and fans who had seen the fight was that Basilio had decisively won it. It was obviously a fix, and some fans demanded their money back. Their demands were met with either deafness or denials. Basilio, having been robbed of the welterweight title, returned to his dressing room. He said he left the arena "with a broken heart."[4] He felt like one who had been mugged in a dark alley; his most important achievement, the welterweight title, had been stolen from him. He was determined to not let it happen again.

After that March 1956 match, Basilio signed to fight Saxton again. It was another IBC-arranged match, but it would be at War Memorial Stadium in Syracuse, close to Basilio's hometown, where he believed his many fans would cheer him on. For reasons no one understood, Saxton reversed his strategy and fought close to Basilio, exposing himself to Basilio's short, powerful lefts and rights, hooks, and uppercuts. Basilio easily outboxed Saxton, who threw wild punches that swung through the air like wayward tennis balls. By the ninth round, Saxton appeared helpless and tired, and Basilio looked as if he could have been belting a rag doll. The referee stopped the fight at one minute and 31 seconds into the ninth round and awarded the win to Basilio by TKO. For Basilio, it was sweet revenge. Several attendees wondered if Saxton had been told to alter his strategy so that Basilio could win.

But because Basilio and Saxton had each won a single bout in their two previous clashes, a third bout, a rubber match, was promoted and would be considered decisive. The two fighters met in February 1957, and Basilio rapidly demolished Saxton in two rounds. Basilio fought as if his fists were sledgehammers smashing a dilapidating wall that crumbled before him. Thus, he retained his welterweight title. No one concluded that the fight had been fixed.

It was finally apparent to even the cynics and the doubters that Saxton was no match for the tough little onion farmer. Sportswriters said there was no question about who was the more skillful, more determined, more aggressive fighter. Basilio had remained a hero to his fans, but he was more than an annoyance to the mob, for people began speculating that a number of Saxton's earlier fights must have been fixed. Even sportswriters speculated that if Basilio's first fight with Saxton had been fixed, then what about Saxton's win over the Cuban Hawk, Kid Gavilan? The mob hated that kind of talk. They and their enablers were always attempting to provide a veneer of legitimacy for the bouts promoted by the IBC. No matter how much cheap cologne the IBC sprayed on the rotting garbage of its stinking reputation, the rancid smell would not fade away.

And what of poor Johnny Saxton? One can look at Saxton's impressive boxing record, and without the testimony of insiders and informants, it's impossible to determine how many of his fights may have been fixed by Palermo. Saxton fought 66 bouts, winning 55, 21 by knockout. He was knocked out five times and fought in two bouts that ended in draws. Similarly, another mob-owned boxer, Primo Carnera, had an impressive record. He fought 103 bouts, winning 89, with 72 coming by way of knockout; he lost 14 times and had no draws. It has been well established that Carnera's bouts were fixed by Owney Madden. In addition to being managed by mobsters, who fixed their fights by paying off judges and opponents, both Saxton and Carnera had something else in common: Once their use to mobsters had expired, they were left to fend for themselves like junkyard dogs. Like many misused and manipulated boxers, they were virtually broke when their ring careers ended.

Poverty stricken Saxton was discarded and ignored by Palermo and Carbo; he lived a hand-to-mouth existence in a New York City apartment without electricity. He occasionally worked as a security guard but couldn't hold a job. He had a mercurial temper on a short fuse, and with only the slightest provocation, he would rage and assault the target of his fury. He was periodically arrested for thefts, breaking and entering, and resisting arrest. He served time in not only jail, but also a mental hospital. Released and left to wander on mean streets with no place to hide from the world, Saxton was rescued by a sympathetic friend who arranged for him to live a life of modest comfort in Florida. He was a beaten relic of what he had been: a promising young boxer whose grace and speed had, just years earlier, reminded some of Sugar Ray Robinson. Before he died in 2008, at age 78, Saxton had been diagnosed with that bane of boxing, pugilistic dementia, otherwise known as punch-drunkenness.

Following his trilogy of fights with Saxton, Basilio was the proud king of his division. He had proven himself against not only Saxton, but also the much harder puncher, DeMarco. Then, just three months after defeating Saxton, Basilio easily disposed of Harold Jones with a TKO. Some thought it was merely a tune-up fight until Basilio could take on the most impressive boxer of the twentieth century. That man, of course, was the inimitable Sugar Ray Robinson, considered the best pound-for-pound boxer of the twentieth century. For promoters, it would be a match made in boxing heaven: The money generated by such a match, especially from television, would be a wet dream for greedy promoters. Basilio, ambitious for greater glory, was determined to wear the middleweight crown. He gained the necessary weight to move up from welterweight to middleweight. Although Robinson was the more skillful boxer, he was 36 years old, an age at which most boxers suffer from diminished stamina and quickness of reflexes. The match would take place on September 23, 1957, at Yankee Stadium, in the Bronx. Every seat in the stadium, from ringside to the stands, was sold.

Basilio had wanted to fight Sugar Ray Robinson for years. He wanted to not only win the middleweight championship, but also avenge an insult to himself and his wife. It began shortly after Basilio and his wife, Josie, had traveled from Canastota for a weekend of fun in New York City. Basilio saw himself as a young sophisticate, a husband who could show his wife a good time and impress her with his new-found urbanity. He was a successful boxer on his way up. He decided to take Josie to Harlem, for that's where Sugar Ray Robinson presided. While Basilio was a tough, young, scrappy fighter ready to take on every welterweight on his path to success, Robinson was the uncrowned king of 125th Street. He was a major celebrity in both black and white

America, frequently appearing on television, where he danced with Gene Kelly. He toured Europe and packed fans into arenas when he deigned to fight local talent. When in New York, Robinson traveled around in a blazing pink Cadillac that could have been the subject of an Aretha Franklin song. Wherever he went, pedestrians waved at him, shouted out his name, and gave him a thumbs-up gesture. On 125th Street in Harlem, where Robinson owned several businesses, he would park his dazzling convertible on the street as if the street had been deeded to him. And why not? Cops never gave him a ticket. Fans flocked to him like iron filings to a powerful steel magnet. Robinson would grin and wave to the crowd. They saw him as an elegant, handsome athlete, a man with plenty of sex appeal and panache.

And there on the edge of the crowd stood Mr. and Mrs. Basilio. They, too, grinned at the famous middleweight. Basilio, with his wife's arm interlocked with his own, managed to make his way through the crowd. He figured Robinson would greet him, one fighter to another, members of the same fraternity. When he reached Robinson, Basilio extended his hand and introduced himself. He said he would like Robinson to meet his wife, and for good measure, he added that he had fought Billy Graham a week ago. Robinson stared at the couple for a moment, then turned his back to them. Basilio felt humiliated. He had expected, at the very least, to be politely received as one boxer cordially saying hello to another boxer. Basilio's wife tugged at his arm, motioning with her head that they should leave. Basilio would never forget the slight, and it would further fuel the fire of his determination to beat Robinson in front of a crowd of his own fans. As they walked away, Basilio said he felt embarrassed. "And I said that someday, I'm going to fight that SOB and kick his ass. That was 1952. It took five years. By 1957, I got my chance at him."[5]

Before their fight, Robinson and Basilio each turned down demands disguised as entreaties from Carbo. While Robinson and Basilio kept their distance from Carbo and Palermo, Basilio's manager, DeJohn, decided he had no choice but to deal with the IBC as a necessary evil, particularly if he wanted to get Basilio in the ring for a shot at the middleweight championship. Robinson, by other means, had decided he would aggressively negotiate directly with James Norris, president of the IBC. Robinson was known as one of the toughest negotiators in boxing, one of the few boxers who negotiated his own deals. An hour before a fight, he would often refuse to fight unless certain additional conditions were met in his contract. He would drive frustrated promoters to rage against him, but Robinson would always remain calmly adamant. He knew his drawing power, and he knew that his demands would invariably be met.

Prior to his bout with Basilio, Robinson visited Norris in his office and insisted that the TV rights for the fight not be given to Theater Network Television but to TelePromptTer, Inc. In addition, he wanted a greater percentage of the gate than he normally received and wanted to be able to sell a large number of tickets. Robinson had taken on the role of promoter à la Mike Jacobs. Robinson was a star, and every promoter wanted some of the profits spun off from his glitter. Basilio, a down-to-earth common man, had his own price, too, and remained as adamant about it as Robinson was in his demands. While Robinson wanted control of the TV rights to the fight, Basilio demanded 30 percent of the gross. He didn't care what Robinson got as long his own conditions were met. The two men proved as hardheaded prior to their fight as they did in the ring. In addition, each looked forward to hammering the other, for they loathed one another. Robinson thought Basilio was a nasty bully, and Basilio thought Robinson was a racist snob.

So, on September 23, 1957, the two men met in front of almost 40,000 boxing fans for a 15-round bout of gladiatorial combat in Yankee Stadium. Basilio now weighed 153½ pounds, and Robinson weighed 159 pounds. Basilio was 5-foot-7, and Robinson was 5-foot-11. Robinson was 36 years old; Basilio was 30 years old. Robinson's speed and reflexes had diminished since his prime. Basilio's disadvantage was his short arms and comparatively short height. It is invariably easier for a tall man to beat a short man. So Basilio would have to box close in to not only connect with Robinson's head and chin, but also avoid his long, devastating jabs.

From the outset, Basilio succeeded in getting in close to Robinson, landing a series of powerful hooks, while avoiding Robinson's jabs. The fight was so fierce that as the bell ended round three, the fighters continued throwing several punches. In round after round, Robinson kept looking for an opening to throw his rapid-fire series of damaging combinations, but Basilio, always crouching and weaving to offset their height difference, was a difficult target for Robinson, many of whose blows landed on the back of Basilio's head. In the ninth round, Basilio had Robinson against the ropes and was pounding away. Robinson looked exhausted. By the 12th round, Robinson seemed rejuvenated, had become the aggressor, and was bringing the battle to Basilio.

Toward the end of the 13th round, Robinson almost sent Basilio to the canvas after a blazing left hook. Then, in the next round, he delivered a powerful right punch to Basilio's body that staggered the smaller boxer. But that was it for Robinson: He seemed to have run out of gas; he had punched himself out. His tiredness showed. One could imagine how heavy his arms must have felt. In the 15th round, Basilio, intent on winning the middleweight title, seemed to be propelled by a hunger that could only be satisfied by taking down Robinson. He went after Robinson with the aggressiveness of a hungry tiger and only came to a heavy-breathing rest after the final bell sounded. Basilio won the middleweight title in a split decision. It was the high point of his career.

Back in his dressing room, Basilio said, through bruised and swollen lips, that he had won the fight because he had been the more aggressive fighter. His face was evidence it had been a brutal battle, for he wore a large bandage on a cut above his left eye. On his cheeks were large, red welts that soon turned to deep purple. When he wasn't talking to reporters, he was rubbing ice along his lips. His face was testimony to the brutality of his encounter with Robinson. Now that he was the middleweight champion, he had to give up his welterweight title; however, he received the Hickok Belt as the foremost professional athlete of 1957. And he had beaten the boxer against whom every middleweight measured himself.

Of course, there would be a rematch. Not only were fans clamoring for it, but also the IBC. There was more than $1 million riding on that fight. The smart money was betting that Robinson would retake the crown. Intent on making sure there would be no detours, no potholes, no bumps in the road to the big-money fight Carbo envisioned, he traveled from Florida to New York. He would defeat any last-minute demands, even if he had to issue threats; before any screwups could spoil his plans, he would rectify each one. He would be the man to make sure that managers and fighters went along with the IBC. Carbo's presence in New York was noted by the DA, Frank Hogan, as was the presence of many other mobsters; they were all planning on flying or taking a train to Chicago, where, on March 25, 1958, Basilio and Robinson would fight again for the title. As mobsters boarded planes and trains for Chicago, they were watched by New York City detectives, who took photos and copious notes. A trio of those detectives also flew to Chicago so they could keep Palermo, Carbo, and their minions under surveillance. There would be ongoing surveillance of Carbo and Palermo until their final trials. The law was determined to put the two of them away and hose off the grime that had adhered to professional boxing.

The rematch got off to a fast start, each fighter aiming his best punches at the other. Robinson repeatedly aimed jabs at Basilio's body and head. Basilio landed a powerful left hook to Robinson's chin. By the fifth round, Basilio's left eye was swollen and partly closed. Robinson continued to jab at that eye, intent on closing it, thus throwing Basilio off balance. By the ninth round, Basilio's left eye was almost closed, and the surrounding tissue and eyelid were swollen to the size of a golf ball. Yet, he rallied with a series of effective left hooks in the 9th and 10th rounds. His punches landed firmly and powerfully against Robinson's midsection. Robinson counterpunched and paced himself more thoughtfully in this fight than he had in the previous one, maintaining his energy from round to round. Robinson, once he completely closed Basilio's eye in the 11th round, went on a powerfully aggressive attack. At that point, it looked as if he would surely win the fight. But they were each growing tired and clinched to slow the pace of the battle. The referee would separate them, and they would clinch again. One time when the fighters clinched, the referee separated them, only to get smacked on the face by one of their gloves—a danger of getting between two men focused on beating one another into submission. The referee was an annoyance for Basilio.

His real problem was Robinson's volley of punches, which Basilio attempted to avoid by crouching and weaving. His head bobbed around near Robinson's midsection. With a limited target to aim at, Robinson's punches landed on Basilio's back and the back of his head. It would not be enough to put Basilio into never-never land. Basilio's tactic of crouching to avoid a possible knockout punch was the only way a man of his short stature could protect himself; however, without being able to trade Robinson punch for punch, Basilio was losing on points. Even when upright, he couldn't see out of his left eye, so Robinson's long, elegant jabs were able to find easy targets of opportunity. Knowing he had to win the last round with a flurry of hard-hitting punches, Basilio tried to punch his way to a victorious decision. Both fighters drew on every ounce of energy they had in reserve and fought on with aggressive belligerence. After the brutal back-and-forth attack and defense of their final punches had been brought to a conclusion by the final bell, each man was bruised and exhausted, and headed to their corners, each a refuge from pain. The ring announcer read the decisions of the two judges and referee: Robinson won back the middleweight title for the fifth time in a split decision. Many sportswriters believed Basilio had won the fight, then speculated whether the decision had been decided in advance so that there would be rubber match. That was certainly on the agendas of Carbo and Palermo.

And why not: The bouts between the two rivals were huge financial successes. Basilio, the gutsy aggressor, had earned more than $500,000 from his two fights with Robinson. Not bad for an onion farmer from the upstate mucklands. Robinson, the dashing celebrity who could rise from the ashes of defeat time and time again, earned a little more than his opponent. Basilio's managers had to increase their contributions to Genovese's bank account just to keep up proportionately with the amount of money their fighter earned. As Carbo's bagman, Genovese delivered enough money to keep his boss happy at least until the next fight. The men of the IBC were as satisfied as a pack of wolves who had just digested a feast. Their satisfaction, however, was soon replaced by their regular hunger for more money.

After the fight, Carbo, Palermo, and Genovese went to Florida, apparently in need of rest and relaxation after witnessing the battle between Robinson and Basilio. Carbo was wanted by law enforcement, but no one seemed to be looking for him in Florida, and he apparently felt safe there. He invited Basilio and DeJohn to meet with him at a home in Miami Beach. There, Carbo explained that he wanted Robinson and Basilio to fight again. DeJohn said Basilio would not take less than 30 percent of the gate, while Robinson wanted more than 40 percent. The negotiations came to a standstill. Later that day, after Basilio had returned to his hotel, he received a phone call from Palermo, telling him to meet with him and Genovese in the hotel lobby. After some perfunctory conversation, Palermo told Basilio they would drive to the home of James Norris. While in Norris's house, Basilio received a phone call from Carbo. Basilio reported that Carbo "asked how I was doing, talking about the Robinson fight. I said I'm asking 30 percent and I'm not going to fight for less. He says 'Good luck' to me and that was that."[6]

The fight never took place. And neither Basilio nor Robinson was threatened. In fact, they were two of only several fighters who never gave in to Carbo.

In an interview with Mike Wallace on October 26, 1957, Basilio claimed that he knew nothing of underworld figures and that Jim Norris, head of the IBC, had been helpful in opening the door for him to become middleweight boxing champion. He did not know that Norris's ostensible decency was an illusion and that Norris was a Carbo puppet. He stated that he hadn't acceded to the mob's demands and that no one had tried to prevent him from getting a chance for a title fight. He owed a great deal to DeJohn and Netro.[7]

Robinson's biographer, Will Haygood, writes,

> Robinson hated the business of the fight game, and as he watched Carbo and IBC officials, his distrust grew. He sniffed graft and imagined conspiracies. He saw sportswriters gallivanting with Carbo and his men; he saw promoters being handed gifts. Low-pitched conversations and overheard whispers fueled more skepticism.[8]

One day, when Robinson was training for a fight, Carbo arrived by car at the training camp. He called Robinson over and offered him a large sum of money to throw his next fight. Robinson politely told Carbo that it was not the way he did business, and Carbo drove away. Robinson was smart enough to keep his distance from Carbo and Palermo, and because he was the best living fighter in the 1940s and early 1950s, he could make his own deals. He didn't need the mobsters the way up-and-coming fighters did or the way down-and-going-further-down fighters did. The former needed the bouts the IBC could arrange that might lead to title fights, while the latter needed mob money just to pay their bills. Robinson remained his own man and took pride in his independence; he was a negotiator, tougher and savvier than most professional managers. He was a celebrity both inside and outside the world of boxing. Whether dancing with Gene Kelly or appearing on *What's My Line?* or *The Ed Sullivan Show*, or singing "Knock Him Down Whiskey" with Earl Hines, Robinson's star shone brighter than any of the lesser stars of pugilism. For Carbo and Palermo, Robinson was a hands-off symbol that could not be tarnished.

Other celebrity boxers were not as fortunate as Robinson. Joe Louis also tried to keep his distance from the mob, although he did get entangled with Mike Jacobs and Truman Gibson, the supposedly squeaky-clean lawyer who fronted for the IBC. Louis knew the mob wanted to get their hooks into him, and he would attempt to placate or avoid them, or simply deny them. He said, "Since 1969, I've had a little trouble with the Mafia. At one time, my life was in real danger. They tried to put me out of the way. . . . They might come back at any time. One thing I know. Your best friends can set you up. Your best friends can kill you."[9]

Another great boxer who avoided having to deal with the mob was Max Baer. Preparing to fight Primo Carnera for the heavyweight championship, Baer was in his dressing room getting a rubdown. Two of Owney Madden's gun-toting thugs entered the room unannounced, their fedoras pulled low over their foreheads, their collars turned up. One had a cigarette dangling from between his lips. The other one told Baer that he better lose his fight with Carnera if he wanted to live. Baer told the two thugs to pound sand, and his manager, Ancil Hoffman, yelled for them to beat it. They did, and strangely enough, there were no repercussions. Baer went on to clobber the hapless Carnera and be crowned the heavyweight champion. That was the end of not only Carnera's heavyweight crown, but also his usefulness to the mob. He was discarded like scraps from a leftover dinner that had gone rancid.

Basilio stands out in the history of twentieth-century boxing as a man who was guided by his principles and dreams, and never forced off the road he chose to travel on. Today, he is less well known than Robinson, Louis, Baer, and the other greats of pugilism, but he remains a man of courage. He came from poverty and made millions of dollars on his own terms. Although his managers felt they had to deal with Carbo, Palermo, and Genovese, they did so for the benefit of the man who was as loyal to them as they were to him. Basilio's resolve never wavered, neither in the face of gangsters nor in the ring. There was never a tougher boxer than the honest man who gave up the mucklands for boxing glory.

After losing to Robinson, Basilio had seven more fights. In three of those, he challenged two others for the middleweight championship. He lost to Gene Fullmer by a TKO in 1959, and again by TKO in 1960. Each was for the National Boxing Association middleweight championship. In 1961, challenging middleweight champion Paul Pender, Basilio lost by a unanimous decision. He had won 56 of 79 bouts and lost 16, and with 16 draws. He was a happy man: He had realized his childhood dream, shamed his belittling teacher, and remained a local hero to the citizens of Canastota. Following his retirement, he worked for the Genesee Brewery Company, found it boring, and resigned. The company did not want to lose Basilio, so he became its goodwill spokesperson and worked in its public relations department. Thereafter, he worked as a physical education instructor for Le Moyne College. He was so respected that he was one of the first boxers to be named to the International Boxing Hall of Fame (IBHOF), which, not coincidentally, was set up in Canastota in 1990. Indeed, the IBHOF was erected in Canastota as a tribute to Basilio, as well as his nephew, Billy Backus, who won the welterweight title in the early 1970s. The IBHOF features bronze busts of Basilio and Backus, even though Backus is not an inductee of the hall.

Each year when the IBHOF sponsored a parade of former champions, Basilio was the one who got the loudest cheers and longest clatter of applause. Films of his fights on YouTube are studied by aspiring boxers, for Basilio was one of the most persistent and aggressive fighters of the twentieth century, along with Jake LaMotta. He received numerous Fighter of the Year honors, and although he suffered terrible injuries to his craggy countenance, he said he didn't like being hurt but had accepted it as the price he had to pay to be a world champion. Winning for him was sweet, while losing was bitter. But when he walked down the main street of Canastota, there was nothing as sweet as being called champ. In 2009, this high school dropout was presented with a diploma in recognition of his achievements by Canastota High School. It was a more hard-earned document than the one he could have earned had he remained a student.

When he died in 2012, at age 85, the town honored its favorite son. He left behind his wife, Josie, who proudly got to see her husband win both the welterweight and middleweight titles. She said she traced her husband's decline in health to heart bypass surgery he had underwent in 1992. She added that an MRI scan revealed no brain damage from his prizefighting days. In addition to his wife, Basilio was survived by four children and many grandchildren and great grandchildren.

During the 1950s, there were a number of great Italian fighters (LaMotta, Graziano, Marciano), and Basilio was as good as any of them. Five of his fights were considered so good they were named fights of the year by *Ring Magazine*: Basilio versus DeMarco II, 1955; Basilio versus Saxton II, 1957; Basilio versus Robinson I, 1957; Basilio versus Robinson II, 1958; and Basilio versus Fullmer I, 1959. In 1957, *Ring Magazine* named him Fighter of the Year.

Looking back at Basilio, there were few fighters who took as much punishment as he did. His craggy, crooked face, scarred and battered, was a visual memoir of what he had suffered through. Yet, he delivered more punishment to his opponents than they delivered to him. He had not only fought for the middleweight and welterweight titles, but also fought his way out of a life that offered few, if any, opportunities beyond the onion fields of Canastota. On the journey, he was a symbol of determination, resolve, and persistence, all of which made him almost unbeatable.

8

SONNY LISTON'S BLUES

Charles "Sonny" Liston was one of 25 children, the second youngest, born to an Arkansas sharecropper, Tobe Liston, and his wife, Helen Baskin, who was 30 years younger than her husband, who was in his mid-40s. They lived on the Moreledge Plantation, which was in Johnson Township. Tobe had 13 children with his first wife and then another 12 with Helen. Since Arkansas didn't mandate the issuance of birth certificates at the time of Sonny's birth, there is no accurate birth date for him. He believed he was born in 1932, while others claimed 1930 as the year. A few even thought it might be as early as 1928. Sonny's early years would put him on a road few Americans would want to travel on. Unfortunately for him, that road had a dead-end sign that the illiterate Sonny was unable to read. That he traveled it as long as he did is testament to not only his love of life's pleasures, but also his ability to outfox the deprivations of fate and the harassments of police.

When Tobe wasn't scraping out a pauper's living from the poor, unforgiving soil of the Moreledge Plantation, he was beating his young son. "The only thing he ever gave me was a beating," said Sonny.[1] Sonny was helpless to defend himself, and Tobe used whatever weapon he could wrap his grimy, gnarled hands around: a leather belt, a slender branch from a tree, a switch found on the ground, the discarded reins from a long-dead mule. The beatings left ugly scars on the mind and body of young Sonny. The burning hatred he felt for his father was later turned against the world of squares and suckers, and those he unmercifully pummeled in the ring.

By the time Sonny was 13 or so, his mother, who had also been slapped and battered by Tobe, decided she had had enough of Tobe's brutality and gathered up some of her children and fled via Greyhound bus to St. Louis, Missouri. Sonny, eager to join his mother and escape the bullying presence of his father, decided to harvest nuts without his father's knowledge. When he had gathered a profitable and bulging sack, he sold his harvest and used the money to pay for a bus ticket to St. Louis. He departed on a hot summer day, happy he would soon see his mother. He had thought that St. Louis was no bigger than a plantation, and so after disembarking from the bus, he asked strangers on the streets if they knew where Helen Baskin Liston lived. People either shrugged or ignored him. One man asked for money. Another man offered money if Sonny would follow him down an alley and into a yard.

Sonny wandered down one street after another, regularly asking strangers the same question. Although he was getting nowhere and seemingly covering the same ground, he would not give up. He had to find his mother. He was finally picked up by cops who found him sleeping amid a collection of garbage cans in an alley behind a greasy-spoon restaurant. They took him to an all-night café and fed him. Afterward, the cops parked the derelict boy in the local jail overnight. Even though Liston never trusted cops, he was treated with kindness that night. Best of all, the cops had located his mother. He happily moved in with her and figured that now life would be easier in St. Louis, living with his mother, than it had been on the plantation. He would never see his father again, and that was just fine with him.

Sonny was bigger than other kids of his age. As he continued to grow like a weed, he also began developing bulging muscles from his part-time work as a day laborer. He was also developing a mean, menacing attitude and stony glare that would intimidate everyone who wronged him. He practiced staring down other kids. His mother thought he should attend school, which he did, but he left after the kids in his class laughed at his outsized presence and illiteracy. The kids thought he was stupid and had been left back several times. They would only cease their tormenting laughter when Sonny glowered menacingly at them. Sonny never did learn to read and write, and until one of his managers taught him to sign his name, his signature was the illiterate's X.

Being a teenager often involves eruptions of rebellion. It may be manifested in the use of drugs, the way one dresses, the friends one chooses, sexual escapades, excessive drinking, and so forth. For Sonny, that rebellion manifested itself in crime. His size and physical prowess led to his being the leader of a small gang of tough delinquent kids, hell-bent on thumbing their noses at the rules of a so-called law-abiding society. They mugged and robbed; they burgled and assaulted. To show his contempt for the law, Sonny always wore an easily identifiable yellow shirt when he committed a robbery. He didn't care if he became known for his yellow shirt. His attitude was "catch me if you can, you suckers." The shirt was his emblem, and so the local cops referred to him as the "Yellow Shirt Bandit." That yellow shirt finally led to his arrest in January 1950.

Cops were amazed at the size of his wrists when they cuffed him. The cuffs barely encircled those thick wrists, biting into the flesh, leaving it raw and red. Sonny was arraigned, tried, found guilty, and sentenced to five years in the Missouri State Penitentiary in Jefferson City. Sonny would later say that because of his size, none of the other inmates messed with him or even tried to mess with him. The few times he got into altercations with other inmates, he arranged to meet them in a dark, deserted place in the prison known as the hole. There, he viciously pummeled his opponents with his enormous sledgehammer fists until their beaten bodies, bruised and bloody, were blacked out to the world. Although prison doctors and guards demanded to know who had beaten them, no one was self-destructive enough to name Sonny. Ratting was not only against the convict's code of behavior, but also would have resulted in an even more severe beating. Victims advised themselves not to provoke Liston in the future. They steered clear of him, and he didn't go out of his way to re-live their punishments.

While enough inmates were sufficiently scared of tangling with Liston, one man was not intimidated by the glowering tough guy. That man chose to see or imagine goodness in Liston. That man was a Catholic priest, and he often befriended troubled inmates in an effort to help them find a useful outlet for their anger. After several conversations with Liston, Father Stevens suggested Liston join the prison boxing squad. Liston liked the idea. He could use his fists and not get into trouble for doing so. Liston was quickly accepted into the squad, for his fistic tough guy reputation had preceded him. Father Stevens arranged for Liston to spar against a professional boxer, who—after two rounds of being repeatedly dazed by Liston's powerful left jab—demanded that

the fight be terminated. "I don't want no more of him," he said;[2] otherwise, he might have been killed.

Father Stevens immediately saw that Liston was so powerful he
could flatten anyone the prison put in the ring with him. Father Stevens
decided Liston needed to become a professional; it would turn his life
around. Through his various political connections, Stevens was able to
arrange for Liston's early release from prison. He was placed on parole
and warned that he better not break any laws. If he did, he would be
back in a cell, a caged tough guy with no chance of making a name for
himself on the outside. Liston merely glowered at the parole officer and
then barely nodded his head.

A St. Louis cop commented, "Going to the can was the best thing
that ever happened to him. If he hadn't gone to the can, he would never
have met Father Stevens, and if he never met Father Stevens he never
would have learned to box, and if he hadn't learned to box he'd be dead
of a bullet in the back."[3]

With Father Stevens as his mentor and greasing the way for him,
Liston went on to box in a series of Golden Gloves contests, winning
each one, usually by knockout. Often his opponents took one look at the
menacing Liston stare and lasted only as long as their dwindling courage. Liston was making a name for himself. Fans couldn't wait to watch
him demolish an opponent with a few quick jabs and uppercuts. Following a string of victories, Liston was booked to box in the International Golden Gloves competition in Kiel Auditorium in St. Louis. The bout
was publicized in local newspapers and on the radio. Liston was
matched against Hermann Schreibauer, a bronze medal winner, from
West Germany. If Liston could beat Schreibauer, then people would
pay big bucks to see him fight.

There was tremendous tension in the auditorium. It was even apparent in the fighters' dressing rooms. The fighters entered the ring to
cheers, hoots, and whistles. The bell for round one sounded, and Liston
came out of his corner like a lion sighting his prey. He threw a series of
devastating punches and knocked out poor Schreibauer in a little more
than two minutes of the first round. There were onrushing waves of
loud approval from the fans. Local sportswriters opined that Liston had
the hardest, most powerful punch of any current heavyweight boxer.
They reported that Liston also had the largest fists of any heavyweight
boxer, measuring 14 inches in circumference. Their comments and Lis-

ton's ring performances were like honey to the hungry bears of the underworld. Ambitious, scheming, and deceitful fight managers, as well as those who controlled them, had their pens poised to sign up the heavyweight colossus. His early managers fell back and then vanished. They were replaced by Frankie Carbo and Blinky Palermo, and their associate, John Vitale, who was the boss of the St. Louis crime family. They proceeded to buy and sell so many pieces of Liston's contract that what was dispersed resembled tranches of sliced and diced mortgage securities. Coteries of shady characters claimed to own percentages of Liston. Some of those percentages may have been as small as fractions. A forensic accountant would have suffered nightmares trying to figure it all out.

Frank Mitchell had been one of the early shareholders in Liston as an enterprise, and he introduced Liston to John Vitale. The following is an excerpt from Mitchell's testimony to the Senate Subcommittee on Antitrust and Monopoly:

> "Did you at one time manage a heavyweight contender named Charles 'Sonny' Liston?"
>
> "I take the fifth amendment."
>
> "Were you the on-the-record manager of Liston from 1952 to 1958?"
>
> "I decline to answer."
>
> "Do you know a person named John Vitale?"
>
> "I decline to answer."
>
> "During this period while you were the on-the-record manager, is it a fact that this person, John Vitale, was the undercover manager of boxer Sonny Liston?"
>
> "I decline to answer."
>
> "You are directed to answer."
>
> "I take the fifth amendment."
>
> "During this period from 1952 to 1958, did you give this man, John Vitale, the proceeds from Liston's purses?"
>
> "I decline to answer the question."
>
> "In March of 1958, did you go to Chicago with John Vitale and meet with a man known as Frank 'Blinky' Palermo?"
>
> "I take the fifth amendment."[4]

Vitale not only owned a percentage of Liston's contract (reported to be 12 percent), but also wanted Liston to be personally beholden to him. So, when Liston needed a regular income between fights for which he was not being paid more than several hundred dollars, Vitale hired him for $65 a week at his cement company. Liston was charged with keeping other black employees in line. Vitale didn't want any strikes or slowdowns, and Liston's intimidating presence meant that cement was poured on time and without disruption. It also meant that Vitale's customers paid their bills on time, for there was no more imposing a collector for outstanding invoices than Sonny Liston. While no debtor ever had to be sued to pay his bill, no one knows if recalcitrant debtors were stupid enough to wind up with their feet embedded in Vitale's cement.

Liston was the perfect muscle for Vitale, a mobster whose reputation meant that no one would mess with him, no one should attempt to compete with him in any of his enterprises, and no one should ever say no to either his requests or demands. The results would have been a beating or death, or a beating followed by death. Many St. Louis residents had heard the story that Vitale had been suspected in the murder of an organized crime figure, Mike Palazzolo, but there was insufficient evidence to bring him to trial. Vitale's police record was also well known: He had been arrested 58 times and acquitted 55 times. It was a batting average that would have been the envy of every thug who used a bat on a victim. Vitale's reputation was sufficient to cause obedience and, in some cases, obeisance.

An associate of Vitale and Palermo, a man named Joseph "Pep" Barone, a Philadelphia matchmaker, took over Liston's management from Mitchell. Following an ongoing series of police harassments (some provoked, some gratuitous) against Liston in St. Louis, Barone figured that the City of Brotherly Love might prove a more congenial environment for his fighter. He brought Liston to Philadelphia and wound up owning 24 percent of him. Palermo took 12 percent, and Carbo took the lion's share of 52 percent. Liston was now a wholly controlled subsidiary of the Carbo–Palermo company. Liston would be easy for Barone and Palermo to keep under their control, to keep away from the kinds of cops who had harassed Liston in St. Louis. Those cops were out to pin every misdemeanor on him and also brought him in for questioning whenever a robbery was committed. He became their go-to suspect from central casting. The cops would not only pick up Liston on the flimsiest of charges, but also further humiliate him by putting him

in a police lineup. They hoped that some guileless witness would identify Liston as the one who had just committed a crime. It never happened.

Why did the cops relentlessly harass him? Because he had beaten up
one of their own. He had badly beaten the cop and taken the cop's gun.
Cops do not take kindly to one of their own being pummeled and then
publicly embarrassed and humiliated. They would never let Liston
know that he wasn't in their gun sights. Liston's managers wanted to
avoid the possibility of their property being incarcerated in some St.
Louis jail cell or even shot by a cop claiming self-defense, and they also
wanted to avoid notoriety that portrayed Liston as a thug. They could
never really succeed in wiping clean Liston's reputation, but they didn't
want to add any arrests to his police record and then have those crimes
made public. It just wasn't good for business. Boxing had already been
portrayed in various media as being controlled by gangsters. Carbo,
Palermo, Vitale, and Barone wanted their boxer portrayed as another
Joe Louis, the man who had been called a "credit to his race" when that
expression was not considered condescending and racist. They looked
forward to the day when Liston would be celebrated as the reigning
heavyweight champion. They believed Liston could easily defeat the
current champion, Floyd Patterson.

Although Patterson was admired as a decent young man, religious
and law abiding, Liston's owners did not want the media to portray a
fight between the two as a battle between good and evil. Patterson was
already being portrayed as a Mr. Clean, a devout Catholic, and a role
model in the black community. President John F. Kennedy; the
NAACP; and Patterson's manager, Cus D'Amato, did not want Patterson to fight Liston. From the point of view of the NAACP, if Patterson
were to lose, the world would have to recognize a felon and a thug as
the new world champion. The organization felt it would hurt the bur-
geoning civil rights movement. The Kennedys did not want a thug to
represent the heavyweight division, and D'Amato hated the mob and
knew they would do everything in their power to get the title. It was
worth millions of dollars to them. He was so worried he thought the
mob might even try to kill him and Patterson. Wherever he went,
D'Amato carried a loaded pistol and slept with it under his pillow. He
even kept an attack-trained German Shepherd as his doorman and burglar alarm.

D'Amato had good reason to fear for Patterson's safety should he agree to a bout with Liston. As heavyweight contender Ernie Terrell stated, "What I admire about Sonny is that he has a fighter's attitude. This separates him from the boys—separates him from every other fighter I know. He's in the ring to 'kill' you, not just beat you or knock you out—but to kill you."[5]

None of this stopped Liston from living as he wanted to. In 1957, he had married Geraldine Chambers, a pretty young factory worker he had met at a prison dance, and he adopted her daughter, Arletha. Few people knew Geraldine's birth date and tried to relate it to her becoming a mother, which she did in 1944. Geraldine's cited years of birth included 1925, 1932, and 1935. The discrepancies didn't seem to bother Liston. He happily moved his family, including his in-laws, into his pleasant two-story house in west Philadelphia.

Meanwhile, he was knocking down tough heavyweight fighters as if they were bowling pins. He defeated such powerhouses as Eddie Machen, Nino Valdes, Zora Folley, Roy Harris, Cleveland Williams, and Howard King, among others. Liston was primed to take on Patterson. Cus D'Amato, meanwhile, was doing everything he could to avoid having Patterson face Liston in the ring. He had previously avoided setting up Patterson to fight Valdes, Folley, and Machen, for fear that his fighter might lose the championship to one of them. Losing to Liston would be an even more humiliating disaster. It's part of a manager's job, after all, to make sure his fighter's opponents are not likely to win, especially if his fighter is a world champion. Arranging for one's fighter to have bouts that will preserve his earning power is an essential motivation for every manager. D'Amato would be not only without a world champion if Patterson were to lose to Liston, but also handing over control of the heavyweight division to the mob. And D'Amato lived and breathed hatred for the mob. Sometime after Patterson had vacated the rank of champion, D'Amato said that managing Liston would be a challenge; but if given the opportunity, he could "make Liston the heavyweight champion again if he divests himself of the people around him."[6]

D'Amato finally seemed to breathe a sigh of relief and express some happiness when Carbo and Palermo went on trial in Los Angeles. The scuttlebutt around the courthouse was that the judge would make sure the two would no longer be able to wriggle free from the iron grip of justice. Once their trial was completed, they would be carted off to long prison terms. When Carbo was finally found guilty, the attorney general, Robert Kennedy, stated, "Frank Carbo has been a sinister figure behind the scenes in boxing for more than 20 years. This verdict will be a great aid and assistance to the Department of Justice and local authorities in taking further action against the attempts of racketeers to control boxing and other sports."[7]

Kennedy may have been a little too optimistic, for Carbo and Palermo, ever clandestine, issued surreptitious orders from their prison cells. Professional boxing was just too good an opportunity to make money, so retirement was out of the question. Aside from that, that's what Carbo and Palermo did for a living. Why stop, when they could get away with it? Even with Carbo and Palermo caged, the aura of mob connections continued to swirl around Liston like a bad odor. For much of white America, Liston was seen as a thug, and he would always be a thug, an unrepentant ex-convict, a man who could not inspire anything but venality in others. He was referred to in the media as a monster, a bear, a primitive animal. Few people commented on the racial resonance of those epithets. President Kennedy, Bobby Kennedy, Eleanor Roosevelt, the NAACP, Martin Luther King, and a good portion of liberal America either wanted Patterson to avoid fighting Liston or beat him. And since there was fear that Liston was a much more powerful boxer than Patterson, there was a chorus urging him to avoid a match with Liston. It would be terrible for black America if Liston were to wear the crown of the heavyweight champion. He would be a despised king. Yet, Malcolm X stood out as a unique voice in the black community, for he rooted for Liston to smash the champion, take away his crown and place it on his own head, and thumb his nose at white America.

Apparently, Patterson had insulted the Nation of Islam, and Malcolm believed he had done it at the behest of white backers. He saw Patterson as an Uncle Tom, always ready to ingratiate himself with the white power structure. Ironically, Liston also disliked the black Muslims, who he had met while in prison. According to biographer Nick Tosches,

> Sonny's loathing of the Black Muslims dated to his earliest exposure to them, at the Missouri State Penitentiary in Jefferson City. Some say it was fear, as well as loathing, as Sonny generally was apprehensive of people who were, or were seen by him as, crazy, and in his

suspicious and unspeaking eyes the Black Muslims were just that—
crazy. He did not like them, and he did not like their ways, and he
did not trust them.[8]

But, he did not publicly express those views. He disliked the strict
morality the Muslims espoused, and he didn't understand their belief
about the separation of the races. He would voice a similar reaction
about Muhammad Ali, although that was before Cassius Clay had become a Muslim and changed his name.

Percy Sutton, on behalf of the NAACP, stated, "Hell, let's stop kid-
ding. I'm for Patterson because he represents us better than Liston ever
could or would."[9]

Yet, Vice President Lyndon B. Johnson invited Liston to visit him in
his office in Washington, and Ed Sullivan invited him to skip rope on
his show, which Liston did, accompanied by his favorite jazz score,
"Night Train." There was obviously a split in America: Patterson represented goodness and religiosity, while Liston represented evil and gratuitous violence, and the world of criminality. One was a symbol of
danger, the other a symbol of accommodation.

How to soften Liston's reputation? How to remove the image of
Liston as a mob-owned fighter? Liston and his advisors decided to
make a show of his changing values. Liston bought back his contract
from Pep Barone for $75,000. It was odd that Barone would sell his
share in Liston when he stood to earn hundreds of thousands of dollars
from Liston's fights. Liston's replacement manager was George Katz, a
respected and politically connected boxing manager in Philadelphia.
While a manager typically takes one-third of his fighter's purse, Katz
agreed to take a mere 10 percent of Liston's net earnings. Net earnings
might be zero, especially after all parties take their cut. Since 10 percent of zero is zero, why would a manager agree to such an arrangement? The deal raised more doubts about Liston than it quieted. Few,
if any, people were impressed by the deal to whitewash Liston's reputation. In view of the cynicism the arrangement caused, it was not surprising that it proved to be short-lived. Katz was replaced by Jack Nilon,
who would receive one-third of Liston's purses.

The match between Liston and Patterson was destined to take place.
The public wanted it, the media wanted it, and Patterson wanted to
prove he was not afraid of Liston.

With Carbo and Palermo in prison, next on board was notorious lawyer Roy Cohn, whose group, Championship Sports, Inc., maneuvered to become the promoters for a match between Patterson and Liston. Robert Kennedy wanted to investigate Cohn and his colleagues, but nothing came of it. Cohn's notoriety was based on not only his work as counsel for Senator Joe McCarthy, but also his vigorous representation of mobsters Carmine Galante and Tony Salerno. They were both interested in the fight game, and Salerno had put up money to promote Patterson's title fights with Ingemar Johansson. The media followed these developments like bloodhounds. Day by day, the odds changed based on the latest news or gossip. As the day of the fight approached, Liston was the 8-to-5 favorite to win by a knockout.

The media played it up as the greatest fight since the second Louis versus Schmeling bout. American boxing fans couldn't wait to see it. The 15-round fight took place in Chicago on September 25, 1962, at Comiskey Park, promoted by Championship Sports, Inc. More than 600 sportswriters attended the fight. At the time, it was the biggest money fight in the history of boxing. For the sportswriters, the fight boiled down to power versus speed. Would Patterson be able to stay away from Liston's long left jab, which had the power of a cannonball? Would Patterson frustrate Liston's efforts for an early win, causing Liston to become enraged and make tactical mistakes that would open him up to a knockout by Patterson? The betting still favored Liston. Yet, he endured derogatory descriptions of himself by many journalists, who referred to him as a beast, an animal, a large bear, king of the beasts, and a gorilla. Patterson, by comparison, was referred to as a gentleman, a well-mannered articulate young man, who was a "credit to his race." By implication, Liston was no credit to his race.

When Liston entered the ring, he was met with choruses of loud boos and jeers. Patterson, in contrast, was met with an explosion of cheers, applause, and whistles. Liston weighed 214 pounds, and Patterson weighed 189 pounds. The 25-pound difference was significant. In addition, Liston had a reach measuring 13 inches longer than Patterson's. As the referee gave his pro forma instructions, Liston directed his tough, hard, intimidating gangster stare at Patterson, who looked down, never once raising his eyes to so much as glance at Liston. He looked like a sensitive young man out of his depth.

The fighters came at one another in the center of the ring. Liston missed with a couple of left hooks, while Patterson attempted to get inside Liston's punches. In clinches, Patterson was unable to tie up Liston, whose hard rights and lefts pounded Patterson's side. Apart, the fighters traded a series of body blows. Patterson weaved and ducked. He was much faster on his feet than Liston, who relentlessly came at him with the determination of a locomotive. At one point, Patterson lunged at Liston, delivering what appeared to be a stinging body blow, but it had little effect on Liston. Then Liston delivered a powerful left hook to Patterson's head. It was the first really hard punch of the fight, and it momentarily dazed Patterson. He continued to duck and weave, causing Liston to miss with his uppercuts and hooks. Patterson then fell against the ropes as Liston delivered a quick left and right to his head. Patterson responded with a left jab and then a right to Liston's midsection. Neither punch had any effect on Liston, who then delivered a left uppercut to Patterson's cheek and another left to Patterson's chin. Liston followed up with two quick rights to the left side of Patterson's head. Patterson couldn't tie up Liston, who delivered a powerful left, a right, and a left that sent Patterson to the canvas. Patterson was only able to prop himself up on his right hand and arm.

The fight ended after two minutes and six seconds of the first round. It was one of the fastest knockouts in the history of professional boxing. In 1938, Joe Louis had knocked out Max Schmeling in two minutes and four seconds of round one. In 1908, Tommy Burns knocked out Jim Roche in 88 seconds. Joe Louis, who was Liston's role model, had accurately predicted the outcome of the fight. Following the fight, the NAACP asked Liston to make a financial contribution. He said no.

The rematch between Liston and Patterson took place on July 27, 1963, in the Las Vegas Convention Center. Patterson, who had slunk away after his first fight with Liston, looked both calm and fearful as he entered the ring. He had not brought along the fake beard and sunglasses he had used to disguise himself after losing to Liston, and he did not try to hide who he was: the former heavyweight world champion. By comparison to the large, muscled physique of Liston, Patterson looked almost trim and elegant, a young man who hadn't fully built himself up. When he entered the ring, he received subdued cheers from the crowd in the arena.

When Liston entered, wearing a hooded robe, he was roundly booed. His cold, hard stare was unperturbed by the unfriendly welcome. He was the 4-to-1 favorite, and bookies and gamblers did not think he would disappoint them. Patterson was not only the smaller man, but also his reach was only 71 inches compared to Liston's 84 inches. Patterson weighed 194½ pounds, while Liston weighed 215½ pounds. In addition to the thousands of spectators in the convention center, the fight was broadcast on closed-circuit TV to 143 theaters and arenas in the United States and Canada. Prior to the clanging of the first bell, the ring announcer introduced an illustrious group of former champions: Sugar Ray Robinson, Slapsie Maxie Rosenbloom, Willie Pastrano, Billy Conn, Rocky Marciano, Joe Louis, and Cassius Clay. The "Brown Bomber" received the loudest and most sustained round of cheers, while Clay was repeatedly booed. Rosenbloom was not in attendance, but the others were, and each entered the ring to shake hands with the fighters. Clay, clownishly, pretended to be fearful of Liston and ran away from the ring and through the stands waving his arms and shouting.

The fight had a mandatory eight count, which the first fight did not. In other words, if a fighter was knocked down, he would have to stay down for a count of eight. It would give that fighter a brief respite during which to clear his head.

The bell sounded for round one. The fighters came out of their corners. Liston threw frequent left jabs, which landed against Patterson's midsection. The difference in their sizes seemed more pronounced as they went after one another. Liston's physique seemed to dominate Patterson's, crowding and almost intimidating the smaller man, who gamely traded blows with the bigger, larger-fisted Liston. Liston exploded with a series of rights and lefts, uppercuts and hooks, which drove Patterson to one knee. The referee counted to eight, and Patterson was up and fighting again. The two men clinched, but Patterson could not keep Liston from punching his body. Separated, the two men traded punches, and Liston was able to hold Patterson by the back of his neck, while he hammered Patterson with his left fist.

Patterson attempted to fight back, but his punches were ineffectual. Following another series of battering rights and lefts from Liston, Patterson went down for a second time. Up on his feet, Patterson did not last long. A third battering sent him to the canvas, where the referee counted him out. It took just two minutes and 10 seconds for Liston to demolish Patterson for a second time and retain the heavyweight title. If there hadn't been an eight count, administered twice, the fight would have ended in less than two minutes, a briefer massacre than the first fight.

After the fight, Liston, always laconic at best with the reporters, was questioned about the bout. He gave answers that seemed to disappoint reporters, for they wanted him to be fulsome in his self-praise. He finally shrugged and left the ring, heading for his dressing room. Now it was Clay's opportunity to rush into the spotlight. He bounded into the ring, shouting to a television announcer that he was the greatest, that he would beat that big, ugly bear Sonny Liston and become the next heavyweight champion. Patterson was history; his absence was not commented on. He was no longer of interest.

Cassius Clay was now in the spotlight. He had been taunting Liston relentlessly, and the media either loved or hated him. He was handsome, quick-witted, and without any felonious baggage. Yet, he was sassy, a wiseguy, a big mouth, and so all of a sudden Liston, the tough stoic, became sympathetic. The media and many boxing fans looked to Liston to teach the young Clay manners, to get him to shut his big mouth. White America was not prepared for a handsome, articulate, loudmouth, wiseguy, "uppity nigger," as men in bars occasionally said. By comparison, Liston had ceased being considered a felonious thug. Yes, he was seen as a hard man, a tough guy, but a man with quiet dignity who knew how to behave in mixed company. Those who disparaged Clay, who denigrated his talents as a boxer, did not envision that he would bring style, elegance, and gracefulness to the heavyweight division. Of course, he would have to win, but it was predicted by the finest minds of pugilism that such a win was an impossibility.

Liston was ingrained in the minds of the public and sportswriters as being virtually indestructible. He had already defeated Patterson as if the former heavyweight champion was a mere journeyman boxer. Even that most respected figure of boxing's bygone glory days, Joe Louis, said Liston was the greatest heavyweight he had seen. If one was foolish enough to opine that Clay might beat Liston, the reaction was one of disbelief or laughter. Pundits on television and radio, and in the newspapers, claimed that Clay could never beat Liston. It was an impossibility. One reporter said that the fight could conceivably be longer than the Liston versus Patterson bout: It could last until the end of the first round. If it lasted longer, it would only be because Liston was playing with Clay the way a lion plays with a wounded antelope before devouring it. The vast sea of boxing aficionados held firmly to that belief.

The only exceptions to the accepted wisdom were secretly whispered by the mob, and only among themselves. They had their hooks in Liston and could pull him in or let him swim for a while. Their hooks were in so deep that Liston was powerless to determine his own destiny.

The fight between Liston and Clay was one of the most anticipated of the year. It had been hyped, promoted, and made to seem like a battle in which the young wiseguy would finally get his comeuppance. It was held in Miami Beach on February 25, 1964. Prior to the fight, Liston had supposedly been receiving cortisone shots in his left shoulder because of bursitis. Yet, it was commonly known that Liston had a phobia for needles. Liston was not in the best shape for a long, drawn-out battle. Since 1961, he had fought only three times, winning each bout with a first-round knockout. He hardly had to catch his breath, never mind breaking a sweat. During that period, he had fought a total of fewer than seven minutes, and he did not train much for his fight with Clay. He had expected to end the fight in either the first or second round with another devastating knockout. His age was also not an asset: Although he claimed to be 32 years old, he may have been 35. Clay was a robust 22-year-old. He had trained assiduously and was terrified of being knocked out and having his career come to an ignominious end.

When polled, 43 of 46 sportswriters believed Liston would win by a knockout in one of the early rounds, either the first or second. They didn't know Clay had been studying Liston's fights, learning that he telegraphed his punches. A smart fighter could see what was coming and get out of the way. And unlike Liston, Clay could move with the alacrity and speed of a cheetah. His camp believed that if their fighter could just dance away from Liston's left jabs, the out-of-shape Liston would punch himself out and become increasingly frustrated, resulting in wilder and wilder swings that would miss the target. In addition to frustrating Liston to bring forth his rage, Clay had also vociferously tormented his laconic opponent. No king likes being lambasted by a young upstart. And Clay was not just a fast talker, he was also a fast thinker, a clever strategist who could execute his tactics, both defensive and offensive, with stunning speed. He had the eye–hand coordination of a magician. While Liston tended to be a flat-footed pugilist, Clay was fleet of foot and hand. Liston would be forced to stomp around the ring, attempting to land punches on the quick-moving Clay, whose reflexes were much faster than Liston's. Clay had all the makings of another Sugar Ray Robinson. Clay had studied films of Robinson's fights and was able to adapt his style; he was Clay's model, and Clay would not disappoint the master.

At the weigh-in, Liston weighed 218 pounds, while Clay weighed 210 pounds. Liston's reach was 84 inches; Clay's was 78. Liston was 6-foot-1, and Clay was 6-foot-3. When they were receiving instructions in the center of the ring from the referee, they each glowered at the other. Clay stood up on the tips of his toes so that he could extend the difference in their heights. He seemed to glare down on Liston, who returned the look. Clay later confessed that he was scared of Liston, but he was going to put up a fearless front to not only motivate himself, but also intimidate Liston. Clay was worried that one of Liston's hard jabs would catch him before he could dance out of range. Were that to happen, one of Liston's sledgehammer punches could quickly end the fight. Although neither Clay nor his cornermen admitted it, Liston was the harder puncher.

When the bell sounded for round one, Liston rushed from his corner seemingly intent on ending the fight as quickly as he had ended his bouts with Patterson, but Clay surprised him with his speed and ability to slip punches. After many attempts, Liston finally delivered a hard right to Clay's midsection. But again, Clay danced away, and Liston missed him with another right hook. Liston was obviously the aggressor, but his aggressive wild swings kept missing the target. What's the point of being the aggressor, if you can't make your opponent a victim? Clay finally hit Liston with a fast and furious flurry of well-aimed punches, but they had little effect on the man who had been beaten over the head by police billy clubs to no effect. When the bell sounded ending the round, the combatants and referee did not hear it. The fighters kept going at one another for more than eight seconds after the first round officially ended. The referee finally heard the repeatedly clanging bell and ended the round, sending the fighters back to their corners.

Liston had been surprised by Clay's speed and ability to avoid being hit. To make matters worse, Clay pretended to yawn while sitting his corner. Liston glowered across the ring. It was obvious he was frustrated, and that frustration ignited explosive anger. He would get him in the next round, his cornermen assured him.

The bell for round two sounded. It was more of the same. Liston landed a left jab to Clay's head, which momentarily stunned him. And Clay landed his left against Liston's head. Liston didn't even bother shaking it off, he just continued trying to nail the dancing image he was chasing.

In the third round, Clay was more confident. He had avoided Liston's big blows, and he saw that Liston was beginning to tire. He decided it was time to bring the fight to Liston. He managed to inflict a cut below Liston's left eye. The announcer was startled: He had never seen Liston cut before. In fact, it was the first time Liston had been cut in a fight. Liston's cut would later require eight stitches. Maybe Clay was going to win after all. Following a barrage of swift blows by Clay, Liston's thick, tree-trunk legs buckled slightly. It did, indeed, seem like Clay might overpower Liston and come away with the heavyweight crown firmly but rakishly angled on his head. Clay's strategy and tactics were working as planned.

Liston threw a number of wild punches that flew through the air like a trapeze artist with nowhere to land. Liston's anger grew, and his contempt for Clay was sketched on his angry countenance. The anger seemed to fuel his punches without intimidating Clay. The punches kept being thrown, and some finally landed, hitting Clay's midsection. Although not apparently hurt, Clay was the one who seemed suddenly tired. Was the tide about to turn?

The round ended; reporters thought it had been won by Liston. In his corner, Liston was breathing heavily like an old man who had just run up 10 flights of stairs. He hadn't had to work this hard in his last three fights put together. What the hell was happening? Why couldn't he flatten this guy as easily as he had flattened Paterson, who also had fast hands? Of course, Patterson was no Clay. Patterson had tried to get in under Liston's punches and couldn't. He didn't skip away as Clay did. Patterson tried to outbox Liston and failed miserably. Now Liston's cornermen stanched the flow of blood below his left eye and iced a bruise below his right eye. He was certainly the more tired-looking fighter, although he had found reserves of energy and fought well in the last round. He was certainly more impressive than he had been in the previous rounds.

In the fourth round, Liston delivered a pair of hard blows that did not prevent Clay from seeming to coast through the round. Liston must have wondered why those hard blows had not slowed down Clay. The blows would have been devastating to any other fighter.

In the fifth round, Clay complained that there was a burning, stinging chemical in his eyes; it felt as if someone had thrown acid on his eyes. He could barely see and tried blinking away the stinging sensation but to no avail. He said he wanted to stop the fight. He couldn't see. Liston would easily beat a blind man. He and his trainer guessed that Liston or one of his cornermen had put some kind of liniment on Liston's gloves. Angelo Dundee, in Clay's corner, wouldn't let him stop the fight. He yelled at Clay. If he forfeited it now, he might never get a second chance at the title. Clay had to continue the fight and wait until he could blink away the caustic substance that was burning his eyes. Dundee poured water from a saturated sponge over Clay's eyes. He put one of his pinky fingers in the corner of one of Clay's eyes and touched his own eye. He blinked furiously from the stinging sensation. He poured more water over Clay's eyes, hoping it would rinse away whatever was there. He also made a dramatic demonstration of trying to help Clay because a cadre of Black Muslims was approaching Clay's corner with murder in their eyes.

Dundee proved rather quickly that he was trying to help his fighter. The Muslims retreated. Clay, like a blind man heading for a cliff, left his corner and went into the center of the ring, where he would have room to maneuver. He could hear Liston's heavy breathing and danced away from the swish of hooks and jabs. When he couldn't dance away from Liston, he extended his long left arm like a pole that kept Liston from getting close enough to land a punch. Clay survived the fifth round with the self-protective instincts of hunted prey. Back in his corner, he blinked his eyes furiously, mitigating the effects of the liniment. He could finally see clearly, and now the temperature of his own anger rose. He would teach Liston a lesson.

By the sixth round, Clay was ready to smash his opponent, to get even for the failed effort at sabotage. His vision cleared, and Clay was now fully in control. He was seemingly hitting Liston at will. He out-boxed the champion and delivered effective combinations that Liston could do little to counter. As Liston retreated, he looked more like a doubtful sparring partner than a champion defending his title. The bell ended a victorious round for Clay, a dismal one for Liston.

Liston could not come out for the seventh round. He sat on a stool in his corner, looking furious and hungover. There are three points of view about what happened: 1) Liston faked the injury to his left shoulder, claiming bursitis, so he wouldn't be defeated; 2) He was genuinely hurt and couldn't effectively punch with that one injured arm; and 3) The mob told him he had to lose and he found what for him was an acceptable way to lose without being defeated in the ring by a young man for whom he had nothing but contempt. The odds, at 8 to 1, so favored Liston that the mob would clean up if he lost. Did the mob force Liston to take a dive? No one will ever know for sure, but it has been noted that Ash Resnick had been in Liston's training camp during his workout and sparring sessions. It was also rumored that Resnick and Liston each took in $1 million from betting on Clay to win. There is plenty of evidence that Liston's left arm had indeed been injured, but there are also sufficient doubts, so that the arguments will continue.

Prior to his rematch with Liston, Clay announced he had changed his name to Muhammad Ali. He was now a Muslim. Soon thereafter, rumors circulated that Black Muslims had threatened Liston, telling him that if he won the rematch, he would be killed. Then, just prior to the rematch, there were also stories that Liston's wife had been kidnapped and wouldn't be released until her husband lost the second fight. If the rumors were true, there wouldn't be a fight worth watching, but it could be a gold mine for those who bet on Ali.

There was difficulty in finding a host city for the fight. Politicians did not want to be seen catering to the Black Muslims, who advocated segregation and armed defense. After a number of failed overtures, including a politic decision by the governor of Massachusetts not to allow the fight to take place within his state's borders, a venue was finally found in Lewiston, Maine, of all places. It did not have the arenas of Vegas, New York, Miami, Boston, and so forth. Lewiston was not known for its mobsters and big-time gamblers. But it would have to do. The big money for the fight would not be earned from the limited number of fans in attendance: It would come from closed-circuit television and betting.

In that first round, Liston shot a left at Ali, who responded with a fast right that seemed to graze Liston's head. Liston fell onto his back, rolled over, got up on one knee, then rolled over onto his back. His entire knockdown looked like a badly choreographed fall performed by a neophyte thespian in front of a class of disbelieving fellow actors. Liston had gone down in one minute and 44 seconds of the first round. The referee, Jersey Joe Walcott, after some confusion, stopped the fight at two minutes and 12 seconds into the round. Ali asked his cornermen, "Did I hit him?" When told yes, he pranced around the ring a conquering hero, a kid who couldn't believe his good fortune. Few others could believe it, too. Fans yelled, "Fake, fake, fake." Others were just getting to their seats when Liston went down. They couldn't believe the fight was over. Some of them had paid top dollar to see the rematch. When they heard people yelling that the fight had been fixed, some of them demanded their money back. The ticket window, however, was closed.

Alistair Cooke wrote that Ali's quick punch that had supposedly dropped Liston seemed no more than "backhanded to [flick away] a bothersome fly."[10]

Wilfrid Sheed, in his book on Ali, writes,

> [Sonny] didn't come out for the eighth [*sic*] [seventh] round because of torn muscles in his arm—quite genuine as it turned out, but such is Sonny's aura that no one in the world believed him. Then in the return match he managed a fainting spell in the first round, which again may have been genuine (microscopes later turned up an actual punch), but when referee Joe Walcott blew the count and gave him all evening to get up, Liston's rendition of a coma wouldn't have fooled a possum.[11]

Newspapers throughout the world regarded the fight as a joke. The *London Evening Standard*, for example, headlined its story "A Piffling Farce."

Sportswriter Larry Merchant, who sat in the press section, claimed years later that he saw the punch that knocked out Liston. Famous ring announcer Don Dunphy believed the fight had been fixed. David Remnick, editor of *New Yorker Magazine*, believed it was a genuine punch that Ali delivered and that it knocked Liston off of his feet. Liston contributed to the theory that the fight had been fixed. He told a *Sports Illustrated* reporter that he thought the Muslims were coming to get him and so he figured he should stay down. If he stood up, he feared he would be shot in the ring. He asserted he hadn't been hit. He just faked being hit. Yet, he had previously said he was hit. What was the truth? John Vitale, who owned a share of Liston's contract, told Johnny Tocco, who owned a Las Vegas boxing gym, that the fight would not go beyond the first round. The FBI claimed it had information that the fight was fixed and overheard a conversation in which Geraldine Liston said that since Liston was going to lose the fight, he might as well go down in the first round. Why take a chance of being hurt?

More fuel was poured on the incendiary controversy by the behavior of the referee, Jersey Joe Walcott, a former heavyweight champion. Walcott never began the count; he was trying to lasso Ali and send him to a neutral corner so the count could begin. That is the rule. Walcott's attention was finally caught by the timekeeper, who told him the fight was over. He had counted Liston out. Nat Fleisher, the founder and editor of *Ring Magazine*, waved his arms like a goalie and confirmed what the timekeeper had said. Some boxing experts believe the fight should have gone on, if only to end the ambiguity of the count. And if it had gone on, would it have ended the same way? If it was a fix, then certainly it would have. If not a fix, then Ali really may have been able to knock out Liston. Some claim that it was too obvious to have been a fix. A fix, they said, is not broadcast for everyone to observe. That is certainly the way the mob wants it to play out.

But there have been plenty of fights where the fix was readily apparent. For example, the bout between Billy Fox and Jake LaMotta could not have been a more obviously fixed fight. Those in the arena who saw that fight expressed their anger about being duped when they shouted the fight was a fix. They had leaped up out of their seats, an angry mob, yelling, "Fix. Fix. Fix. Fake. Fake. Fake." It was only years later, after Ali had become a media darling, a symbol of resistance to the war in Vietnam, and was recognized for his wit and lack of obeisance to white authority figures, that it became unfashionable to say that the fights with Liston had been fixed. If they were fixed, Ali had no part in it. He probably wouldn't have even known it. It only takes one boxer to fix a fight, and his opponent need never know. As long as Liston agreed to take a dive, there was no reason for Ali to be told that Liston was paid and prepared to hand him the heavyweight title. After all, why would Ali have asked his cornermen if he had hit Liston, if he thought his punch had been as soft as flicking away a fly? He was as unsure of what had happened as were the fans and many of the reporters. Once he was declared the champion, why should he question his good fortune? And once he became media darling, why would the media want to tarnish his usurpation of the heavyweight crown?

Following his loss to Ali, Liston's reputation as a towering figure of power was burnt to ashes. He was once again considered a thug, an ex-con, a venal man who sold his title. Once a criminal, always a criminal. He began drinking heavily; his sense of failure and humiliation was too much to bear. In addition, there were rumors that the great Joe Louis had led Liston into the pharmacological nirvana of heroin, and since Liston had a needle phobia, he probably found other means of absorbing the drug. While Liston's reputation was on a downward spiral, he still had his fans, especially among those who admired his outsider credentials as an ex-con, a former strong-arm collector for the mob. America frequently has love affairs with those who survive outside of the law, men like Al Capone, Willie Sutton, John Gotti, Jesse James, Billy the Kid, Butch Cassidy, and so on. Gangster movies are some of the most popular films ever made. And Sonny Liston seemed all gangster to many of his fans.

Liston had 16 fights following his loss to Ali; he lost only to Leotis Martin by knockout. His last fight was against the inimitable Chuck Wepner, known as the "Bayonne Bleeder," who he beat on June 29, 1970. Wepner was sure to lose. The fight was not going to be a big moneymaker, unless, of course, there was an unexpected outcome. Liston may have been told to lose, but his fists did not obey such orders. With a powerful body blow, he dropped Wepner in the fifth round. The fight did not end there. Liston finally bloodied Wepner so badly the referee had to stop the fight following the ninth round. There were so many cuts on Wepner's face that it looked like a map with crisscrossing red road lines.

On January 5, 1971, Geraldine Liston returned to the Liston's Las Vegas home following a two-week visit with relatives. She was initially disturbed by the sight of old newspapers collecting dirt around the front door. Upon entering the house, she was nauseated by the reek of Liston's decomposing body. She found his corpse slumped against their bed; a broken footstool lay in shatters nearby. She immediately phoned her husband's lawyer and doctor, but she did not notify the police for at least two hours. When the police finally arrived, they decided that Liston had died from a fall brought on by a heart attack. Later, they would conclude that Liston had died from a heroin overdose, although no drug paraphernalia was found in the home. The police had found a small amount of heroin in the kitchen and a small amount of marijuana in one of Liston's pants pockets.

Many think Liston was given a drink that knocked him out and then given a hotshot of heroin, which killed him. There have been a number of theories about why Liston was murdered, and each of the theories lays the blame on the mob. Reasons include that Liston was about to go public about the fixed second Ali fight if he wasn't paid the money that had been promised to him; that Liston had double-crossed a local shylock and tried to take over his business; that Liston, although he had promised, did not take a dive in the Wepner fight; and that Liston had cheated a gang of drug dealers out of the money he owed them. Whatever the truth might be, Liston's end seemed to have been etched in his early life. He had moved from associating with small-time hoods to associating with big-time gamblers and mobsters. He, along with many other boxers, owed not only his success to the mobsters who had guided his career, but also his downfall. Whether he won or lost, the mob made money from the "Big Bad Ugly Bear," as they had from many others who were owned like chattel.

9

WHY GIVE UP A GOOD THING?

The mob is attracted to money as sharks are attracted to blood in the water. It's why the mob was involved in boxing for decades; however, it seemed as if the world of boxing would change after the Kefauver investigations into fixed fights, unlicensed managers, crooked promoters, and venal referees and judges. And, of course, the trials of Frankie Carbo and Blinky Palermo had alerted the public to the role the mob had played in boxing from the 1940s through the 1950s. Articles in newspapers and magazines revealed how the mob had formed a monopoly and manipulated the careers of boxers and guaranteed the outcomes of their matches. The mob stopped at nothing to get its way: Broken knees and noses, as well as cracked skulls, were the emblems of those who resisted the mob. Corruption was rife, and untaxed money poured into the safe deposit boxes and offshore bank accounts of those who controlled the monopoly. Money was also laundered into seemingly legal businesses that the mob controlled, especially construction and real estate.

The public was fascinated by the reports about Frankie Carbo (former Murder, Inc., hit man) and Blinky Palermo (the numbers king of Philadelphia), and the alliances they had formed with promoters, matchmakers, managers, trainers, and even some sports reporters. The public heard the stories of Jake LaMotta. They saw the movies *The Harder They Fall, Requiem for a Heavyweight*, and *On the Waterfront*; the first two were based on the sorry career of Primo Carnera. They read revelatory articles in *Sports Illustrated* and the columns of a few crusading reporters who wanted to help clean up boxing. They learned of courageous boxers who refused to go along with Carbo and Palermo, and so were excluded from participating in important fights and certainly could not get championship matches. Kefauver said that his purpose had been to drive the racketeers out of boxing. But there was still blood in the water, and sharks, other than Carbo and Palermo, not only swam to the feast, but also took jailhouse orders from the two imprisoned impresarios. After Carbo and Palermo were carted off to prison, Attorney General Robert Kennedy, who had been instrumental in prosecuting mobsters, said he hoped the mob would no longer be involved in boxing. One can only wonder if the two criminals cynically snickered in response to Kennedy's optimism.

Thirty years after the Kefauver hearings and after Kennedy's hope expired, the mob was being investigated by a new senate committee, for there was talk that the mob had returned and the waters were as bloody as ever. The Senate's Permanent Subcommittee on Investigations of the Committee on Government Affairs, in March and April 1993, under its chairman, Senator Sam Nunn of Georgia, heard from dozens of witnesses. One of them was FBI agent Joseph Spinelli, who testified that in 1980, the FBI had initiated a multifaceted investigation known as the Crown Royal investigation into the corruption of professional boxing. Spinelli and two undercover agents, plus a pseudonymous informer, explained that they had formed their own boxing company and were eager to promote professional bouts. It was the bait that would attract the sharks. And sure enough, the sharks swam right into the FBI's net.

The possibility of earning money off of ambitious boxers had grown extremely enticing, as big money was now part of the boxing scene. Television, particularly pay-per-view, had the dazzlingly golden lure of a bonanza. The ersatz company was contacted by representatives of organized crime groups: guys who looked and talked like mobsters. They could be charming but also threatening when necessary. Their promises were so fulsome that one was expected to salivate at the thought of the vast amounts of money that would pour in; however, if their promises were met with demurrals or doubts, their hard-fixed stares would drive home the point of how important they considered their offer. Their offer was not meant to be rejected. And to close the deal, the mobsters promised they could provide access to promoters and assist in putting together copromotion deals. The money would be phenomenal. All the ersatz company had to do was produce the boxers, train them, and get them ready for their fights. The mob would take care of their rankings, even if it meant paying off certain officials.

The agents appeared to go along with the mobsters, nodding their agreement, stating that they looked forward to enjoying the fruits of their cooperation. All the while, however, the agents were compiling files and files of incriminating information that contained declarations that several organized crime families were eager to control some boxers and managers. The mobsters wanted to move forward with their plans, and the agents did too, as once the mobsters started their illegal operations, they would be met by prosecutors at the doors of the courthouse. The agents were set to throw a net of indictments around the sharks, but when they presented their evidence and plans to the director, there was concern. The agents waited for a favorable response, but no such thing was forthcoming. They expressed disappointment that nothing might come of their undercover investigation. Then the FBI informed them that it did not want to be party to any boxing promotions for fear that severe injuries suffered by a boxer might result in liability claims against the agency. That liability was not only financial, but also could result in negative publicity. For an image-conscious federal agency, the possibility of being sued for its own misdeeds was not welcome. Following years of diligent efforts by J. Edgar Hoover, the FBI had a reputation to protect and keep from being tarnished. Thus, there would be no grand jury investigations, no arrests, no indictments. The plug was pulled, the respirator was turned off, and the investigation died a quick death.

Although the Crown Royal investigation came to a nonfruitful end, the Senate Committee intended to move forward. It intended to shine a light into the dark corners where several boxers, managers, and trainers may have developed ties to organized crime families. When names of alleged associates of organized crime families were mentioned, those individuals, as expected, indignantly denied any such ties. The committee neither voiced agreement nor disagreement with those denials. It simply made the names public, alerting law enforcement to areas officers might want to investigate. The committee then drove down a different route looking for signs about how the mob evaded rules and regulations. The committee learned, for example, that numerous boxers had unlicensed paid advisors. By calling oneself an advisor rather than a manager, a boxer's advisor was able to avoid having to obtain a state license. Yet, they often negotiated contracts on behalf of their boxers and worked with their trainers to assure boxing commissioners and doctors that their boxers were physically prepared for their bouts. In other words, they performed the duties of managers without being formally identified as managers. Without licenses, such advisors did not have to worry about violating state boxing commission rules. Definitions, evasions, and semantics became clever ways of flouting the rules and avoiding sanctions.

The committee then heard testimony that if a boxer is not ranked by a sanctioning body, he will not be approved for one of its sanctioned bouts, and he will certainly not be permitted to fight in one of its championship bouts. Thus, he will be denied the opportunity to earn the enormous sums such bouts command. In fact, some boxers who are not ranked may find it difficult to simply earn a living. To stay in the game, they may fight here and there for a few hundred dollars per bout. After a few months or years of scraping by on the outskirts of professional boxing, most boxers will leave the sport and find other means of supporting themselves.

In addition to rankings, there is the issue of managers and promoters who are supposed to remain at arm's length from one another and not share common interests. While the manager earns a third of a fighter's purse, the promoter is incentivized to pay the fighter as little as possible so that he can fatten his own take from a match. What happens then if a promoter is related to the manager and the manager has contracts with each of two fighters who are ring opponents? There are ways and means of making such deals that fly under the radar of the various state boxing commissions.

The Senate Committee learned that if there is collusion between a manager and a promoter, they may arrange for rankings that result in lopsided mismatches, where a truly proficient fighter is matched against either a neophyte or an over-the-hill journeyman. The result may be a quick win for the proficient fighter, but it also might mean death for a fighter who is either a little better than an amateur or one whose speed, reflexes, and skills have been diminished by age. In fact, numerous deaths have hurt the reputation of boxing and periodically resulted in demands for its elimination as a sport.

A touching example of a fighter who was mismatched is Ricky Stackhouse, whose story, as related by Senator William Roth, was one of poignancy. Stackhouse was a middleweight boxer who began boxing professionally in 1984. Senator Roth said,

> Stackhouse was banned from boxing in New York because he was considered as no longer having the ability to adequately defend himself. Stackhouse was also banned in Florida for the same reason but nevertheless was subsequently allowed to fight in Detroit, Michigan, not just against any fighter, but against IBF middleweight champion James Toney, and, predictably, Stackhouse was knocked out in the third round of the fight.
>
> The New York commissioner testified as to the travesty of a regulatory system that would allow this boxer to continue to box anywhere. Seated next to the New York commissioner when he testified was the New Jersey boxing commissioner. And where did Ricky Stackhouse next appear in the ring? In Atlantic City, New Jersey, four months after our August hearing, where he was knocked out again in the third round. Well, so much for health and safety.
>
> Boxing has, for decades, provided opportunity to young men, many of whom are underprivileged, to advance themselves. These young men deserve much better assurance that their health and safety, as well as their financial earnings, will be better protected than under the current inadequate regulatory system.[1]

In another case, the senators heard testimony from the chairman of the New York State Athletic Commission, who told them that in 1982, there was a match between Billy Collins and Raheem Tayib that was held on board the USS *Yorktown* in Charleston Harbor. The bout was televised on ESPN, and Tayib was knocked out. The chairman of the commission said that Tayib was actually a boxer named Eddie Flanning, and he had been knocked out just six nights earlier in New York. As a result of that earlier knockout, Flanning was suspended from boxing for 45 days. Although the commissioner had told the promoter and the local commissioner what had transpired, the fight with Collins was not stopped. That, too, didn't stop promoters from booking Tayib/Flanning for a third fight several days after being knocked out by Collins. Flanning, according to an article in the *New York Times*, used as many as seven aliases in his career.

The committee learned that numerous fighters used aliases so they could fight frequently, although they may have been medically unfit to do so or suspended from boxing. The motive those boxers shared with their managers was to earn as much money as they could and as frequently as possible. The health of the boxer was not an issue.

The committee also heard a humorous, rather than tragic or poignant, story that occurred in 1979, when Mexican bantamweight boxer Carlos Zarate was matched to fight an unknown boxer from Africa. No one was permitted to interview the African boxer, and no one was permitted to watch him train and work out. When the fight commenced, Zarate was bemused by his opponent's unusual style. He thought it was an act. He thought he might be suckered into getting close and then being knocked out. He stayed out of range and continued to observe his opponent's style for two rounds. He had never seen such a strange style exhibited by another boxer. By the third round, Zarate realized that his opponent didn't know how to box. He moved in and quickly knocked him out.

In an October 2001 article in *Nation* magazine, entitled "The Shame of Boxing," Jack Newfield, a journalist and boxing fan, writes that a number of boxers had been killed in the ring as a result of mismatching, as well as negligence by ring doctors and referees. He notes the mortal fates of Benny "Kid" Paret, Beethoven Scottland, Willie Classen, Stephan Johnson, Jimmy Garcia, and Bobby Tomasello, tragic victims. Newfield notes that from 1970 to 2001, 50 boxers died in the ring, and it never should have happened. Newfield asserts that as long as the mob controls fighters, their only concern will be how much money they can make. If a fighter can breathe and walk on his own, he may be considered healthy enough to tie on a pair of boxing gloves and be led, like a sacrificial goat, into a ring. There, he may die, but he will have served his purpose for some people making big money.

Adding to the malaise of the witnesses and the pessimism expressed to the senators regarding the future of boxing, World Boxing Association cruiserweight champion Bobby Czyz, on August 11, 1992, told the committee, "There is more honesty, loyalty, and decency among common criminals and street thieves than among promoters and managers in boxing today"; however, "without these managers and promoters, the fighter has no vehicle to succeed and to get the necessary fights to earn a living."[2]

The Senate Committee, after hearing solo statements from senators Sam Nunn, William Roth, William Cohen, Byron Dorgan, and John McCain, was about to take a dramatic turn, as it was set to call a notorious expert witness, a man who had dominated tabloid headlines for months. The choir of senators was about to hear the singular song of a rock star of the underworld, and his testimony would rock the world of boxing—or at least that's what the senators hoped. The Senate's Permanent Subcommittee on Investigations, under its chairman, Senator Sam Nunn of Georgia, announced that Salvatore "Sammy the Bull" Gravano would testify. The senators may have been skeptical of their star witness, worried he would omit or distort certain valuable information, but whatever they could derive from him would be more than they currently had. Reporters from major newspapers waited and watched.

Senator Roth then made the introductory announcement about the star witness:

> [Gravano], the underboss of the Gambino crime family, will state that in addition to controlling the construction industry in New York, the family was involved in professional boxing. Mr. Gravano discussed a $10,000 bribe with reference to moving a fighter up in the rankings of the WBC. This convenient step would have assured a big payday in the future after fixing the outcome of a fight.[3]

Gravano was then a member in good standing with the U.S. Federal Witness Protection Program. He existed in a cocoon of protection. When his name was finally called, it was as if a Hollywood star, making his comeback, had been beckoned to come before the cameras. As reporters must accommodate themselves to the cramped, busy schedules of stars if they want to interview them, so the Senate Committee members had to wait for an available date in Gravano's busy schedule before he could testify. He was an in-demand witness, for he was testifying for the government from coast to coast. Prior to Gravano's heralded arrival, room 342 of the Dirksen Senate Office Building was searched by FBI agents and by bomb-sniffing dogs. The hush in the room was like that in a Greek temple while a petitioner awaits to hear the voice of an oracle. No one was permitted to leave, no unauthorized people were allowed in the visitors' gallery, no photographs were permitted, and no audio or video recording devices were authorized. Gravano was wanted by not only the senators, but also the mob, which had reportedly issued a $2 million contract on his life. At the time, he may have been one of the most infamous men in the United States, interviewed on national TV, excoriated as a rat in the pages of tabloids, the subject of countless newspaper and magazine articles; he was the man who had brought down John Gotti, head of the Gambino crime family.

Gravano, in an understated, elegant suit and tie, his hair neatly cropped, was sworn in and as polite as an altar boy. He looked like a prosperous executive, a sincere spokesman for corporate America. The questioning quickly got under way, and Gravano stated his expertise, role in the mob, and various responsibilities. His résumé was not new, as his activities had been widely reported in the media.

When asked how he got involved in boxing, Gravano surprised the committee members by telling them he had been something of an amateur boxer in the 1960s. He often worked out at Gleason's Gym, one of the most popular boxing gyms in the country. The committee shouldn't have been surprised, as many mobsters had been boxers. Mickey Cohen and Vincent "The Chin" Gigante, among various others, had boxed professionally when they were in their 20s. Other boxers, for example, Tony Canzoneri, were associates of various crime families throughout their careers.

Gravano explained that the mob not only owned boxers, but also used them as dramatic walk-ons in courtroom dramas. Celebrity boxers were invited or instructed to attend trials of mobsters, who sat at defense tables as they listened to prosecutors and defense attorneys present evidence, accusations, excuses, and inspired performances of theatrical indignation. A celebrity boxer would smile several times in the direction of a defendant, who would return the smile. It was as if the defendant was saying to the jury, "Did you see that? That's my pal. He knows I wouldn't hurt a fly. The champ loves me because he knows I'm not guilty. You must vote to acquit me." But such simple methods were usually not as effective as simple jury tampering.

Although the Gambino family had not been involved in boxing for two decades, Gravano said he attempted to interest John Gotti in getting involved again. Gravano said Gotti instructed him to look into the possibilities. Gravano had an interest in a fighter for whom he wanted to get a high ranking to make him attractive to matchmakers. Gravano told the committee such a high ranking could be arranged if he paid $10,000. He then told the committee that out of respect for John Gotti, the amount could probably be lowered to $5,000. Even the check stubs issued to boxers have included a deduction for a withholding payment to sanctioning bodies. (It's all done legally so as not to inflame the interests of the IRS.)

Gravano stated,

> The Gambino family had basically gotten out of boxing sometime around or before 1960. We were involved in other things that made more money. But I have always had an interest in boxing. I boxed a little when I was in the army, and I picked it up again a few years before I was arrested. I would go to Gleason's Gym in Brooklyn every week and work out. Sometimes, I would go a few rounds with other people who trained there. I often attended fights in New York and New Jersey, including the Mike Tyson–Larry Holmes fight in 1988, in Atlantic City, which I attended with John Gotti.
>
> You should know that our involvement in boxing has changed from the way it used to be. A lot of people think that organized crime makes money by fixing fights and betting on the winner. That really doesn't happen anymore. The purses have gotten so big that it doesn't make sense to fix a fight in order to collect a bet. While we would consider fixing a fight in order to set up for a big payday fight, the money is in the purses, not in the betting. Besides boxing is a risky business for bookmakers—you couldn't bet big money on a fight even if you wanted to.[4]

When asked what sums would be considered big money, Gravano said such amounts as $40,000 to $50,000. Bookmakers would not undertake the risk of accepting such large sums. He said it would be more likely for bookmakers to accept bets ranging from $1000 to $2000, although some more adventurous bookies might agree to accept $5,000, but certainly no more than that. They might accept large amounts for a bet on a boxer being knocked out in a certain round, since the odds on such a bet favor the bookie.

He explained how the mob's interest in boxing has changed from the days of Carbo and Palermo. He said,

> Interest today is in getting a piece of a successful boxer. Until a boxer reaches a certain level, there is not much money to be made because purses are small. But once a boxer becomes successful, the family that has him can profit from that success. Now, because the size of

the purses has gotten so big over the past 20 years, organized crime is more and more interested in getting back into it.[5]

Asked by Senator Cohen of Maine what would happen to a boxer who, after learning that a percentage of his earnings was going to the mob, wanted to break away, Gravano responded, "Traditionally, we have given people a hard time with that situation, senator. We aren't too fond of them walking away from us."[6]

Asked by Senator Cohen the best way to keep organized crime out of boxing, Gravano said the only way to do so would be by keeping the purses small. He added that there would be little the federal government could do to keep the mob out of boxing. He said now that big money was involved in boxing, we can expect the mob to return, for they go where the money is. While the mob may have returned to boxing, it does not exert the kind of all-encompassing influence it did in the days of Jake LaMotta and Billy Fox.

When asked by Senator Nunn when the mob got back into boxing, Gravano said,

> Well, over a period of time recently, we have had an interest. Again, talking about my own family, going down to [the gym], I met some fighters and tried to put something together.
>
> In that period, I found out that we would be able to reach certain people who are rather successful in the boxing industry, and I felt that given enough time, we would be able to go back into it.[7]

Asked how the mob would get paid from a boxer, Gravano went on to explain that they might start by owning a prominent gym, one where many boxers train. Then they would hire some trainers. They would groom certain fighters and arrange matches for them. When the purses got really large, the money would supposedly go into training expenses and promotional work. Then they would put a captain in charge of the boxing and branch off into other related industries.

During later testimony, Gravano was asked by Senator McCain, "Have you noticed in the past on other occasions that someone is moved up in the WBC rankings in time for a fight, and then that person disappears or drops way down again; have you seen that happen before?"

Gravano responded, "Well, it is common knowledge. I'm not surprised by it. I don't really follow that part of it, but it is basically common knowledge that it can be done."[8]

When it was Senator Cohen's turn again to ask questions, he wanted to know how the mob could ensure that a fighter would take a dive. Senator Cohen asked,

> What deterrent do you have if they don't live up to it? Let's suppose he got in the ring, he felt pretty good, and, suddenly, victory is a couple of punches away. Does he take a look out from the ring and see you out there or maybe John Gotti or somebody else, and take a fall, even though he smells victory and the other fighter may have unintentionally walked into a roundhouse punch? What deterrent exists, either expressly or implicitly, to make sure someone lives up to an agreement?

Gravano responded, "I believe our whole background, John Gotti's and mine, our reputation of what we did and what happened. I believe if he would have knocked him out by accident, he would have picked him up." (The senators and reporters all laughed.)

Senator Cohen next asked, "Is it clear in the boxing industry that the boxer—let me put it this way—have you ever heard of a boxer being threatened with injury because he was unwilling to give organized crime a cut of his winnings?"

Gravano responded, "I have never heard that personally. I know that's talked about not only in boxing, but in a lot of industries, and I don't find that really happens all that much. I believe it's a two-sided greed. Organized crime, from what I have seen, has a history of sharing."[9]

Senator Cohen next wanted to know how the money is moved from person to person when the mob has control. Gravano stated,

> Well, it would go through the trainer or manager, trainer-manager. He has a percentage of the fighter. He would get a percentage of that. One of the ways—there are a few ways—would be that when he gets his check and he cashes it, he sends his piece up, what his deal may be—20, 30, 40, or 50 percent, whether he is partners with John Gotti—whatever his specific deal is, he'll send his end of the cash up after taxes, because he obviously can't duck that.

But there are other ways where we could cheat or duck, if I could use those terms. We would set up a gym, and if we were talking about real big money, then we could talk about padding training expenses, we could put people to work, we could go into promotional. We can go into a lot of areas to absorb part of that big purse, especially when you are talking about purses that go into the tens of millions of dollars, we would really be able to—I don't know the word—we would really be able to lunge into that.

The conversation then focused on what the mob would do to a fighter who didn't want to go along with them.

Senator Cohen asked, "So, once organized crime has an interest in a fighter, even though the fighter may not know that he is owned or at least influenced by organized crime, he can't walk away?"

Gravano explained,

Well, I wouldn't say that. If his manager was with us, he couldn't walk away. If the fighter really knew nothing, I don't really know how we can go after him, except that he would lose his power base and connections, and we would try and cut him off that way. If he himself shook our hand and made a deal with us, it would be a lot harder for him to walk away.

Senator Cohen continued, "So if he didn't know he was in any way associated, you might try perhaps to reduce his ratings and rankings?"

Gravano said, "We would use whatever tactics we could use short of violence, because he really doesn't know what he is involved with. If he knew what he was involved with, we would use just about any tactic, including violence."[10]

Senator Cohen concluded by asking once again what the government could do to keep the mob out of boxing. "Make the purses very small," stated Gravano, eliciting laughter again from the senators and reporters.

Following the end of their questioning, the Senate Committee issued the following statement about the role of organized crime in boxing:

While organized crime elements do not currently exercise the pervasive control of professional boxing uncovered by the Kefauver hearings, members and associates of organized crime groups do remain heavily involved in boxing. There is evidence that the greatly increased amount of purse money now available to top professional boxers makes the sport more attractive to organized crime. On the other hand, current state regulatory efforts to limit organized crime infiltration of professional boxing have continued to be little more effectual than they were 30 years ago.

The committee further stated,

Despite numerous congressional hearings and other calls for the boxing industry to police itself, both the boxing industry and the current regulatory structure have failed in the effort. Most industries, when subjected to federal scrutiny, would attempt to address problems voluntarily in order to obviate the need for any federal involvement. However, one can only conclude, as did Senator Kefauver more than 30 years ago, that states are unable to adequately regulate professional boxing. [11]

Senator Roth of Delaware reiterated some of the committee's conclusions and added his own assessment:

Today, the mob is less likely to fix fights and more likely to seek control of individual boxers, managers, and promoters, and thus collect its share from their big paydays. The boxer may even be an unwitting dupe in the whole scheme. However, as with the other problems we have found in boxing, it is the boxer and the public who lose, whether the boxer knows it or not. [12]

While the Senate Committee seemed to have affirmed that boxing was no longer ruled by the mobsters who set the sport's illicit agenda in the 1940s and 1950s, a new generation of mobsters inserted themselves into the sport and maintained a poisonous presence in professional boxing. As long as the amount of money for hyped, hotly contested bouts increased, the mob schemed to get its hands on a significant portion of the money. The committee acknowledged that as long as the mob used its ability to operate by stealth, it would continue to evade the eyes of law enforcement agencies. After the committee issued its conclusion, there seemed to be little interest in going after mobsters involved in boxing. State boxing agencies were not known as attack dogs with sharpened teeth. Indeed, they were barely seen even as watchdogs. In addition, there were numerous individuals who were able to front for the mob, giving illegal activities the appearance of being entirely aboveboard.

In 1961, Rocky Marciano, the undefeated heavyweight champion of the world, had told legislators that the sport of boxing could only be cleansed by the appointment of a boxing czar with the authority to protect boxers and keep the mob out of the sport. He was ahead of his time, as the mob was as integral to the sport of boxing as punching bags and jump ropes. When the Senate Committee issued its report on the role of the mob in boxing, few people thought its diagnosis would be followed by a cure for an apparently chronic condition. The infection was too long lived and too pervasive. It had taken up permanent residence in the body of boxing. Then, just three years later, to much fanfare, President Bill Clinton signed the Professional Boxing Act. Unlike the committee, it did not make recommendations: With the president's signature, it became the law of the land. It would change the world of boxing, for it mandates that every professional boxing match be sanctioned by state commissions.

If a state does not have a commission, it must adopt the rules and regulations of a state that has one. The act also requires that all boxers register with a state boxing commission and maintain up-to-date identification cards. Each card is to contain a recent photo of the boxer and his social security number. That was supposed to eliminate the problem of suspended boxers hiding their identities using aliases. A boxer's suspension could no longer be hidden from boxing commissioners, and promoters couldn't claim they were unaware of the suspension.

And from the point of view of boxers and their families, the most important new regulation was designed to ensure the health and safety of boxers before they enter a ring. To wit: The act demands that every boxer be deemed physically able to engage in a boxing match and carry adequate health insurance. Furthermore, professional boxing matches must be held in the presence of a medical doctor and an ambulance service. Prior to a boxer entering the ring, his health and physical capabilities must be certified by the doctor. This is especially important if the boxer has been suspended following a series of consecutive losses or injuries. And, of course, no boxer may engage in a boxing match while under suspension.

To help boxers remain free from the grip of the mob, the act authorizes the attorney general to bring civil actions against individuals who violate the act. And since the mob signed boxers to onerous contracts that tied them to ongoing contests with less-than-generous payouts, boxing service providers may not require a boxer, according to the act, to grant anyone future promotional rights as a requirement for competing in a professional boxing match.

As beneficial as the act proved, it was just one step in the right direction. In 2000, the Muhammad Ali Boxing Reform Act was passed by Congress. It is an amendment to the earlier law. It expands on the 1996 act with legislation against exploitation and conflict of interest rules, while providing the means for enforcement. The Ali Act, as it came to be known, was written as a result of the continued and widespread abuse of boxers through exploitation, artificial rankings, rigged mismatches, fixed fights, and pressure from shadowy figures who attempted to control the careers of numerous boxers. The Ali Act also outlaws coercive contracts that are judged to be a restraint of trade and thus unenforceable.

While good intentions may result in suitable laws being enacted, the mob always finds ways to avoid adherence to laws they find objectionable. As long as there are multimillion-dollar purses for hyped boxing matches, the mob will find a way to cash in. Those vast sums of money, rather than the contents of matches, inspire headlines on not only the sports pages of newspapers, but also the business pages. It was said of Paul Castellano, former head of the Gambino crime family, that he read the pages of the *Wall Street Journal* on a daily basis. If he were still alive, undoubtedly he, too, would want to get his family back into the business of boxing. The big money would prove a target too attractive to ignore. And there have been whispers and murmurs that the sharks are circling, ever hungry for a big payday. Have they started feasting? Some surely know, but no one is talking to law enforcement. And why should they? Are law enforcement agencies even watching? If so, what will they do? They, too, are not talking. The mob is extremely adaptable and opportunistic. If there's a way for them to get back into boxing, they will surely do so. Maybe they already have.

NOTES

INTRODUCTION

1. David W. Maurer, *The Big Con: The Story of the Confidence Man* (New York: Anchor Books/Doubleday, 1999), 12.

1. THE MAN WHO FIXED THE 1919 WORLD SERIES

1. Leo Katcher, *The Big Bankroll: The Life and Times of Arnold Rothstein* (New York: Da Capo, 1994), 22.

2. F. Scott Fitzgerald, *The Great Gatsby* (New York: Charles Scribner's Sons, 1953), 48.

3. Katcher, *The Big Bankroll*, 15.

4. Katcher, *The Big Bankroll*, 12.

5. Katcher, *The Big Bankroll*, 20.

6. Katcher, *The Big Bankroll*, 28.

7. David Pietrusza, *Rothstein: The Life, Times, and Murder of the Criminal Genius Who Fixed the 1919 World Series* (New York: Carroll & Graf, 2003), 53.

8. Katcher, *The Big Bankroll*, 42.

9. Nick Tosches, *King of the Jews* (New York: Ecco/HarperCollins, 2005), 227.

10. Katcher, *The Big Bankroll*, 44.

11. Katcher, *The Big Bankroll*, 45.

12. Katcher, *The Big Bankroll*, 102.

13. Katcher, *The Big Bankroll*, 137.

14. Pietrusza, *Rothstein*, 173.

15. Pietrusza, *Rothstein*, 182.

16. Pietrusza, *Rothstein*, 235.

2. FROM BOXER TO BAGMAN TO GAMBLER

1. Monte D. Cox, "Interview with Legends of Boxing," *Cox's Corner*, http://coxscorner.tripod.com/interview2.html (accessed 14 March 2016).

2. Interview with the author.

3. OWNEY MADDEN AND FIXING THE HEAVYWEIGHT CHAMPIONSHIP

1. Donald L. Miller, *Supreme City* (New York: Simon and Schuster, 2014), 96.

2. Herbert Asbury, *The Gangs of New York: An Informal History of the Underworld* (Garden City, NY: Garden City Publishing Company, 1928); T. J. English, *Paddy Whacked: The Untold Story of the Irish American Gangster* (New York: Regan Books/HarperCollins, 2005).

3. Graham Nown, *Arkansas Godfather* (Little Rock: Butler Center for Arkansas Studies, 2013), 39–40.

4. Asbury, *The Gangs of New York*, 345.

5. Asbury, *The Gangs of New York*, 352.

6. Asbury, *The Gangs of New York*, 354–55.

7. Miller, *Supreme City*, 105.

8. Miller, *Supreme City*, 95.

9. Nown, *Arkansas Godfather*, 158.

10. "Primo Carnera, Italian Boxer," *Encyclopedia Britannica*, June 25, 2018, https://www.britannica.com/biography/Primo-Carnera (accessed 15 August 2018).

11. Joseph S. Page, *Primo Carnera: The Life and Career of the Heavyweight Boxing Champion* (Jefferson, NC: McFarland, 2011), 204.

12. Page, *Primo Carnera*, 2.

4. THE MACHIAVELLI OF PROMOTERS

1. Kevin Mitchell, *Jacobs Beach: The Mob, the Fights, the Fifties* (New York: Pegasus, 2010), 17.

2. Barney Nagler, *James Norris and the Decline of Boxing* (New York: Bobbs-Merrill Company, 1954), 9.

3. David Margolick, "The Beach of Jowly Men," *New York Times*, 9 October 2005, City section, 4.

4. Mitchell, *Jacobs Beach*, 17.

5. Mitchell, *Jacobs Beach*, 224.

6. Budd Schulberg, *Ringside: A Treasury of Boxing Reportage* (Chicago: Ivan R. Dee, 2006), 206.

7. Schulberg, *Ringside*, 267.

8. Mitchell, *Jacobs Beach*, 144.

5. THE GRAY CZAR OF BOXING

1. Barney Nagler, *James Norris and the Decline of Boxing* (New York: Bobbs-Merrill Company, 1954), 20.

2. Jimmy Breslin, *A Life of Damon Runyon* (New York: Ticknor and Fields, 1991), 5.

3. Carl Sifakis, *The Mafia Encyclopedia* (New York: Checkmark Books, 1999), 310.

4. T. S. Eliot, *The Complete Poems and Plays* (New York: Harcourt, Brace and Company, 1952), 164.

5. Kevin Mitchell, *Jacobs Beach: The Mob, the Fights, the Fifties* (New York: Pegasus, 2010), 96–97.

6. Jack Roth, "Carbo Released on $100,000 Bail," *New York Times*, 8 August 1959, 12.

7. Jack Roth, "Carbo Sentenced to Two Years in Jail," *New York Times*, 1 December 1959, 31.

8. Nagler, *James Norris and the Decline of Boxing*, 221–22.

9. Nagler, *James Norris and the Decline of Boxing*, 222.

10. "Frankie Carbo, Underworld Figure Once Known as the Czar of Boxing," *New York Times*, 11 November 1976, 46.

6. THE BIG FIX

1. Jake LaMotta, with Joseph Carter and Peter Savage, *Raging Bull: My Story* (New York: Da Capo, 1997), 59.

2. LaMotta, *Raging Bull*, 78.

3. Barney Nagler, *James Norris and the Decline of Boxing* (New York: Bobbs-Merrill Company, 1964), 31–32.

4. Kevin Mitchell, *Jacobs Beach: The Mob, the Fights, the Fifties* (New York: Pegasus, 2010), 94.

5. Chris Anderson and Sharon McGehee, with Jake LaMotta, *Raging Bull II: Continuing the Story of Jake LaMotta* (Secaucus, NJ: Lyle Stuart, 1986), 12.

6. Anderson and McGehee, *Raging Bull II*, 17.

7. Anderson and McGehee, *Raging Bull II*, 27.

8. Arthur Daley, "Sports of the Times," *New York Times*, 16 June 1960, 42.

7. UP FROM THE MUCKLANDS

1. "The Times of Your Life," Carmen Basilio interviewed by Jim Roselle, February 1966, https://searchaol.com/video;_ylt=A2KLfsbt96buuMAi (accessed 26 September 2018).

2. "The Times of Your Life."

3. Barney Nagler, *James Norris and the Decline of Boxing* (New York: Bobbs-Merrill Company, 1964), 183.

4. "Fighting the Mob: The Story of Carmen Basilio," *ESPN Classic*, https://www.youtube.com/watch?v=DZbWEMy6HY (accessed 26 September 2018).

5. "Fighting the Mob."

6. Nagler, *James Norris and the Decline of Boxing*, 185.

7. "Mike Wallace Interview: Carmen Basilio," *Harry Ransom Center, University of Texas at Austin*, October 26, 1957, http://www.hrc.utexas.edu/multimedia/video/2008/wallace/basilio_carmen.html (accessed 28 February 2018).

8. Will Haygood, *Sweet Thunder: The Life and Times of Sugar Ray Robinson* (New York: Alfred A. Knopf, 2009), 119.

9. Kevin Mitchell, *Jacobs Beach: The Mob, the Fights, the Fifties* (New York: Pegasus, 2010), 277.

8. SONNY LISTON'S BLUES

1. Nick Tosches, *The Devil and Sonny Liston* (New York: Little, Brown and Company, 2000), 34.

2. Tosches, *The Devil and Sonny Liston*, 53.

3. Rob Steen, *Sonny Liston: His Life, Strife, and the Phantom Punch* (London: JR Books, 2003), 22.

4. Tosches, *The Devil and Sonny Liston*, 82–83.

5. Steen, *Sonny Liston*, 93.

6. Tosches, *The Devil and Sonny Liston*, 224–25.

7. Tosches, *The Devil and Sonny Liston*, 148.

8. Tosches, *The Devil and Sonny Liston*, 136–37.

9. Steen, *Sonny Liston*, 99–100.

10. Steen, *Sonny Liston*, 200.

11. Wilfrid Sheed, *Muhammad Ali: A Portrait in Words and Photographs* (New York: Thomas Y. Crowell and Company, 1975), 42.

9. WHY GIVE UP A GOOD THING?

1. Hearings in front of the Permanent Subcommittee on Investigations of the Committee on Government Affairs, U.S. Senate, 103rd Congress, First Session, March 10 and April 1, 1993. Corruption in Professional Boxing Part II. Roth, 3.

2. Permanent Subcommittee on Investigations, Bobby Czyz, 39.

3. Permanent Subcommittee on Investigations, Roth, 72.

4. Permanent Subcommittee on Investigations, Gravano, 76–77.

5. Permanent Subcommittee on Investigations, Gravano, 77.

6. Permanent Subcommittee on Investigations, Gravano, 87.

7. Permanent Subcommittee on Investigations, Gravano, 78–79.

8. Permanent Subcommittee on Investigations, McCain and Gravano, 83.

9. Permanent Subcommittee on Investigations, Cohen and Gravano, 85.

10. Permanent Subcommittee on Investigations, Cohen and Gravano, 87–88.

11. Permanent Subcommittee on Investigations, 62.

12. Permanent Subcommittee on Investigations, Roth, 71.

BIBLIOGRAPHY

Alexander, Michael. *Jazz Age Jews*. Princeton, NJ: Princeton University Press, 2001.

Allen, Merl L. *Welcome to the Stork Club*. New York: A. S. Barnes and Company, 1980.

Anderson, Chris, and Sharon McGehee, with Jake LaMotta. *Raging Bull II: Continuing the Story of Jake LaMotta*. Secaucus, NJ: Lyle Stuart, 1986.

Asbury, Herbert. *The Gangs of New York: An Informal History of the Underworld*. New York: Vintage, 2008.

Brenner, Teddy, as told to Barney Nagler. *Only the Ring Was Square*. Englewood Cliffs, NJ: Prentice-Hall, 1981.

Breslin, Jimmy. *A Life of Damon Runyon*. New York: Ticknor and Fields, 1991.

Dickie, John. *Cosa Nostra*. New York: Palgrave Macmillan, 2004.

Downey, Patrick. *Gangster City: The History of the New York Underworld, 1900–1935*. Fort Lee, NJ: Barricade Books, 2004.

English, T. J. *Paddy Whacked: The Untold Story of the Irish American Gangster*. New York: Regan Books/HarperCollins, 2005.

———. *The Westies*. New York: G. P. Putnam's Sons, 1990.

Fitzgerald, F. Scott. *The Great Gatsby*. New York: Charles Scribner's Sons, 1953.

Fontenay, Charles L. *Estes Kefauver*. Knoxville: University of Tennessee Press, 1980.

Haygood, Will. *Sweet Thunder: The Life and Times of Sugar Ray Robinson*. New York: Alfred A. Knopf, 2009.

Katcher, Leo. *The Big Bankroll: The Life and Times of Arnold Rothstein*. New York: Da Capo, 1994.

Kefauver, Estes. *Crime in America*. Garden City, NY: Doubleday, 1951.

Kelly, Robert J. *Encyclopedia of Organized Crime in the United States*. Westport, CT: Greenwood Press, 2000.

Kimball, George, and John Schulian, eds. *At the Fights*. New York: Library of America, 2011.

LaMotta, Jake, with Joseph Carter and Peter Savage. *Raging Bull: My Story*. New York: Da Capo, 1997.

Maas, Peter. *Underboss: Sammy the Bull Gravano's Story of Life in the Mafia*. New York: Harper Perennial, 1999.

Maurer, David W. *The Big Con: The Story of the Confidence Man*. New York: Anchor Books/Doubleday, 1999.

Miller, Donald L. *Supreme City*. New York: Simon and Schuster, 2014.

Mitchell, Kevin. *Jacobs Beach: The Mob, the Fights, the Fifties*. New York: Pegasus, 2010.

Nagler, Barney. *James Norris and the Decline of Boxing*. New York: Bobbs-Merrill Company, 1954.

Nown, Graham. *Arkansas Godfather*. Little Rock: Butler Center for Arkansas Studies, 2013.

Page, Joseph S. *Primo Carnera: The Life and Career of the Heavyweight Boxing Champion*. Jefferson, NC: McFarland, 2011.

Permanent Subcommittee on Investigations of the Committee on Government Affairs, U.S. Senate, 103rd Congress, First Session, March 10 and April 1, 1993. U.S. Government Printing Office, Washington, DC, 1993.

Pietrusza, David. *Rothstein: The Life, Times, and Murder of the Criminal Genius Who Fixed the 1919 World Series*. New York: Carroll & Graff, 2003.

Schulberg, Budd. *The Harder They Fall*. New York: Random House, 1947.

———. *Ringside: A Treasury of Boxing Reportage*. Chicago: Ivan R. Dee, 2006.

Sheed, Wilfrid. *Muhammad Ali: A Portrait in Words and Photographs*. New York: Thomas Y. Crowell and Company, 1975.

Sifakis, Carl. *The Mafia Encyclopedia*. New York: Checkmark Books, 1999.

Steen, Rob. *Sonny Liston: His Life, Strife, and the Phantom Punch*. London: JR Books, 2008.

Sussman, Jeffrey. *Max Baer and Barney Ross: Jewish Heroes of Boxing*. Lanham, MD: Rowman and Littlefield, 2017.

———. *Rocky Graziano: Fists, Fame, and Fortune*. Lanham, MD: Rowman and Littlefield, 2018.

Tosches, Nick. *The Devil and Sonny Liston*. New York: Little, Brown and Company, 2000.

———. *King of the Jews*. New York: Ecco/HarperCollins, 2005.

Turkus, Burton B., and Sid Feder. *Murder, Inc*. New York: Da Capo, 1992.

Young, Anthony. *New York Café Society*. Jefferson, NC: McFarland, 2015.

NEWSPAPERS

Chicago Daily News
Chicago Tribune
Los Angeles Times
Miami Herald
New York Daily News
New York Post
New York Times
Newark Star Ledger
San Francisco Chronicle
Washington Post

MOVIES

Body and Soul
The Boxer
Boxing and the Mafia
Carmen Basilio: Fighting the Mob
Hands of Stone
The Harder They Fall
Raging Bull
Requiem for a Heavy Weight
The Set Up
Somebody Up There Likes Me

INDEX

ABOUT THE AUTHOR

Jeffrey Sussman is author of 13 nonfiction books. In addition, he is president of Jeffrey Sussman, Inc. (www.powerpublicity.com), a marketing/PR firm based in New York City. He has been a boxing fan since the age of 12, when his father taught him the elements of boxing and signed him up for 10 boxing lessons at legendary Stillman's Gym. Sussman writes for several boxing websites, one of which is www.boxing.com. His latest books are *Max Baer and Barney Ross: Jewish Heroes of Boxing* (2016) and *Rocky Graziano: Fists, Fame, and Fortune* (2018).

CPSIA information can be obtained
at www.ICGtesting.com
Printed in the USA
LVHW092211010420
651898LV00003BA/5

9 781538 113158